HOAX!

THE DOMESDAY HIDE

HOAX!

THE DOMESDAY HIDE

ARTHUR WRIGHT

Matador
5 Weir Road
Kibworth Beauchamp
Leicester LE8 0LQ, UK
Tel: (+44) 116 279 2299
Fax: 0116 279 2277
Email: books@troubador.co.uk
Web: www.troubador.co.uk/matador

FRONT COVER A Saxon four-ox plough, the key to the Domesday statistics with a timber built motte-and-bailey
Norman castle of the type shown on the Bayeux Tapestry.

BACK COVER a one-inch to one-mile map of part of Essex in 1086 drawn from the statistics listed in the Lesser
Domesday and other evidence.

ISBN 978 1848761 650

British Library Cataloguing in Publication Data.
A catalogue record for this book is available from the British Library.

Typeset in 11pt Bembo by Troubador Publishing Ltd, Leicester, UK
Printed and bound in Great Britain by TJ International Ltd, Padstow, Cornwall

Matador is an imprint of Troubador Publishing Ltd

Dedicated to all those clever people who made me think and to the few friends and family whose faith encouraged me to speak.

CONTENTS

INTRODUCTION

Error Qui Non Resistitur, Approbatur –
an error which is not resisted, is approved.

In Essex we have been unfortunate. Several eminent thinkers and researchers who were students of Domesday Book made this shire their home and the intensity of their deliberations has blinded their acolytes to the value of discussion or further research. If people do read what I have written I hope they will discuss it freely and I certainly hope they will not just repeat it blindly. To teach the text but not the method is failure, I want people to study the methodology. If they can fault it, good luck to them, it will make a change from the failures who won't make the effort. Not being a 'clever person' or a learned scholar I have tried to write a book for people like myself. It is an ordinary little book which has, at times, to name some of the engine's parts but which really tries to explain in simple terms what the mechanism does. Thirty years ago I tried very hard to submit papers and open up discussions on this subject but, with the exception of the late Professor Henry Loyn, no-one wanted to encourage me. Others rubbished, scoffed, even lied about my questions, they hid behind privilege and refused to enter into public or private debate. I think these people saw my questions as a threat to their comfortable lives and reputations and resolved to silence me at all costs. They were right.

Any 'clever person' reading this book will deem its references too light-weight for an academic work. I do not say this by way of apology, quite the opposite , I am in this respect unrepentant. It is a type of book quite unfamiliar to those who write long, sententious panegyrics destined to be consigned to library shelves before they can be sold, 'references' packed with references to other people's opinions which, by association and repetition, make the writer a person of importance. Only a kernel of such work is usually readable and what is said in them has often been better expressed, in scansion and in style, by their exemplars. To the 'man in the street' such works mean nothing, they are impenetrable Abelardian audits. I have tried instead to be readable rather than formal but above all original (without being condescending) and, as footnotes tend to impair reading I have used them only when essential. 'Clever people' will know the sources anyway and have their own, favourite editions. I have tried to write a work of *original* research, a book of new ideas and fresh formulae. It should be quite a novelty in this field.

Scientific method, it has always seemed to me, is that foundation of formulae and devices designed to encourage good sense in the analysis of practical problems. Sadly unscientific writings are often more attractive reads. Thus I have attempted to add some facility to the scientific structure I have been obliged to apply to the subject presented here; I hope I have succeeded in making it more readable even if it does not look polished and academic. In forty years of close contact with academia I learned that the 'clever people' will contrive whatever they can to discredit a book like this, so they are hardly going to be the auditors who matter. Knowledge has nothing to do with education, or at least history does not need to rely on tuition to impart knowledge. What it really needs is common sense, but they don't do degrees in that.

For forty years in the historical field I laboured at the coalface of education. When I began I believed two things, that we had a duty to do our best and that we could change the world. Age and experience have shown me that both these things were fallacies and that few (either in formal or informal education) retain evangelism, even when they start with it. Just occasionally one may see pupils build on the knowledge imparted but it is unlikely that others will allow them to retain this for long. The National Curriculum is designed to kill enthusiasms. I may be wrong but it seems to me that there is now much less enthusiasm about for learning than when I was a child and I attribute this to the lack of stability in human affairs, knowledge and relationships which characterised the last century. The effort required by reading, counting, discovering is superficially much less attractive than letting a picture tell us what a machine has been programmed to do. I can sympathise: what was the point of much that we learned at school and which we saw swept away in favour of another and yet another novelty of system or politically correct structure, of all the sealed packets of information technology which have discouraged the modern student's thirst for knowledge? Why were we required to learn so many things which would be abolished and discredited within a few years? Some ascribe this to 'progress', but progress builds to advance, it does not vacillate and destroy. As yet, the machines have no initiative by which to advance to human knowledge, but while we wait for such developments many humans go half way by seeking to emulate the machines. Let us be consoled by the comfort of those claims to scientific methodology which are provided by the cosmetic applications of technology. Domesday Book experts love them.

What I have done in this little book is to take original material, study it and come to novel conclusions, conclusions based on simple arithmetic, which anyone can replicate and whose statistical significance is undeniable in honest circles. At the end of this production line of information is a new artefact for Domesday Book and its ilk, it becomes *an entirely readable*, comprehendible and addible inventory. It was painstakingly researched because I became convinced, over thirty years ago, that for the last century scholars had (and have) been led astray by a hoax. Prior to 1900 academics believed that Domesday Book could be converted to just such an obvious and open format, after 1900 they accepted that this was impossible, so that it was also pointless to make any more attempts. (Incidentally it also made them look very clever when they said *why* it could not be done.) This abnegation of hope and belief was the result of a hoax, though whether it was accidental (in the sense that it began as a temporary expedient) or intentional I cannot say. Its originator can be identified, but whether others encouraged and mislead him I am not qualified to say. I can only say that it became permanent and it is the current state of knowledge. Of course, I would like to change this so that our state of knowledge *can* move forwards.

For my Domesday Book references I generally used Professor Morris' Philimore series as the concurrent text makes rechecking easier, though I started by using the Victoria County History studies and ended with the Allecto edition where it sufficed. The scholar who impressed me above all others was Professor Maitland though I respect others, some before him, who cut a path through the wilderness in the right direction before coming to the hoax. After it many able and educated researchers wandered around in circles with, here and there, a flash of steel even if it was not in a profitable direction. By the 1970s no one had the courage to admit that there might be any first principles, though Henry Loyn remarked to me that we might have too readily dismissed the Victorian scholars and their contributions. The idea of *original* research was, to the 'good and the great', incomprehensible so I make no apology for being original now. I think that more historians (*if* that is what I am, which many will dispute?) should have a go at it.

I know that I must, inevitably, disappoint not only academics but also documentary and film producers and re-enactors when I propose that feudal society (in England at least) was not an alliance of King and magnates to exploit 'the masses', the proletariate, but did they really think such a 'system' could ever work outside a modern surveillance state? No doubt the Church will be upset by the worldly emphasis I have given to the temporal preoccupations of prelates and saints just as much as by the perception and suggestion of a spiritual dimension among monarchs who held by divine right? It cannot be helped, this is what the evidence suggests, though I have not been dogmatic. For those incensed in case I stop the scholarly gravy train I say, 'cheer up, see it as an opportunity instead'. Just think of all the new areas of debate I have opened, it will take more than a working lifetime to rewrite English history and so many allied disciplines. Will we learn anything useful about sustainability from finally knowing the accurate and measurable picture of early agriculture, well I feel an affirmative in my bones but I am not an expert and the 'experts' haven't yet read and reconstructed what I have said. It removes some agrarian and demographic 'comfort rags' but there should be personal reward available to many in reanalysing modern methodologies against the real eleventh century.

Inevitably there will be detractors who say that I am bitter and vengeful after thirty years of persecution. Well, if they find it comforting they may believe it, I cannot stop them, but I am old enough to know that neither ability nor effort ensure success in any human activity. Life is a matter of luck and I have been lucky. That I lost thirty years of potential enlargement on my discoveries may, perhaps, matter to someone, but for myself I spent my energies and abilities pursuing other fields with just as much reward, so why should I care? Were it not for the jealousy and stupidity of others I would be a very different person and this text would not be so thorough, for it is a fact that long reflection often clarifies perceptions. What is disappointing to me is the knowledge that so many others who could contribute to society are treated in the same way, have been treated in the same way, and the experience of my working life has been that education and science, or what we might encapsulate under the description 'personal discovery', are denied to so many youngsters by those who can only be described as proponents of politics in education. These are the people who replace discovery and enthusiasm with the cheap package tour, as an educational prescription. We lived in a wasteful and foolish century. It seems to me that the Victorians had a better idea of how to engage students and I even wonder whether the children of 1086 had happier lives and a better education? If you think this strange, read this book, it will show you how much our ancestors *could* comprehend and that we have forgotten, and how adept they were at solving problems without even those basic systems which *we* deem essential.

Our natural world, it seems, is reciprocally running out of control as our technologies are allowed to overload flimsy systems, whilst our absence of science to guide us seems an overwhelming and undeniable argument. To survive as a species, we are told, we need to change things now which should have been changed long ago and the hoax I have discovered and the reality masked by that deception, which wasted a century of research, may seem to some insignificant. Can it have any direct application to climate change and sustainability to know that nine hundred years ago a large population could sustain itself without modern agricultural methods? Well, I hope it will help and I hope that the further discovery of the way in which such societies were structured, taxed and administered may enlarge our knowledge of ourselves, dismissing mythologies in favour of real histories. Moreover, as we shall see, a great deal has been built on convenient interpretations of what Domesday Book should say in order to be politically useful. Such mythologies need to be challenged and the record set straight. It is a truth universally acknowledged that the world may be divided into 'developed' and 'undeveloped' economies. On the one hand are those who have (so far) sustained debt and on the other those succumbing to it and these divisions are largely coincident with urbanisation and industrial and vehicle pollution, and with subsistence and self-reliance without option. We throw it all together under the heading of 'global economy', thus ensuring that in the absence of localised economies we have no buffers against universal economic collapse, but this certainly does ensure that our political masters can survive in either of these major economic divisions by using similar formulae in order to wield power.

Could it just be that our definitions are misleading, that 'development' is not a sustainable goal *or* maybe not one that all should seek to attain? Might it just be the case that 'history' has misinformed our grasp of reality and that exploitation with debt and derivative creation is not a system for economic development? The catastrophic collapse of economic theories which coincided with my conclusion of this work suggests, for those of us who always doubted the feasibility of commercial Cockayne, that economists may also have been long a-building on similar sands in order to gratify their political masters? Of course, all knowledge is illusion, but illusions should serve some durable and beneficial purpose, one greater than placing money in the pockets of those who, through serendipity, can exploit the gullibility of others. No doubt the Greeks would have smiled to hear that ethics is sounder philosophy? Historians have cast beyond *and* levelled at the moon[†] in coscinomantian frenzies and, yes, how Cobbett would have laughed to see the fall of 'stock-jobbers' who cried and jumped over the moon. One wonders whither that vessel of clay which doubted the existence of a surly tapster has taken the treasure it purloined[Φ]? One thing now seems certain, without the mirage of a global economy such exploitation and domino effects would have been impossible.

One question, perhaps above all others, has taxed students over the centuries, what was the purpose of Domesday Book? The answer is that almost everything anyone else has said is right, but it would be wrong to make any of these things mutually exclusive. Yes it was a geld book, a feodary, an inventory, a cadastre, it was (as I demonstrate) also a lot more, including a sort of atlas. The question might actually be rephrased and put into two parts. First of all, for what purpose or purposes was it conceived, second what purposes did it serve? Even then we have a corollary: what were its consequences? As no one up to now has known what it is saying, so no one has explored this last question. Half a century from now I hope we will have a few ideas about its consequences. I hope we will also appreciate the consequences of the hoax!

It is an over simplification to say that Domesday Book was conceived as an updated, new and comprehensive form of the much older 'hidages' and that it was intended to serve only the judicial purpose set out in chapter six. Ultimately it served as a tax calculator and a paradigm by which to formulate even more inventive projections of tax liability, in which sense it was the humble tool of all the systems that came after it, none of which had its scope. The first is always original. Eventually its use both as a paradigm and terminus post quem were forgotten and it became a curio with tangential legal value, though its consequences were to act as a catalyst for many events and chains of thought. We can see the roots of the Reformation and the Dissolution of the Monasteries (etc.) discussed in the final chapter.

Years ago I, half joking, wrote a recitative (as a Stanley Holloway monologue) suggesting that Domesday Book was the origin of the Civil Service and because it was too large for 'King Billy' to read "right away" they are still involved in précising it down today. Now I have convinced myself that this is correct, except that instead of simplifying the surveys the civil service are now vastly increasing the many volumes of detail which they think they require. So, the real legacy of Domesday Book is, in a nutshell, information technology and the surveillance society. If you don't believe me, read this book.

CHAPTER ONE

IDENTIFYING THE HOAX

When Professor Cantor wrote his book and gave it the title 'Inventing the Middle Ages' he certainly did not have Domesday Book in mind[1]. His beautifully crafted analyses speak of the affinities and, in particular, the political imperatives which have motivated medieval historians to approach medieval history ('middle ages' is surely tongue in cheek and provocative) from their own and individual view points. Ultimately one can even attempt to synthesise such divergent views in order to reach a modus vivendi, though nothing like a consensus by which student, layman or jobbing academic could present this period to others. It has continually changing definition. In particular, there is really nothing by which to present this period for the benefit of examiners or auditors of knowledge although, of course, its acolytes try to make a fist of it. What he did not appreciate was that the very foundations of this discipline had been fatally flawed by a hoax.

Although medieval historical interpretation may be particularly susceptible to political suggestions and so to interference, and to academic idiosyncrasy, we should not imagine that it is unique in this respect, which is to say that it is not unique in the presentation of 'alternative objectives'. All academic fields ultimately win their war for recognition by this strategy; the 'way to win wars' (to borrow Liddell-Harts' terminology) *is* the alternative objective, the indirect approach, this is what the world deems 'balanced argument'. Only by discussion and consensus can we validate any field of study, so the analogy with warfare is not inapt. However in many fields there arise, from time to time, disastrous and maybe deliberate by-ways that create dead-ends in research, even though at the time of generation and pro hac vice, they appeared to be solutions to what was otherwise imponderable. Under such a poor light even the deliberate hoax may be perpetrated with the best of intentions: not all confidence trickery sets out to criminally deceive, a 'little white lie' may serve (pro hac vice) to advance study and scientific progress? In fact it *is* often represented as a scientific advance. If its author receives scholarly recognition thereby, he (or she) may not have been entirely motivated by such desires, or not motivated primarily by the academic vice of honour seeking for recognition. There is always Schroedinger's cat. Of course, it is the nature of a hoax to deceive, to deceive the generality as well as the dupe on whom it is foisted, so that he (or she) is flattered, until the hoax is exposed. Strictly speaking, therefore, a hoax is a trick played on another and, by extension, the perpetrator need not necessarily be the dupe, though it can take modified form: it might also be that the perpetrator, for the best of reasons, dupes everyone else and himself? Piltdown ceased to be a hoax because the hoaxers succeeded in duping everyone, in the case of Piltdown it was Dawson's colleagues who encouraged his gullibility but academia was also gulled. The Domesday hoax certainly includes a large measure of gullibility but it was more likely to have arisen from the desire of others to share reflected glory than of the originator to maliciously encourage or deceive. I can see no evidence of suggestion by some subordinate, though I have not looked very hard for one.

Thus, I say, Professor Cantor did not have in mind a hoax and much less the perpetuation of a super-Piltdown hoax when he took up his pen and gave us all so much pleasure. I doubt whether even a fraction of today's academics, even of today's medievalists, understand that their knowledge base has been corrupted, structured and confined by a super-Piltdown hoax? Their training has not included such a possibility. Those few who have been told in the past are understandably reluctant to give credence, or yet to permit expression, of some minority view that the major bones of English medieval history are fabrications altered by clever pigmentation and substitutions from their true value! This is because our hoax does concern the *very bones*, the fundamental structure of our history. Piltdown itself completed a series and a picture, a 'missing link', so did the hoax I now wish to explore but this was even *more* serious. Initially it appeared to make further and apparently fruitless searching bootless and in so doing comfortably secured the further progress of study in English history, especially social, economic and legal history. It began, we might say, as a working hypothesis but it quickly became a marble monument and a tomb. Eventually, of course, with Piltdown we had to rewrite everything again, but that didn't matter at the time and who remembers it at all today? It is a footnote in anthropology. What matters much more to us is that our present hoax *has never even been identified* yet what I am about to expose is the foundation on which *all* English history has been prospectively and even at times retrospectively constructed. This is not merely what Piltdown was to anthropology it is undoubtedly the *biggest single hoax* in the history of history, in historiography. Was it deliberate, I don't know, was it honestly intentioned, I believe so? I stand to be corrected by those who know better, but wasn't Dawson's creation honestly intentioned, just like Frankenstein's? A hoax should, by definition, be good natured, not an outright fraud. Most important of all, where would we be today if Eoanthropus dawsoni were still part of our evolutionary sequence? *Did* its exposure make one iota of difference, or (instead) did it change the world for research and human progress? Depending on your answer, do we need to know of a hoax which, in its sheer scope, eclipses even that one? I think we do, but the hoax has taken such a root in the uncritical soil of scholarship that it will be difficult to eradicate.

This 'invention of the middle ages', with its imprecision of medieval history, whilst fun for the historian does little to impress the man (or woman) in the street who, if they are interested at all, are actually, naively, prepared to accept the most outrageous parodies and the most simplistic of political messages from a barely variable diet, often the menu set out on film. The plain staple of this diet is, indeed, most readily accepted: life was rude, crude, violent, uncomfortable and short, as were the people themselves. Thus we are lucky to live in our modern society. Academics speak of the importance of 'peer group review' as a means of ensuring that mythology is not promoted but the evidence is dead against them. The mythology of medievalism flourishes, Hollywood is the proof. It is this very 'peer group review' which ensures its perpetuation for no dissentient voice, especially one questioning a deep-seated hoax, may be heard, dissenters do not belong to the peer group, QED. Review from first principles (let alone revision) is effectively barred by the uncritical acceptance of a hoax and by complete lack of scientific methodology, by which I do not mean superficial or cosmetic pseudo-scientific methodologies ("innovative applications of modern technology") but such simple and demonstrable formulae as may be (and should always have been) provided by arithmetical reconciliation. Medieval history has no simple mathematical formulae to hand and why, because the most important of all the scientific precautions, review from first principles, *is not permitted*. At least it is not permitted in mainstream studies. The Medieval 'experts' could do worse than to emulate the patient methodology of those who research the history of medieval technologies, who usually do make use of scientific models. The (this) hoax, which sustains so much mythology, is at the statistical core of our foundation for medieval studies, Domesday Book, itself a statistical matrix but one which arithmetic must not be allowed to pollute!

Ultimately even those indoctrinated in the Piltdown view of history were persuaded to permit analyses of the physical material in question, so why (you may ask) is this not possible for Domesday Book? Well, you see, no one is questioning physical material such as the substitution of a bone, a folio or membrane. What is in question is the lack of scientific methodology, the refusal to apply the simple and obvious test of arithmetic which alone could validate all theories. In the second place, our Victorian ancestors actually *had the wisdom* to ask for such a test and such evidence, but their sensible precautions were swept aside by rhetoric and academic legerdemain around 1900: the proponents of such scientific foundations and methodology were deliberately discredited and so we have had to live with the result for a century. We can return later to the question 'why', but in essence it was because an answer of the conclusive type required by Victorian methodology was not forthcoming and such a failure did not accommodate the hubris of the age, which had its own expectation of a false dawn of enlightenment attending the birth of the new century. Those of us who lived through the Millennium should appreciate the political pressures generated by such events. Then, thirdly, there is the sheer scope of the hoax thus perpetrated on academia for, as a result of this decision to accept a hoax that was an indemonstrable hypothesis, by which to calibrate all subsequent analyses of Doomsday Book and its attendant and dependant archives, almost every aspect of English history has been 'explained' and corrupted.

Progress in so many (allied) fields hinged upon a resolution of the Domesday enigma that once success had been *claimed* (broadly by 1900) it subsequently informed all that was dependant on it. Thus a politically acceptable though indemonstrable hypothesis led to unsubstantiated hypothecation in every related field. Where Piltdown could only claim anthropology the core issue of Domesday Book, as identified by antiquaries, the Domesday hide, has exercised a major influence in the fields of topography, cartography, demography, social and agrarian history, constitutional convenience, political constructivism and social stability, aspects of jurisprudence, ecology, the appreciation of pre-Conquest history in its entirety and of post-Conquest history in its substantial and progressive hypothecations and in its consequential constructs of human development. In a nutshell, if we demolish the indemonstrable hypothesis lying at the heart of this hoax then we will need to reconstrue and rethink *the whole* of English history! The conception and perspective we have of Domesday Book really is *that* important to every aspect of what we *think* we know. That is why I called it our foundation and the skeleton for medieval studies, these are the foundations of all subsequent interpretations of history. Indeed, in the recipe book of the humanities alone there is hardly a dish in which Domesday does not figure, either as an ingredient or as a flavouring. Moreover, it is still of use because it provides an insight into the evolution of present practices and contemporary systems. If you actually make it to chapter 9 you may understand what I mean by the consubstantiality of governors and governed.

Any academic with expertise in (what is) the arcane field of Domesday studies, any medieval doctorate, knows that to remove this chip of information (the indemonstrable hypothesis) and replace it with another will invalidate almost every programme by which the machine of scholarship operates and the task is, therefore, perceived to be too difficult to attempt. Instead there is a self-congratulatory culture that commends, rather than criticises, repeated failures to produce simple answers, one which ring-fences present assumptions with repetitions. This is only because iteration has been permitted to grow and to subsume, for so long, an appalling prospect, it has been allowed to adopt the potential of a cataclysmic collapse of knowledge, a collapse not so far removed from that of our global economy. What no one appreciates is that, if this is true, if it is true that a hoax has undermined the basis of much of our present 'knowledge', the disaster is not irretrievable. You see, although in the first instance we have to admit a fraud, it is only after its exposure that we can hope to recover sufficient composure to enable us to rectify it. The ship need not sink if we acknowledge it is so badly damaged that its integrity is threatened, but it *will*, ultimately, sink if we do not acknowledge this fact. Which ship will sink? Obviously the ship of medieval studies, but also the academic value of English historical studies, but then and finally the most important ship of all is humanity, for if you believe that the study of the past has value in charting our course for the future (and is not just a waste of time and effort) it is essential that our foundations should be sound or 'right'. How, for example, do we validate our economic well-being today if all our knowledge of the past is no more than 200 years old? Even then, how much of our 'knowledge' was hypothecated on what we believed to have happened before those 200 years began? Domesday casts a long shadow for its penumbra even covers modern economic assumptions.

Academics often speak of "taking the information of Domesday Book at face value" but this is precisely what *they do not do*. By their training they are indoctrinated in the need to study and accept interpretations of Domesday Book, *the most important of which* focus on the doctrine of the variability of all the units to be encountered in the surveys – the hides, virgates, ploughlands, even the acres. The surveys are, let's face it, nothing but units, great lists of statistics, but because academics have never had to make sense of these units they say that they are obviously irreconcilable and contradictory. If this was always the case, why were they ever collected? Differences in particular groups of totals they dismiss as 'proof' of this doctrine. I have never yet found one who had even attempted to distinguish between different types of meadowland, so it is not at all surprising to me that they *deny* constant units yet *apply* consistent definitions – 'of course everyone knows what a wood is!' Do they, most people don't know the difference between wood and timber, let alone wood and trees and even today *who* has a definition which will separate a copse or spinney wood from a wide hedgerow or shelter-belt? The truth is that these savants cannot 'do' the arithmetic and so they avoid it by saying it doesn't exist. No, no, this will not do, their first lesson as students should have been *to answer the question*.

Which is not to say that they have not applied themselves to their creations. Volume after learned volume testifies to the patient and ceaseless task of verifying the immaterial, of giving substance to mirages. Indoctrination has reached such a pitch that anyone trying to present a simple arithmetical analysis or reconciliation is deemed to be 'ignorant', unschooled in the 'major advances made by modern scholars', those very studies which have failed to support the fantasies of scholars or even to reconcile the Domesday statistics. It is wonderful what fantasies can be built for succeeding centuries when we start from the certainty of *no* specific knowledge. And if these people are not abject failures, why are they so frightened to debate what I have to say in this book and why do they want it hidden from ordinary people, from students and from other disciplines? Are they solicitous for my reputation, well *I* am prepared to stand up and dispute the case, I am prepared to tell others how it is done. Together you and I are going to take a journey (if you read on) into the past and where no one has trodden for nine hundred years. The most important part of this trip is that once you have been there and you have the trick, you can do it again and again and you don't need 'clever' people to act as your guides. The 'Tardis' will be yours. I won't ask you to believe what I shall show you, I shall ask you to disprove it! After all, *this* hypothesis *is* demonstrable.

In Domesday Book we have a choice of 13,418 places, some large, some small and all in detail[2]. Not one of our Domesday 'experts' can take us to one of these places and then transfer the ancient writing to a modern, mapped topography, so we are going to do it for ourselves. We are going to turn woods, meadows and arable land into one inch to the mile maps, we are going to rebuild 'dead' landscapes and meet long dead people. We are going to show that these resurrected landscapes covered the same areas 200 years later, 500 years later, even 800 years later! Then, from late Victorian maps we can look to our more recent maps to see what has happened in modern times. We are going to read and reconcile the entries made in Domesday Book with modern equivalents and no one can stop us nor yet deny what we shall achieve. Then we are going to learn a lot more. Never think that figures can't be fun, it's like riding a bike. Screw up your courage and you, yes you, can challenge the cleverest historians in the world.

Once you accept that the fabric of history is not yet a compilation of 'facts', a thesaurus of definitions, but (instead) a heap of hypotheses, an asseveration of assumptions, it is easier to understand the commonly held 'brick upon brick' concept of human progression. Remove the lower courses of brickwork and the foundations are undermined, so down it all falls. Now every generation, we are assured by this concept of progress, must have a 'better' experience of life than the last. Is this so? Accepting that the concept *is* one of progressive development, then it becomes easier to comprehend that we may not ascend if we do not know where we actually began? Indeed, there is evidence that we are already relegating history, especially medieval history, to the irrelevance of entertainment rather than treating it as a serious subject, a dismissal led by those who set educational standards for English primary schools. Should we not ask ourselves why it has been marginalized? Did we never decline from some peak of civilisation and then ascend again, I will ask, for such an hypothesis *would* destroy our faith in 'progression' and yet make the study of history essential to our understanding of success and failure in building modern societies? 'Civilisation' as we know it, so we are told, is only possible if we pollute and destroy the earth, if we create materialism and erect it on the back of fossil fuel industrialisation, history 'proves' this.

Let us suppose for a moment that this is not necessarily the case, let us suppose that it is not necessary to destroy our children's futures to gratify ourselves? Supposing we found that some part of our past had been one of ecological balance and concomitant happiness (though not necessarily in the 11th century), what would that do for our present political structures? It would surely be disasterous? Let us suppose that we really do need food more than we need cars and cheap flights to countries we can still exploit? Would our politicians have the courage to tell us this? The provision of an indemonstrable hypothesis for Domesday studies allowed all the fields which I enumerated above to continue to create themselves according to their most convenient hypotheses, which was (of course) entirely acceptable to politicians, but it prevented us from *exploring the reality of the past*, at least in English history. So it was convenient for all concerned, and the question must arise, was it wrong to accept convenience? Well, Schroedinger's cat is an expedient not a solution and, ultimately, it cannot exist in a pragmatic world. Only one decision can be the valid answer and that decision is the one which ultimately does least harm. The evolution of human affairs has a way of pragmatising sophistries, often by a direct route. I think we need to get the past right before reality sets us straight. Besides, a hoax is a hoax, whether by intention or by default, whether the result of vainglorious pride, of hubris or of political legerdemain. This book is actually about the 'three R's' and how a failure to understand them has resulted in ignorance of the 'four E's', that is education, economics, ecology and the English heritage. So reading, (w)riting and (a)rithmetic have only been important if they served political ends, among which is the comfort of a progressive economic history? We appear to have discovered not only a hoax but hoax upon legerdemain?

The indemonstrable hypothesis of Domesday Book appeared to be the endorsement required by the politicians of 1900, validating industrialisation, urbanisation and materialism. It provided the keystone for a superstructure far beyond its inventor's imaginings by recognising the ancient and potential conflicts of governed and governing, for from its simple invention whole fields of human development could unroll securely under the spell of history. As a hoax it was ideal, it provided both the acceptable and the expected, it validated the form of democracy approved by authority *and* its concomitant economy, without any need to consider consequences. It is only now, a disastrous century later, that we can see how extensive and irrevocable was the damage already sustained by our earth in 1900. Now reality is being forced upon us, and yet, even in the urgency of survival, we have lost sight of even the pseudo endorsements of 'the past' for we are, indeed, altogether losing our belief in the value of history as an aid to navigation. It has not warned us of the dangers. It is not surprising that when an emergency arises it is now the short-term solutions, and not informed, longer-term structures or strategies, which form the straws at which we grasp, but short- term solutions are *not* what we require. What we *think* we know from history apparently, sadly, has nothing to offer us. What we do require, instead, is an *informed* and universal view.

Our ancestors, I suggest to you, were not mistaken in supposing that *their* ancestors may have formulated some wisdom. They had biblical injunction, of course, to instruct their 'honouring of father and mother' but it is also typical of the arrogance of youth to dismiss prudence in favour of change for changes' sake. It has always been so and perhaps it was the very immaturity of western society that encouraged men in 1900 to dismiss their ancestors as fools when they themselves were the dunces? They have been doing it ever since. Worse still, academics, those who should have known better, have done it ever since, basing their dismissals on fantasies created by invented 'history'. These are the derivatives and debentures of scholarship, claiming their validation from differential coefficients, changes of function based on a variable and then repackaged and sold on to buyers who never suspect their insubstantiality. It is all too easy for the popular historian to become a wolf in sheep's clothing, ignoring the economic lessons of a case study (from which we might actually benefit) in favour of some fool's gold of 'peasant freedom' and 'female emancipation'. Such politicians pretending to be historians invariably conflate villein with serf, serf with slave, liberty with bondage, affluence with destitution for effect and because what matters is not the reality of the past but the opportunity the past gives us to influence the present through uncritical, mentally inactive audiences. So many of the media's 'authentic voices' of our ancestors are really Lorelei with personal agendas, out of context and time, who would be unknown to themselves could the original testators but return from the dead to listen. And many of *us* might well resemble serfs to them, thanks to our subservience!

This present study is, therefore, an analysis of one, small, aspect of English history, yet I propose that it has had immense consequences far beyond its obvious and immediate sphere of application. It may not be the only fallacious construct in all the sophistries that have brought the world, our earth, to its knees today, but it happens to be the one that I have studied. That is all I can claim. What I set out to do, thirty years ago, was to solve a problem which Victorian historians and scholars had found irreconcilable by any simple arithmetic; what I found was *a simple arithmetical reconciliation*, the key they had been looking for. The opposition which I then encountered made me realise the extent to which this one, apparently trivial, substitution of political fantasy (however innocently intended when it began), how one hoax, could alter our view of history and the way in which we use it in our attempts to justify and manipulate human endeavours. The indemonstrable hypothesis was a convenient way of isolating and abandoning what the wit of (intelligent) men could not explain at the time and it *appeared* to work. Strategically, like blitzkrieg, it bypassed the difficult bits and so demoralised the whole 'enemy front'. Today, with the benefit of hindsight, I suggest to you that it has done more damage than, perhaps, any other palliative or convenience in history? Will you permit me to justify what I have said? Then take up the challenge, read the evidence and the method and, please, *prove* me wrong.

CHAPTER TWO

THROWING OFF THE HALTER

Our first task is to convert the units entered in the Domesday Survey of 1086 into those of a modern agricultural survey. Once this has been accomplished we can turn these statistics into local, regional and national maps, not just guesses at intensities or pie charts but *real areal surveys*. In our search for maps there will inevitably be gaps (scholars call them 'lacunae', which sounds impressive) but these will not be inexplicable and they may provide evidence of their own. Large parts of the north of England were 'harried', that is laid waste and terrorised, in 1068-70[3]. Such evidence as we have suggests that King William felt great remorse for this by 1086 and that he may even have blamed his half-brother, Bishop Odo of Bayeux, for some reason unknown to us? Where populations were massacred and homes and crops burned, we may expect recovery to be slow and evidenced by new introductions and we might find evidence of refugees on the periphery. Anyway, we want to read Domesday like a book and to do that we must begin by 'transliterating' the statistics of which its conglomerate is composed. This was the task set by Victorian scholars and they identified the key element as the numerical value of 'the hide', a unit used in Domesday to define 'something' in very many shires and one apparently related to several other units.

For those who have never attempted this before it may seem easy, theoretically obvious. For those with some experience in the field it will be an eye-opener. For those qualified in such studies it will be both heresy and bitter wormwood. If you haven't encountered all the strange and archaic language of Domesday Book before, *don't worry*, you will soon get used to the weird nouns (like 'hide') and you will realize that they are only a giant set of building components, then you too will become excited and even eager to know more. As for those who are expert in such things already, no I'm not sorry that all the mystery and secrecy is being taken out of your world, it's about time ordinary people had a chance to read it and a chance to unravel it when you couldn't! Not all professors are windbags, but neither are they all the clever, eccentric yet approachable academics of C.S. Lewis' 'The Lion, the Witch and the Wardrobe'. Come on all you explorers and children-at-heart, all you scoffers at history and children's stories, all you geeks with more ram than you can deliver, come along too all those who seek an eternal winter of frozen arcaneties, we're going into Narnia! This is the real thing, not Lewis or Tolkien fantasy but *a real and secret world* .

Indeed, we have worlds upon worlds to explore. There are strange, even to some students frightening, documents which are only 50 or 100 years old, others 200 or 300, but we *are* going to set foot in a documented landscape almost 1,000 years old, think of that. The maps and directories, surveys and statistics of 100 and 200 years ago which now seem so daunting (because you never knew of them before) are only echoes of the world we seek and shall assuredly find, but being only a hundred or so years old they are not so far away or the people so different from us, why we can even look at photographs of the people who lived then. Now we will travel back to 900 years ago and, behold, the world will not seem so different − on the landscape itself − from that of the people of the photographs. So people like those in the photographs but much, much older and in other clothes (and speaking other tongues) lived in a − well a not-so-different world. Now that *is* exciting, isn't it? Most archives are alarming because only 'clever' people understand them, they are not accessible by 'us'. We are amazed when we hear the knowledge of clever people and the erudite language they use. Is this not so? O.K. forget it. 'We' are the ones who are going to run rings around them and when we have finished, they won't be able to answer our questions, not until they join us. Not until they become like us, travellers in another dimension, inheritors of knowledge rather than of fantasies or guess-work.

All journeys begin and end. *This is where we begin*: if you like we are brushing through the old fur coats in a wardrobe and ahead we see light and we drink-in cold air. We scrunch into snow and our feet are cold. We are now in 1086 and, as yet, we aren't going to discuss how all these figures came about (that can come later), we are going to list them and apply them instead, for we must look about us and try to understand what no-one has seen since about 1300, maybe even longer ago than that? No university, not even the Public Record Office, can do this or has done it. We are the first, because we have refused to believe in fantasy and we seek reality.

ACRES − Here we are, looking out of a wood onto snow-covered fields below, mostly larger ones divided into long rectangular strips. When it rains the water will follow the dividing furrows to irrigate the fields before emptying into boundary ditches. These ditches take the excess water to meadows and rivers and tenants who fail to scour them are fined. In some places the acres of land will

11

belong (administratively) to different parishes and different people, so did they have a common unit by which to buy, sell, value and discuss land? Of course they did, it's only common sense. You can't have acres of different sizes! It was always the, so-called, 'statute acre' (set down in later law) of 22x220 yards. It isn't difficult to remember or to visualize such a strip of ground, in fact most of our field strips visible below snake along the contours of the land in 22x220 yard acres. It would be plain silly if fields met at a property boundary and were of different sizes for the same measure, wouldn't it? It would be plain silly for any unit to be infinitely variable!

Some historians have argued against any standard units, against standardised or enforced metrology, yet without them (even prior to 800 A.D) *there could not have been* a money economy in England or in Frisia or in Carolingia, yet we know there was just such an economy[4]. Money and land, they *do* go together don't they, standard coins and standard acres. That is our first surprise.

HIDES – this is a big landscape, for we are looking out across a plain and a large valley. Down below, not always easy to see because they blend so well into the landscape, are cottages and houses: we can see the smoke of wood fires rising on the crisp, still air. A dog is barking, somewhere sheep are bleating, a voice is singing.

'If all four acres belong in different manors, are they each worth 2d the acre?'
'Am I buying, selling or insuring?'

How on earth can one measure such a landscape and how do you count up in large numbers? Remember, most of our counting here is done with counters and only written-up in Roman numerals. X=10, L=50, C=100, D=500, M=1000: well 1,000 acres won't cover much of this scale of values, so where do we go from here? Besides, it's easy to miss a unit or two when the numerals themselves don't add. Remember, we have no zero, no '0', we can't make columns for our arithmetic (not yet). Only the Arabs know about Arabic numerals. Scribes are always getting the counters wrong, striking out the Roman numerals and redoing the sum! Sometimes we see dots in the margin where they have made a swift recalculation. *We must have bigger units*, only then can men count their land in acres up to 'the big unit' and pass on the total simply, in big units. From ancient times we have had 'households' or 'mansi', now called 'hides', land enough for a group of people to live on and off. Each hide is 240 acres. Anciently a 'five hide' man is a man of some status, well he does farm 1,200 acres. The hides are our big units and the most commonly encountered, and that is why the Victorians wanted this value above all others, though they never found it. Well, here it is, 240 acres. Later we will discuss the evidence but for now we need to understand how this works.

The trouble is, if you own (or let) a hide or two, or five, the King and his advisors (the government) know about it. It's very difficult to hide a hide (forgive the pun). If you have such status all your neighbours know it. When the Vikings were at their worst, raiding, stealing, burning, raping, murdering, the King said it would be a good idea to pay protection money so that they would go away. He did so and they came back for more. Silly king! So tax after tax, called danegeld, drained the silver pennies from men's purses *according to how many hides they had*. So much on each hide. Now, was that fair? I mean, if I have a lot of woodland and water, I don't make as many silver pennies in a year as my neighbour who raises lots of wheat and barley and sells it for a fortune to the bakers and brewers. Wouldn't it be more reasonable if we only paid tax on the arable land? Of course, but I need my neighbours to agree with me, otherwise I will be reported to the King – for treason! Round about the year 1000, in some counties, men began to count *only* their arable in hides. Meanwhile, in blissful ignorance, or (perhaps) loyalty, other counties continued to pay it on every acre and hide they could see, which sometimes included acres of water and sometimes did not. After all, *it is easy to set a numerical standard* but *it is harder to set a definition*. Tell me, back there behind us, did we come out of a wood or out of the trees? See what I mean? Remember this for it is the key to the indemonstrable hypothesis.

CARUCATES – Not much ploughing today, in this hard frost. But then as Walter of Henley said in c.1260, when you have done with holidays and other encumbrances, you will scarcely get 260 days of work out of a ploughman in a year. These peasants really ought to work harder (we will return to this). The 'caruca' is the plough, a wooden soil-slice drawn by a team of eight oxen, often as a four 'up' and four 'down', for speed, but all of them together on heavy clay going. Oxen pull slow but steady, they don't fail you like a horse will and they are cheap to feed and easy to breed. Provided soldiers or Vikings don't eat them, you can change a stott every two years, so there is usually plenty of beef for stewing. Sadly you can't eat old tractors and they don't breed, so this ox-power is a sensible arrangement. *A carucate* is the area which a plough team can reasonably till in a year. Of course it varies, soil to soil, but ancient practise gives a 'rule of thumb' average of 120 acres. Half a hide (a carucate) is sensible for at least half your ground needs to lie fallow and recover from cropping, unless you want the soil to become exhausted. Later we will deal with such things in detail but it is also the case that 'carucates' often measure the lord's arable (demesne), not that of his tenants. Well, if you want tenants to work your land *they* must live on something.

Of course, the whole basis of society here is self-sufficiency, but a surplus can be traded. This means that every village, or vill, has to grow its own cereals; why, even townsmen at Cambridge have fields outside the town on which to grow their staple crops. If you want to know the local economy, *just ask how many carucates there are*, for although the distinction between long term fallows (wareland) and a 'course' (change of crops) may not always be easy to follow, although some plough-lands represent the lord's own profits and some the tenant's sustenance, few men will tell you that *all* of their hidated area is tilled, not unless they are tax-dodging anyway. Some land is suitable, some is not, some people leave long fallows while others have a simple grasp of courses that might even be like rotation, but you can't plough up everything without courting disaster and you can't plough woodland or water without some drastic effort of labour. Neither can you hold all your plough-land 'in demesne', not unless you want to plough it yourself! So our landscape has plough-lands and ditches, heaths and commons for grazing, meadows, scrub in places, trees where trees grow best and crops worst. Each land use has its economic value and its effect on topography.

TYPES OF HIDATION – By 1086 not everyone acknowledges the same logic for the employment of hides – and we know why, don't we? Quite apart from those shires where men feel they should not pay geld on a gross assessment (hidation), but should only pay it on the arable (carucation), the kingdom has also been divided by the 'Danelaw', which was a division into 'English' and 'Danish' areas long ago in King Alfred's day. By this device the different ethnicities learned to live in peace, until both had been attacked by a

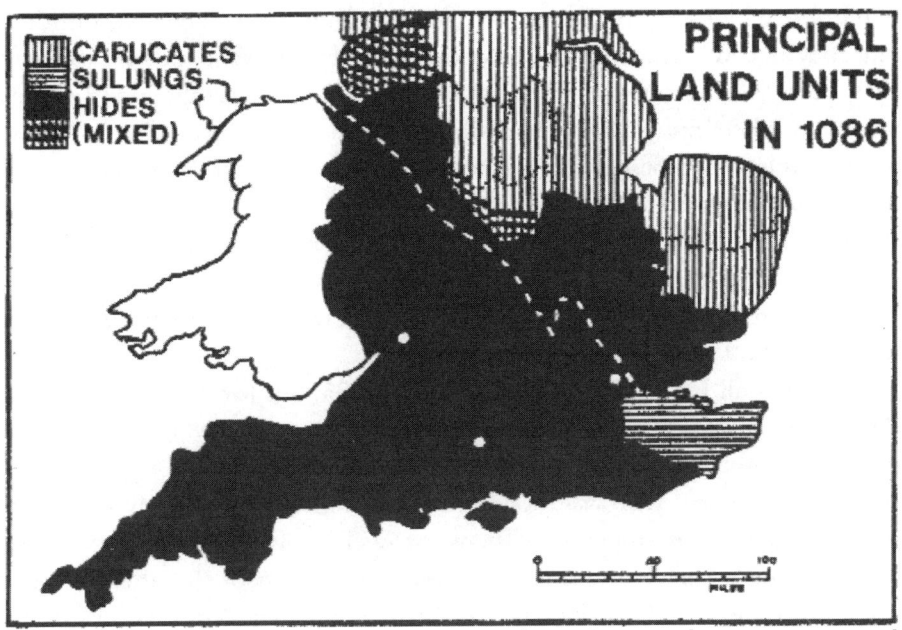

new wave of Norsemen – the Vikings. Now, in the Danelaw, where the former Danes live, in northern and eastern shires, the Danes count land by carucates. They only acknowledge what they till, while in the south and west the English stick to the tradition of counting in hides, so that they know the whole area which they occupy. No doubt the English were influenced by their education long before the Danes arrived, or perhaps they were just loyal?

Thus we can speak of *different* hidations by 1086. We have what tradition demands in some shires ('traditional hidations'), an areal gross: places like Middlesex, Surrey, Oxford and Berkshire. We shall certainly deem their inhabitants honest and loyal servants of the king. Then we have the old Danelaw shires such as Leicestershire, Derbyshire, Nottinghamshire, Norfolk and Suffolk, who only declare what they till, their arable (='carucations'). We cannot say that they *intend* to deceive the King. Finally we have shires like Essex, Sussex, Dorset, Huntingdonshire, Gloucestershire and Rutland where landowners didn't want to be left out of a good thing or where (maybe in Essex, half in and half out of the Danelaw by 1000) men were confused. Let us be kind and call these 'revised hidations'. Well we might term both of these groups 'selective hidations' as that is what they do, they select? Obviously, when we are told of manors that are not hidated in 1086 and which *never* paid geld (if true), we are looking at estates carved from some sort of set-aside (wareland) or even royal estates, where the memory of a hide as a comprehensive land measurement had been lost through long abeyance. When there was no written record medieval courts reckoned 90 – 100 years as 'time-out-of-mind'. By the time of Domesday the hide's original purpose was becoming 'time-out-of-mind'. Yet, just occasionally, we find a note in the margin of Domesday Book (they had to be careful for, as we shall see, the hide was to be treated as a 'state secret') which is essential to our comprehension. In the Golden Valley of Herefordshire we find that 112 ploughs *could* plough Stradelie (= 112 carucates), and then interlined above this total the words "56 hides". Apparently there were no ploughs here but there *was* capacity for 112 and 56 hides of geld must not be overlooked[5].

So, it has all become a bit of a mess by 1085, but for very good reasons. Maybe this is what King William thought at Christmas 1085 when he had, 'mycel getheaht and swithe deope spaece' with the wisest men in the land. Maybe he wondered who was fooling him? We think he had already shut up his (half) brother Odo on suspicion of the worst? Well, we will come to that, in time.

Well now, we have found (as we should have guessed) that there is rather more to this new world of snowbound farmers and rich lords than just paying taxes or dying. Life must go on, so what about the smaller, the important and specific, agricultural uses of this beautiful landscape? Not textbook theories: no one wrote them and, anyway, few of those who could read Latin (the only real written language) had enough practical knowledge to even attempt a day's work! Hm, sounds a bit like a barge-load of dons on a convivial outing: at least the guy steering the boat has to know what he is doing.

PLOUGHS – Well, a plough is a plough-and-team, we know this works out at 120 acres by rule-of-thumb: rather less for poor devils on Wealden clay but more on Essex loess and, in the middle, about right. Sustainable agriculture and subsistence are about knowing how to survive, not how to go begging for food-aid. The land must not be exhausted, however light and fertile the soil, however tempting the profits to be made.

This is the really, really clever bit, diabolical you might say? I'll bet King William didn't spot this one, no, some clever civil servant (we used to have them) sidled up and whispered in his ear once the coast was clear. Clear of whom? Why, of barons and bishops of course, the people who wished to keep secrets from the King: we'll also come back to this later on. Who else had so much to gain? Pay attention, I know it's cold but just keep walking while I talk. We need to go down to the river.

What was really clever about the Domesday surveys and what hadn't been done before in any earlier survey, was *the inclusion of the ploughs*. Still puzzled? Well you can't give a nod or a wink to a blind horse, can you? Ploughs I said, ploughs, motive-power units with a rule of thumb value. Just like saying 'tractors'. Yes, now you understand don't you? A man says he pays tax on his hides or his carucates. Leave aside the difference for the moment, how do we verify whether he is calling one 'the one' or, instead, 'the other'? You can really get bogged down searching for meanings when definitions are hard to find, let alone when clever men are dishonest, so ask them a nice simple question. 'How many ploughs do you have, sir?', he says 'six' and after some other chat and looking up an older document, you note that he claims to pay tax (geld) on four ploughlands. No, as a good clerk (camerarius) you don't need to say anything to him or to the lords who are your presiding 'inquisitors' or 'commissioners' (legati), they are probably *his* mates even though supposedly acting for the King. What you do is smile, wink at your colleague, ask the peasants later how many ploughs their lord has and make sure that all these statistics appear *very* close together in the record. Your boss, what we would call a 'mandarin', won't miss the relevance and neither (thanks to the word in the shell like orifice) will the King. Four does not equal six, but it seems such an innocent question to ask.

In Middlesex in 1086[6] we read of 81,150 acres of land, with 79,920 being accepted as arable, yet only 68,040 were actually under arable cultivation (= ploughs). 'Room for more' was the laconic comment when Domesday Book was finally engrossed (written up) by the 'mandarin', an observation also made at other places. Yet the innocent question was in two parts: 'how many ploughs belong to the lordship' (demesne, the lord of the manor's personal profits) *and* 'how many ploughs belong to the men' (the tenant farmers' own subsistence and profits)? Is tax being paid on all the arable or only on the demesne, or maybe on less? In other words, '*who* is telling me the truth and (I wonder), if not, who is making a profit (and at this date tax evasion is treason)'?

SULUNGS or SOLINS – this is the Kentish equivalent of a hide. Back in c.600 A.D the ethnicity (so the noun) was different from the rest of England. As Domesday Book itself says, '400 acres and a half' (= 600 acres) 'makes 2 sulungs and a half' (viz. 2x240 + 120 = 600 acres). Beautiful logic, it had to be, this Bernard was giving Sir Humphrey a hidden message: 'thank you, Bernard'.

VIRGATES – these were quarter hides, in other words 60 acres of land, arable or not, when the term was properly used. Thus a 'virgator' was a farmer on the scale of an English 18th century farmer. An awful lot of scholars have gone round and round in circles trying to 'prove' that this unit had no fixed value, or only a local one, but the acid test is "does it work" and this one does! Still, for those committed to the Domesday hoax it provides a spurious 'test' of scholarship: snigger, snigger, "he doesn't know where it says 25 or 30". Oh yes he does and it's rubbish! In Somerset, Devon and Cornwall a quarter virgate was called a FERDING. At Huntingdon FERDING was used to distinguish a quarter, or farthing, of the city, just as the noun 'shire' was used at York of the city's quarters.

JUGUM – a quarter sulung, or 60 acres (a virgate), in Kent.

BOVATE – from the root 'a beast/beasts' it meant a quarter carucate or a quarter of a plough-team (of 8 beasts), a pair (or yoke) being the smallest number you could use as motive power for harrowing or light work. The basic motive-power unit, in fact, or half a virgate (half a jugum), 30 acres.

SO THERE WE ARE, in a word, in one word, we can now say : 240, 120, 60 or 30 acres (but in Kent the word is likely to be different) .

MEADOW – right, now that we are approaching the river (mind that ditch filled with snow, if you break something these people don't have doctors, even *if* they want to be friendly to strangers) we can see meadows of one sort. These are water meadows. Whatever sort of meadows they are, meadows are usually listed, often expressed in acres (because they are valuable), they are used as a special feeding resource for over-wintering livestock and that includes the essential stotts. In some shires Domesday Book tells us of meadows in small units and then (as at the present) we know we are looking at riverside water meadows: open the sluices and flood them in February so that silt, detritus, organic nutrients, seeds, all settle with the flood waters and, by May or June, you have a fine crop of mowing grass. Carry this and let the animals graze a while, then (with a little luck) by September another rich after-crop of grass mixed with clover. When fresh this is bad for the sheep, but it makes a super winter-feed for stotts. Otherwise, just one rich hay crop will have to serve for the haystacks and winter feedings, but without any hay, no stotts.

But what do farmers do when there are no flat valley bottoms and flood plains with leats and sluices? Do *all* men think of winter feed stuff in the same way? Well, in hilly areas one has upland or alpine meadows, lenses of soil or even the richest fallows, often near the top of the valley slopes. Where conditions are bad and the land too poor to crop or to fallow one might use it as 'meadowland' out of necessity, though in truth it is more like rough grazing and rough pasture. Anyway, in Surrey[7] meadows were measured down to half an acre (being so valuable) while in Middlesex all the meadows were in larger units – thus the logic changed as one crossed the river Thames in 1086. Excuse me, one might say, are you trans-or cis-pontine? Where we are told that meadow is measured in plough teams, as in Cambridgeshire and (rarely) Gloucestershire, we may be sure that it is not any special meadow but rough pasture and fallows, for in such cases it is the ability to expand the ploughed areas into the long-term fallows that is being measured as much as the hay.

PASTURE – not so many pastures in Domesday Book, so (as we look around) we are guessing what we are looking for. Well now, how would (how do) *you* define the difference between meadow, fallow, grazing and pasture? We believe that non-arable land was already coming under population pressure by 1066/1086. 'Pasture' can be anything used for grazing something. Remember, some creatures will eat anything and some creatures will not tolerate others: goats and geese 'taint' (make foul) the pasture for deer, causing 'slinking' (abortion) in particular. This is worth remembering when we think we are on the edge of pastures used specifically for the farming of deer, such as royal forests. (Yes, venison was farmed, but as wild creatures.) In other places 'pasture' may mean the open wilderness, land fit for nothing else unless fit for 'forest'. Forest need not mean trees. At Blingsby Gate (in Derbyshire) there was, "woodland not for pasture", just to emphasise the confusion. It all depends, as I have said, on definitions and not on units. And then there is what has been termed 'permaculture' or even 'horticulture', the elision of husbandry with hunter-gathering, the use of woodland pastures, assarts and wide shelter-belts to combine arable, pastoral and woodland cultures. Such survivals were perhaps still possible in 1086 and may have added to the complexities recorded by the Domesday commissioners and their clerks?

SHEEP PASTURE – specifically those pastures beneficial to sheep, maybe even exclusive to their use? Sheep do not damage woodlands but they don't like boggy ground. When sheep are 'folded' on fallows they are, of course, manuring the land and these people have an obsession with manuring and folding, so it is unlikely that a reasonable number of useful sheep kept on the arable of this manor will be of any great interest to the commissioners. However, when pasture is *specifically set aside* for sheep, then someone is making a profit; it is a good thing for the King to know, from his point of view, where profits arise. Even today the rule of thumb of one acre per sheep is a good one, as they are normally pastured on rough and unimproved land, like the moor up there, under the woods, or on the littoral. They are not always beneficial on dedicated pasture-lands.

SWINEWOODS – not all woodlands are suitable for pigs, and the other way about, but those pigs up there have a swine herd with them and we can see his charges (those who survived the winter slaughter) rooting around in spite of the snow, so no-one is worried about the trees there. Swine, of course, can root up and eat just about anything, so they are the enemies of the coppice wood. But where there are pollarded trees or maybe mature oaks or beeches rooted in a forest 'lawn' they can do no damage to the precious tree resource. Indeed when the autumn is right, a fall of acorns or beech mast will fatten them up in no time, ready for slaughtering: it is good pannage. Of course, swinewoods like sheep pastures betoken a *deliberate enterprise* for profit, at two acres per pig. The peasant's pig is unlikely to be included in this, he is simply a garbage converter and one essential for the peasant's survival, so the pigs recorded are on the demesnes or pastures.

SWINE PASTURES – in Sussex and Surrey they speak of pastures not swinewoods, but they are much the same, specific areas used for farming pigs as opposed to the peasant's pig in its sty or tethered on the village green.

SWINE-RENDERS – in Sussex they also make 'renders', that is they pay an in-kind rent to the owner of the swine pasture, which is a useful thing for him *and* useful for the King to know.

UNDERWOOD & WOOD PASTURE – in Huntingdonshire and Derbyshire they use these terms instead of swine pasture, which is sensible as sheep or cattle can also be 'agisted' on the ground set aside for pig pannage. It all depends on market forces, one doesn't want to miss the wood for the trees, does one?

WOODLANDS – how shall we know the difference between wood and trees? Over on our left are coppice woods, closed to all grazing, rooting and browsing animals. By the river the trees are pollarded. Coppice woods contain valuable crops of coppice poles mixed in with larger standard trees and need to be protected. So, not all trees are woods for pigs (or even for sheep) and in some places they do not even distinguish any difference. Woodland, they say is woodland, nice and simple, or is it? How do *you* define a wood? How many trees to the acre, what sort of trees, how mature should they be and what about bushes, underwood and bracken in between. How do *you* distinguish between a 'common' and a 'wood'? The easiest solution to such knotty problems is to take linear measurements each way (this can be easily done, even on irregular shapes) and say it is 'so much woodland' – either singly or double linearly expressed – that is, for so many acres: thus one cuts the 'Gordian knot'. The single linear expression is probably estimated as a length x one unit (viz. 'two leagues' = 2 x 1 leagues) and the moorland and rocks in the middle are incidental for the real meaning is, 'not cultivable'. If it is fit for *nothing* (but hunting over) it generally says so and in the West Country we have 'moorlands'. In Oxfordshire they even defined 'spinnies' of 8 acres, 'groves' of 2x2 acres or 3x3 furlongs, as well as 'woods' down to 20 acres.

Woods 'for fencing', or 'a spinny', are accidental inclusions in Domeday Book, they keep the manor working but they are not profitable. Sometimes an entry included 'royal forest' or 'demesne forest' (there is an important legal difference here) but such entries are mere luck. The King accounted to no one for his own properties. When in Oxfordshire we learn that he had 9 x 9 leagues and 4.5 hides (= 325,080 acres, note the precision) for his own hunting use, the precision of the entry is important because he is laying claim to sole *hunting rights* over all this land (some 56% of this shire in 1086). Woe-betide any usurper, any poacher, lord or no lord, owner of the soil or no! There may, or may not, be many trees. One imaginative chief tenant at Rayleigh (Essex) disguised his own woodland preserves (without saying whether they included arable assarts) as 'a park for woodland beasts … now one parkland and six arpents of vineyard', a neat little fudge. Another at Ware (Hertfordshire) had a park and four arpents. In Bedfordshire they extracted bog iron from boggy woodlands and they paid their dues in iron; 300 years later Caxton (in his 'Description of Britain') claimed as much for a lake "near Winchester". In front of us we now have the frozen river.

WATERS – in among the reeds it is hard frozen but in the deep water of the mill pool the draw of the wheel has kept the centre of the river clear. Of course, Domesday Book also recorded terraqueous appurtenances in many places, but the logic applied is always local. No one was enforcing a standard vocabulary for fishing. Rents for waters are mostly paid in eels or in money with an apparent conversion of four eels to the acre of water and one silver penny to seventy eels. In Shropshire we hear of the 'stick' of eels, said to be 25 in number. No doubt eels and lampreys were all the same for most purposes?

In some areas, instead of fisheries, there are whole territories (like our 'hunting rights') over which there were rights to fish. In Wyfold Hundred in Berkshire there were 23 square miles of fishing rights over an area now measured at 23 square miles. At Ganfield in Berkshire similar rights covered 25.5 square miles over an area now measured at 25.125 square miles. They were pretty good at measuring in 1086 and we can bet our miller knows *exactly* the area of his waters and the yield in fish and eels to be expected in an average year. This is a very comfortable, balanced and profitable landscape even if it is cold, but the people who live here aren't fools or bumpkins. Give them security and they will make a good living *and* turn a penny. The pennies, however, go to the sheriff for the King's taxes, like as not. Rich and poor alike resent the geld, but they fear the Vikings even more!

CASTLES – look up there, on the crest of the far slope, what do you see? Is it a crude stockade or a thatched cottage? No, on an artificial mound (motte) stands a solid, wooden boxwork, just like the castles pictured in the Bayeux Tapestry (and *not* like a Wild West stockade). No-one will get into that in a hurry and, judging by the wood smoke, it's lovely and warm inside. Still, if Vikings do turn up the garrison will have to send out a flying column.

There were few castles mentioned in Domesday Book and the impregnable ones, Colchester and London, built of stone, are not mentioned at all. But then, as we have said, the King didn't need a record of what he owned, he knew that. He needed to know what everyone else claimed to hold from him as honest subjects. He owned the Kingdom and, after all, not everyone was telling him the truth when it came to taxes. That is how our story begins, with a search for 'the truth', just as we too seek the truth.

VALUES – are (next to people) *the* most fascinating pieces of historical information, everyone wants to know rents and commodities in order to prove how affluent we are today and thus 'superior'. Sadly conversion scales are notoriously difficult and they are *not* the business of this book. Therefore I will only include this note in order to assuage curiosity, though I am far from confident about the results.

It all comes down to relative purchasing power and just how *do* you calculate such things when there is *no like for like* comparison, for example no tomatoes or potatoes, when spices (though not herbs) were so much more expensive and when silver is, today, comparatively so plentiful and cheap? One can only crudely calculate such basics as bread, cheese, beef, beer, barley, wheat, oats, peas and beans. Farmyard fowls were scarcer (because not intensively reared), beef was common (thanks to stotts), 'keeping cheese' was more expensive (as hand worked produce), cloth was tremendously labour intensive to produce, unskilled and semi-skilled labour was cheap (hours were long and few were idle), fresh and salt water fish and fowl were plentiful but rabbits and pigeons were farmed and so protected, premises were unrated and homes largely self built, daub and thatch were free and handcrafts common place, bloodstock was prohibitively expensive and pigs were unrestricted garbage converters. Back in 1980 I concluded (and many will dispute this) that a silver penny in 1086 (1d) probably had a purchasing power value of £30.00, so a shilling was equivalent to about £360.00 and a pound sterling about £7,200.00! The coinage was, of course, made of silver and its value was more than a few pounds to the ounce, thanks to supply and demand. Vikings didn't work for peanuts, peanuts didn't exist.

Since 1980 inflation has pushed most prices up maybe sevenfold, property (up to September 2008) increased tenfold, but in 1980 terms a (not uncommon) 1086 manorial value was around £150,000.00 p.a. If this was 'income', pause for a moment and consider the total value of 34 English shires? To add it all up was certainly beyond 11th century 'systems limits', which is why major accounts aggregated sums. Domesday Book has no 'bottom line' yet we could attempt it today. I hope someone will. I have heard '£73,000' banded about – say £525,600,000 p.a. in 1980 values but I think this is probably low. Neither did they have our inflation fuelled by purposeless pursuits of pleasure and indulgence wrapped in paper promises and fed by usury. In the meantime my business is to prove to you that we can now recover *real history* because we can now read the statistics; we must find the truth and render it certain, then everything else will fall into place. "Certum est quod certum…", as the lawyers say.

CHAPTER THREE

OCCAM'S RAZOR

The principle behind this book was first set down in the 14th century and it has upset bigots (including 'bigot servientes') ever since. As there are no reasons (or grounds) to hypothesise anything which can be readily interpreted without resorting to assumptions, one simply disregards all twaddle in order to start again from what is known. Most problems are solved by this simple expedient: go back to first principles and use your common sense.

Domesday Book, all the academics will tell you, is not a subject for the beginner, it is just too intellectual and abstruse. How very flattering for the cognicenti, how very convenient for deflecting enquiry. Well, these same clever, academic people can tell you very little about the new world we have just entered, beyond the wardrobe, other than to say that any numerical reconciliation between 1086 and 1886 or 1986 *must* be coincidence as *simple arithmetic isn't possible*. As Douglas Adams said, 'where there is a discrepancy between the 'Guide' and reality, reality has got it wrong'[8]. Clever chap that Douglas Adams. So, in 2008, we have now arrived at the stage where most people can see no practical purpose in studying Medieval history, with all its inventions and fantasies, and most universities seem dedicated to proving that these critics are right! Standing by our frozen water meadow and river let us take a giant pin and puncture the bubble of delusion; we stick it into our frozen picture and it vanishes, poof, the perpetual winter 'and never Christmas' dissolves and instead we have sunlight, leaves and people. This is not a frozen frame any more for with our units *we* can begin to travel in time and space. Let's make some maps, as if we were flying over England in a helicopter in 1086. Off we go.

Using our conversions from chapter 2 we will make tables of statistics. This isn't as bad as it sounds. These tabulations we will then compare to Victorian county surveys, surveys that contain statistics of their own (directories are very good sources) and then we will 'place' our Victorian statistics on to Victorian, one-inch, Ordnance Survey maps. Finally if we place our Domesday statistics onto these same map matrices we will find what we are looking for. No problem, you will say, historians and archaeologists always find what they are looking for and that is, of course, true. Well, in many cases we will find that areas and units at all the three dates we mentioned above coincide (1086, 1886, 1986), often broadly and sometimes exactly, while discrepancies can usually be reconciled after a little work in the local record office examining 16th, 17th or 18th century evidence, such as old estate maps. Of course definitions can change with people and with cultures, our much laboured 'woodland' is a good example, but events like the Napoleonic Wars also caused major changes, for example massive woodland clearances to make way for an increase in cereal farming. But many of these changes changed again, even maybe rebalanced, while in some places nothing changed much, even over thousands of years. In Essex there were 'relict' landscapes still around in the early 20th century whose field and track boundaries had remained the same since the Iron Age, or the Roman or the Medieval periods, though *had* the ditches and hedges been abandoned (for even a generation) these features would have vanished for ever![9] When woods are felled their boundaries may remain; sometimes even modern housing developments follow ancient field boundaries. Land is sold in parcels and often according to those ancient boundaries which originally defined the parcels. Above all, the terra firma, the local area, doesn't move, *it is always there.* Let us just hold on to this fact, however incredible it may seem that people in the past could count or measure! We have to discard our indoctrination in order to perceive the truth.

ESSEX – THE WITHAM HUNDRED.

If we aggregate the areas of 'woodland', 'arable', 'meadow', as entered for the whole of this hundred in 1066, we can recover 30,135.5 acres. In 1845[10] the hundred was surveyed at 36,000 acres and in 1894[11] at 35,000 acres: so we can see that there were discrepancies even in the 19th century, due to boundary changes and due to bureaucracy. Moreover, in 1066 we cannot find two of the manors or parishes (we can usually treat these as synonymous and call them 'estates') listed in 1845 and in 1894 so, *if we now subtract* these two (in 1894 called parishes and not manors) from the 1845 and 1894 totals, we find that (hey presto) 1066 and the 19th century have become (for all practical purposes) identical in names and in acreage! Remember, according to the clever people *such coincidences just aren't possible*. It must be a fluke. Really, we just did it *and we'll do it again*.

If we now look at the manors of Ulting, Hatfield Peverel, Witham, the Braxteds, Rivenhall and the Coggeshalls in 1066 and then at the same parishes in 1845/1894, we find that they are very close in area despite changes which must

Estates	Hidation	Arable+Woods+ Meadows in 1066	Recent Parishes	
			1845	1894
Ulting	285	1060		1162
Small Lands	480	129		
Hatfield Peverel	3957	4450	3830	4746
Howbridge Hall	720	903		
Benton Hall	255	480		
Blunts Hall	720	504		
Witham	1491	3004½	3280	3633
Powers Hall	960	486		
Braxteds	980	2365	2920	3231
Terling	1340	1502	4190	3220
Ridley Hall	270	204		
Fairstead	70	720	1590	
Faulkbourne	367½	485		1151
Rivenhall	1025	2869½	3240	3601
Kelvedon	2040	2170	3160	3101
Coggeshalls	1091	3758	3600	3600
(Bradwell – jC)			3210	1161
(Cressing)			2960	2519
Notleys	1912	5045½	4390	4164
Slampseys	15			
Totals:	**17978½ acres**	**30135½ acres**	**36370a.**	**35289a.**
(less Bradwell and Cressing)		30135½	30200	31609

The Witham Hundred

necessarily have occurred in the centuries in between. As we have said, things rebalance themselves over the years, though clever people won't believe this.

Now for the information of especial use to King William. The hidation of 1066, the area admitting liability for taxation, was broadly 81% of the arable land we have entered here and so some areas were going untaxed whilst others were over rated and over taxed. While 73% of the 1066 area was being used for arable farming only 60% was paying hidation, so more (geld) *could* be had and more ploughs might be employed and those were some of the specific questions set out by the king. Obviously the change of owners had not improved production. It also suggests that these Saxon farmers were not amateurs if they were successfully farming so much of their land.

ESSEX – THE HARLOW HUNDRED

Estates	Hidation	Arable+Woods+ Meadows in 1066	Recent Parishes.	
			1851	1898
Epping (Part)	390	388		
North Weald	725	5089		3423
(Nettleswell)			1830	1552
Latton	2220	2705	1380	1625
Roydon	2700	1992	2995	3031
Parndons	2320	2169	2970	2751
Harlow	1670	2897	4490	4015
Sub Total		**15240**	**17065**	**16397**
Matching	680	1299	} 2530	2416
Housham Hall	600	996		
Sheering	1230	952	} 1520	1646
Quickbury	720	680		
Hatfield Bd. Oak	5412	7720	} 8810	8810
Ryes	120	163½		
Hallingburys	1760	4722	} 4251	4344
Wallbury	240	584		
Sub Total		17116½	17111	17126
Grand Total	**20787 acres**	**32356½ acres**	**34176a**	**33613a**
(Less Nettleswell)		32356½ acres	32346a	32016a

Doing the same calculation for this hundred we find that in 1066 it returned 32,356.5 acres and in 1851/1898[12] was surveyed as 33–34,000 acres. However, we find that the place called Netteswell was not listed in 1066, so once again we subtract it to find (hey presto) that in 1851/1898 this area was identical to its area in 1066 (as near as 'cossit' is to 'dammit', as my grandfather used to say).

The burden of taxation, hidation, was just larger than the arable at 64%. Maybe they had once been the same? North Weald (next to Epping Forest) had a lot of 'woodland' but had also taken in a lot of arable, more than it was paying for. Latton and the Parndons appear to have been declaring their total areas and not just their arable for hidation, for their arable areas were only 33% and 50%. In other words, for some reason they followed their own logic and not that of their fellows. And in the centre of the hundred, the arable was being intensively worked.

ESSEX – THE WALTHAM HUNDRED

Here a comparison between 1086 and 1845 reveals a hidation of 75% but an arable of only 35%. At Waltham itself 48–49% was under the plough compared with only 42% of Epping and Nazeing in 1066, which by 1086 had fallen to 36%. But then the King 'loved the tall stags as though he were their father' and so in 1086 no recommendations were made to restore the missing ploughs. Anyway not everyone wanted to live next to a royal game preserve where the royal game beasts were allowed to destroy crops with impunity: this was the reality of the king laying claim to areas over which he hunted, forest law. Here the deer took precedence, they could eat your wheat.

In 1066/1086 we find the 'woodlands' of this hundred (Waltham) stated as 3,208 acres. In 1777 Chapman and André published an accurate map of Essex and using this we can put together the woodlands, commons and 'greens' of Waltham (Epping) Forest (those found in the Waltham Hundred), in about 1777, to total 3,360 acres. Not bad, eh, over 700 years? Then we can look even more closely at the 650 acres of Nazeing Marsh in 1086, which appear to have been the '669 acres of Cowleazes' listed by Fisher in 1887[13].

ESSEX – THE CLAVERING HALF HUNDRED

In 1066 Clavering with Langley, Berden, Farnham, Manuden and Ugley were totalled as 13,661 acres and as this 'half hundred'. In 1851 the same area was surveyed at 14,161 acres but by 1899 it had shrunk to 13,991 acres due to changes on paper. Once again, not so dusty, but the best is yet to come in the heart of the shire.

Estates	Arable+Woods+ Meadows in 1066	Recent Parishes	
		1851	1899
Clavering with Langley	5715	5417	5526
Berden	502	1570	1796
Farnham	1894	1966	2018
Manuden (with Peyton and Pinchpools)	2288	2488	2531
Ugley (with Bollington Hall)	3262	2720	2120
Totals	**13661 acres**	**14161 acres**	**13991 acres**
Bentfield (later in Uttlesford Hundred)	1646		472
Pledgedon Hall (later in Freshwell, then Uttlesford Hundreds)	1530	1190	
Total	**16837 acres**		

The Clavering Half Hundred

ESSEX – THE CHELMSFORD HUNDRED

In 1086 the Chelmsford Hundred returned 86,800 acres. In 1875[14] it was surveyed at 86,650 acres. Manors and parishes also conform rather well between these two survey dates, though in 1875 we can trace 'detachments' (parcels of land administratively belonging to another hundred) so we suspect that 'detachments' or 'berewicks', of special agricultural use, may have had a very long history, maybe right back to Saxon times? Such parcels of land might well account for some of the small differences in totals that we see from time to time in the intervening centuries, if only because people sold their parcels of land? Here, at Chelmsford, we can plot parish and berewick boundaries, woodlands

Place Name/Parish		Area in Acres		Reconstructed Areas
		1875	1086	1086
Springfield	SP	2900	1800	1000a. were in Chelmsford
Chelmsford, Moulsham, Galleywod & Widford	CM	3550	5700	+ 1000 +1100a. later in Springfield & Writtle
Writtle & Roxwell	WR	13300	11000	1100a. were in Chelmsford
Boreham & Walkfares	BW	3800	5000	+ 1200a. later in the Leighs
The Leighs	L	4200	2800	1200a. were in Boreham
Broomfield & Patching	BP	2300	3260	+ 500a. later in the Chignalls
The Chignalls	C	2000	1500	500a. were in Broomfield
The Walthams	W	9700	7700	
The Baddows	B	6600	6300	
Sandon (Bedenested)	S	2300	2610 }	300a. of Sandon's woods physically situated in Danbury in 1086.
Danbury (& Berewic)	D	3000	2600 }	
Rettendon	RE	3900	5400	
Runwell	RU	2000	3780	
Stock	ST	1800 }		+ 400a. later in Margaretting and Ingatestone
The Hanningfields	H	6900 }	9000	
Margaretting, Ingatestone and Fryerning	MIF	5000	4600	400a. were in Hanningfields
Mountnessing, Cowbridge & Blackmore	MC &B	6800	6350	
Buttsbury	BU	2100	2400	
Woodham Ferrers	WF	4500	5000	500a., later a detachment of Dengy Hundred, incl. in 1086
Totals		86650a.	86800a.	

The Chelmsford Hundred

mapped in the 18th and 19th centuries, roads of proven antiquity and even some traces of relict landscape around Moulsham and Baddow, all sorts of corroborative evidence. We can, in fact, *produce a one-inch to the mile map of Domesday Chelmsford!*

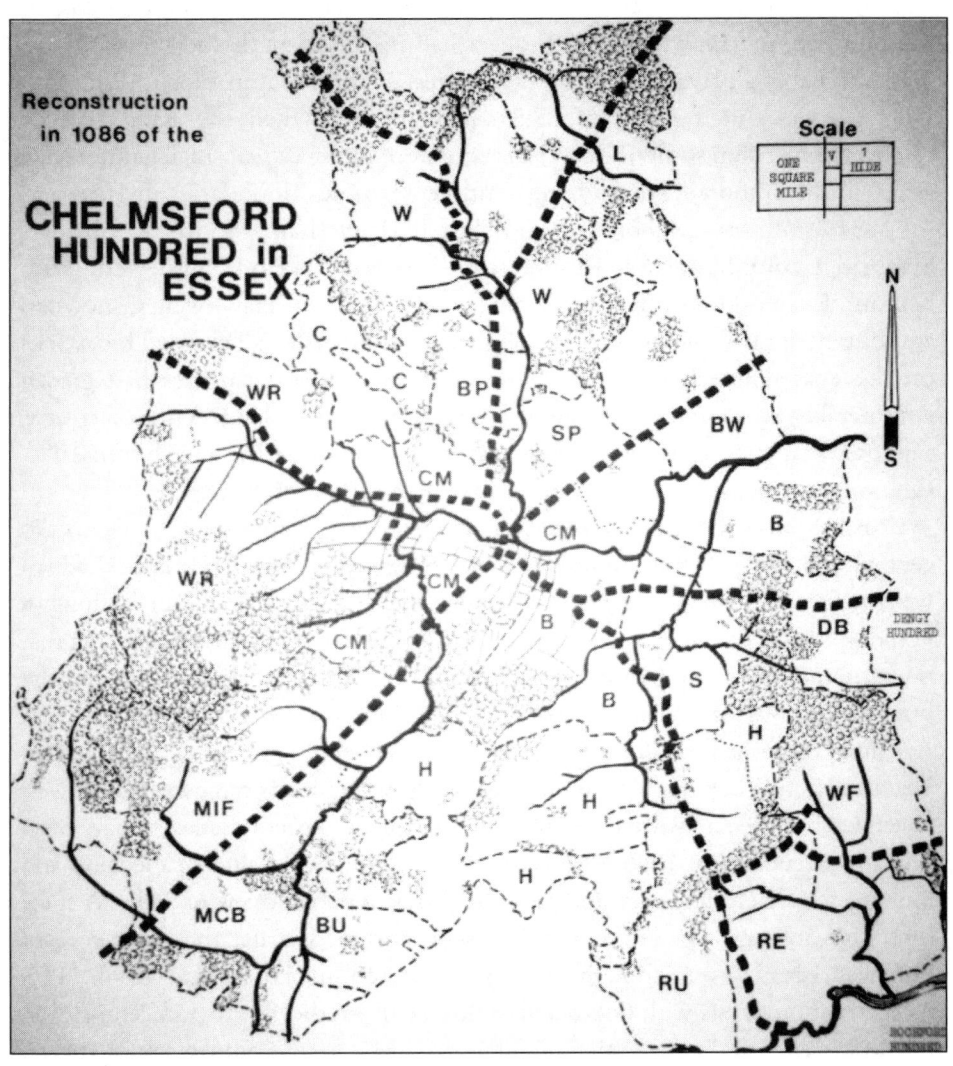

ESSEX – THE ROCHFORD HUNDRED

Now that we have accomplished the impossible we will go south. Here we are going to have rather *more* fun as its much indented, marshy coastline (on two sides) is supposed to have been extensively reclaimed in recent centuries, so how can we *possibly* reconcile Domesday with any Victorian statistics? Well, it will make a test, won't it? Have helicopter will travel.

We find that in 1086 there were 36,053 acres enrolled but by 1851 the area was surveyed at 45,400 acres: well, 80% isn't a bad start. Smack in the middle of the hundred, in 1086, Suen fitz Robert had his castle, park and vineyard, the 'park' probably a private forest of 5,600 acres. We find that in North Wales Earl Hugh carved out a forest of 67.5 square miles (which the King's survey discovered in 1086) so fitzRobert's nine miles of preserve was small game. Once again, in this hundred, we find apparently coterminus boundaries in 1086 and in 1851, such as Shoebury, Southchurch, Paglesham, South Fambridge, Stanbridge and Shopland. In the later Medieval period Prittlewell (with Milton), Eastwood, Ashingdon, Rochford, Hockley and Hawkwell, Canewden and Putsey, the Wakerings, Barling, Leigh and Thundersley all claimed berewicks on the coastal marshes. By 1851 the areas of all these parishes had grown considerably, so perhaps they grew on reclaimed marshland? This, of course, supposes that they were not just hiding the existence of the marshes in 1086. One might well ask what use a lot of marsh and mud might be?

Apart from woodlands and roads, including those we have found shown on 17th century estate maps[15], this hundred also had an extensive relict landscape by which we may frame a map or topography. Only on the east does it peter out, nothing of Foulness Island (or of Canvey on the south) can be detected in 1086, nothing that is but mention of sheep pastures which could equally be here or in Kent (over the water): we know some 'detachments' were in Kent in the 19th century and in 1086 Aylesford Lathe had pasture for 200 sheep 'in Essex' but appurtenant to Chalk in Shamwell hundred, Kent. If we remember that Mersey Island's causeway (north west Essex) has been securely dated to c.690 A.D, we might expect Foulness to have been similarly occupied by 1086[16]. Now, by plotting the areal value of the hide and looking for the boundaries and seawalls shown on old maps to help us trace successive 'innings', we can actually guess-fit and reconstruct the older core of Foulness Island, even though it is not entered in Domesday Book. This reconstruction attests with documentary sources from the 13th to 15th centuries to provide a very good guess-estimate of the original core of Foulness Island. It is an interesting question whether we should add our guess-estimate to the enrolment for the Rochford Hundred in 1086 or, as it was more readily accessible from the north by water, to the Dengy Hundred? Water was the fastest highway.

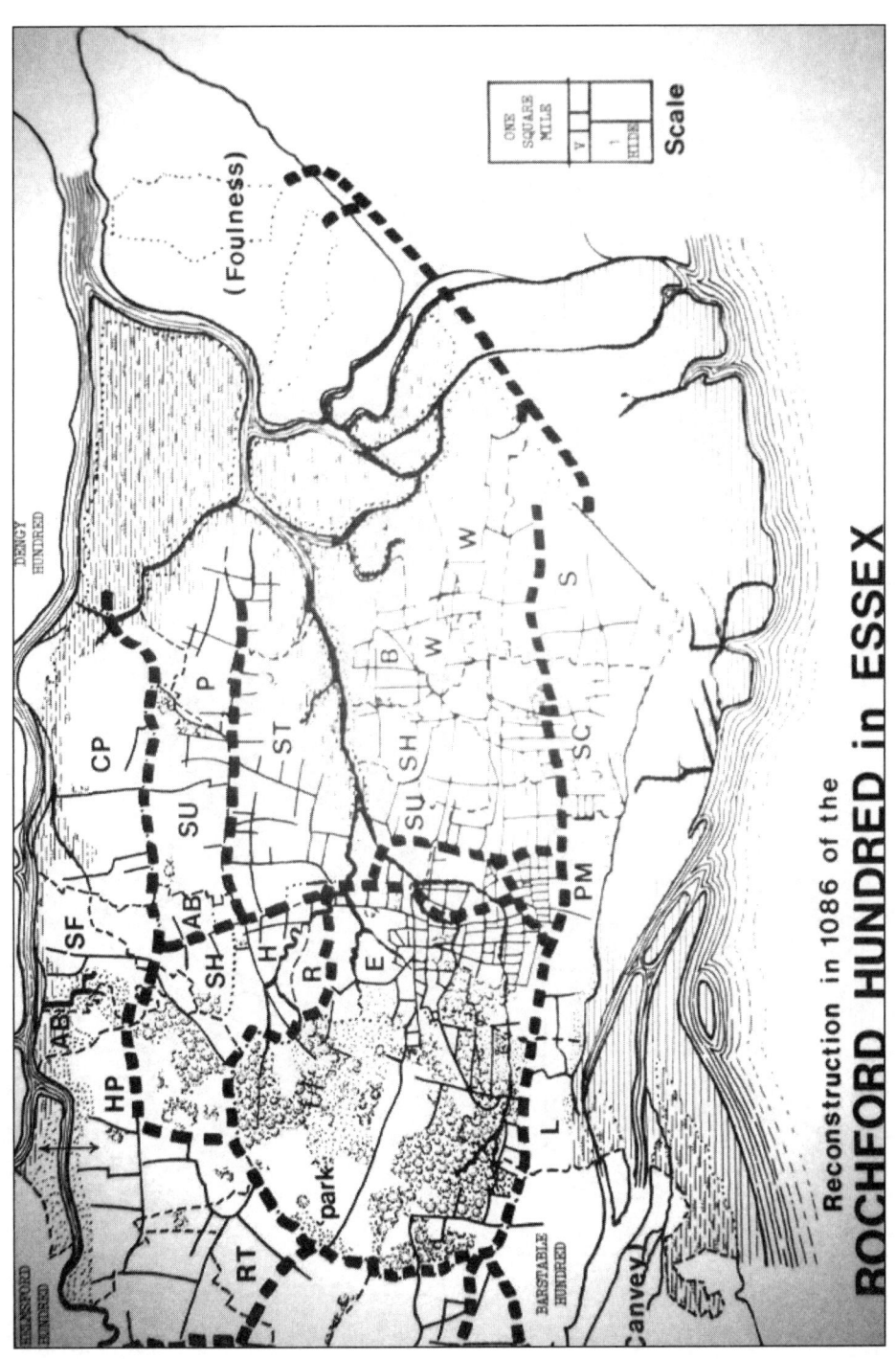

Reconstruction in 1086 of the

ROCHFORD HUNDRED in ESSEX

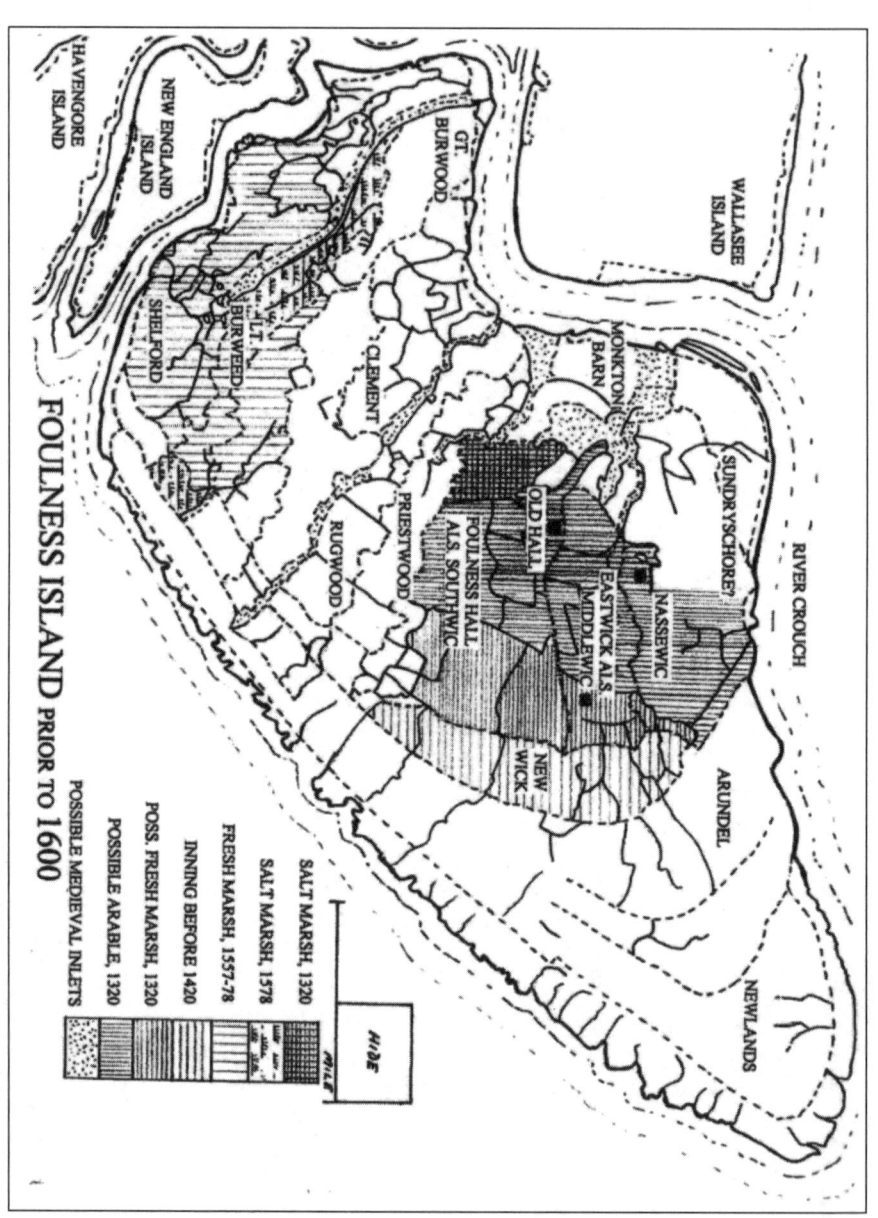

FOULNESS ISLAND PRIOR TO 1600

HAVENGORE ISLAND

NEW ENGLAND ISLAND

SHELFORD

GT. BURWOOD

LT. BURWEED

CLEMENT

PRIESTWOOD

RUGWOOD

MONKTON BARN

OLD HALL

FOULNESS HALL ALS. SOUTHWIC

MIDDLEWIC

EASTWICK ALS

NASSEWIC

NEW WICK

SUNDRYSCHOREY

WALLASEE ISLAND

RIVER CROUCH

ARUNDEL

NEWLANDS

SALT MARSH, 1320
SALT MARSH, 1578
FRESH MARSH, 1557-78
INNING BEFORE 1420
POSS. FRESH MARSH, 1320
POSSIBLE ARABLE, 1320
POSSIBLE MEDIEVAL INLETS

MILE

HIDE

ESSEX – THE DENGY (WITBRICTESHERN) HUNDRED

This was another marshy habitat in 1086, then (as now) generally devoid of woodlands and, like Rochford, today heavily evidenced by a relict landscape. In this hundred, though, we discover an alternative logic at work for here the hundred court and the inhabitants did not think like the men of Chelmsford *or* of Rochford, they also were quite individual. Rackham touched on this paradox when he asked why some shires had so many bridge names in 1086 while others did not?[17] Why (he asked) was it that heath names were absent in some places and moorlands were only found in the West Country? He noticed the etymology of 'leah' and 'maed' *but he fell into the trap* of assuming universal definitions of terms in 1086 (which would need to be supported by some universal education and accepted textbooks). We know better and we do not make such assumptions. In fairness to him, we have a carefully tabulated and mapped arithmetic for our framework (which he did not have) so, for him, the logical parallax was not apparent. For him the accepted view was that nothing could reconcile (perhaps because there were no village schools to teach such units), so numbers were never challenged and assumptions never questioned, yet it is this dynamic which ultimately enlarges human knowledge. What we are looking at is evidence of the logic of those thought processes which distinguish one group of men from another, processes which in time must be agreed with other groups if common problems *are* to be solved. What follows below is how men worked out the problem of the coast for themselves in the Dengy Hundred in 1086, and they did it *in a different way* to the men of Rochford.

In 1086 the area of the Hundred came to 79,246 acres but in 1875 the surveyed area was only 60,000 acres. Why? Well in 1086 the total (enrolled) agricultural asset (as we might call it) was only 42,080 acres with perhaps another 5,010 acres of sheep pastures. The largest woodland, inland at Purleigh, was only 458 acres (used for sheep). All in all this amounts to 70% of the 1875 surveyed area yet, still, *we* will not accept this as satisfactory for it leaves us with 19,000 acres missing, an area for which the hundred court was prepared to 'answer' (and pay taxes) in 1086 and, thanks to our other examples, we now expect greater accuracy, at least in this shire. No, 70% accuracy will *not* do. Once again we should ask why the totals are not closer, as close as elsewhere?

If we make an estimate of the littoral area, mostly to the east of the hundred, we do have an area of fresh marshes, especially those defined by a geological feature known as the Shingle Ridge (viz. not salt but inned marshes) and its mudflats, something like 19,000 acres in all, even more of which was inned or reclaimed in later centuries. Can we validate this? Well, looking at Southminster we see only 6,300 acres of land in 1875 whereas it was said to be 12,830 acres in 1086, yet here we have the widest belt of mud and salt marshes on this whole coast and *the mud could not have been less* in 1086. Well, why not the mud? In the reign of Edward IV Tillingham had 4,000 acres of arable, 3,000 acres of "moor and pastures", *4,000 acres of marsh* plus various messuages and tofts[18]. In 1086 it had had 5,200 acres (of which 2,480 were under cultivation) and 400 acres of sheep pastures. If (for argument's sake) we add to these an estimated 4,000 acres of foreshore or marshes (which is the recent area of mud and salt marsh) we can then propose a grand total of 10,000 acres for 1086: thus (in summary) by c.1480 this had become 11,500 acres. Not so bad? No, say the scoffers, it is contrived for *we* cannot be proved wrong and *we* say it is nonsense. Well, without even making Foulness a berewick of Dengy we can certainly account for the 19,000 acres we seek.

There is one further piece of evidence for this paradigm. As late as 1786 (700 years after Domesday) there was still no Ordnance Datum. As a result the County of Essex was actually estimated as a quarter of a million acres *larger* than its surveyed area was to be in the 20th century. This was because the Admiralty was *including foreshore and salt marshes below even the present limit of habitable land throughout the county*, and so I rest my case for mud. It all depends on your definitions of 'land' and 'water'?

What *does* this inclusion of mudflats mean? From other sources we know that the Saxon interpretation of 'divine intervention' was quite literal. Shipwrecked vessels, flotsam, jetsam *and* mariners were there by divine will and in 1086 slavery (in its true sense) had only just been abolished under English law. Thanks to Vikings, traders were only allowed to come ashore at specified ports, where they paid dues. The 'ordinances' of the city of Chester exemplify the shipping fines and forfeits at a recognised port. Landing outside a port was highly dangerous. At Saltfleet (Lincolnshire) Domesday tells us that, "the sergeant receives the customary dues of ships which come, willingly and unwillingly…and they began this as a new practice…", so others had the same idea. Viewed through a dark glass the dangerous Essex coastline by Buxey and inshore of the Gunfleet Banks, with prevalent winter easterlies, was a *very profitable appurtenance* to whoever owned the foreshore rights .In this hundred everything had a price and what had a price had had (at some time) to pay taxes, so the men of the hundred were prepared to pay for a lucrative perquisite in order to retain it. Maybe they were wreckers and ghouls, but they were honest men to the King. Would that his other subjects were so tractable about land, profits and taxes!

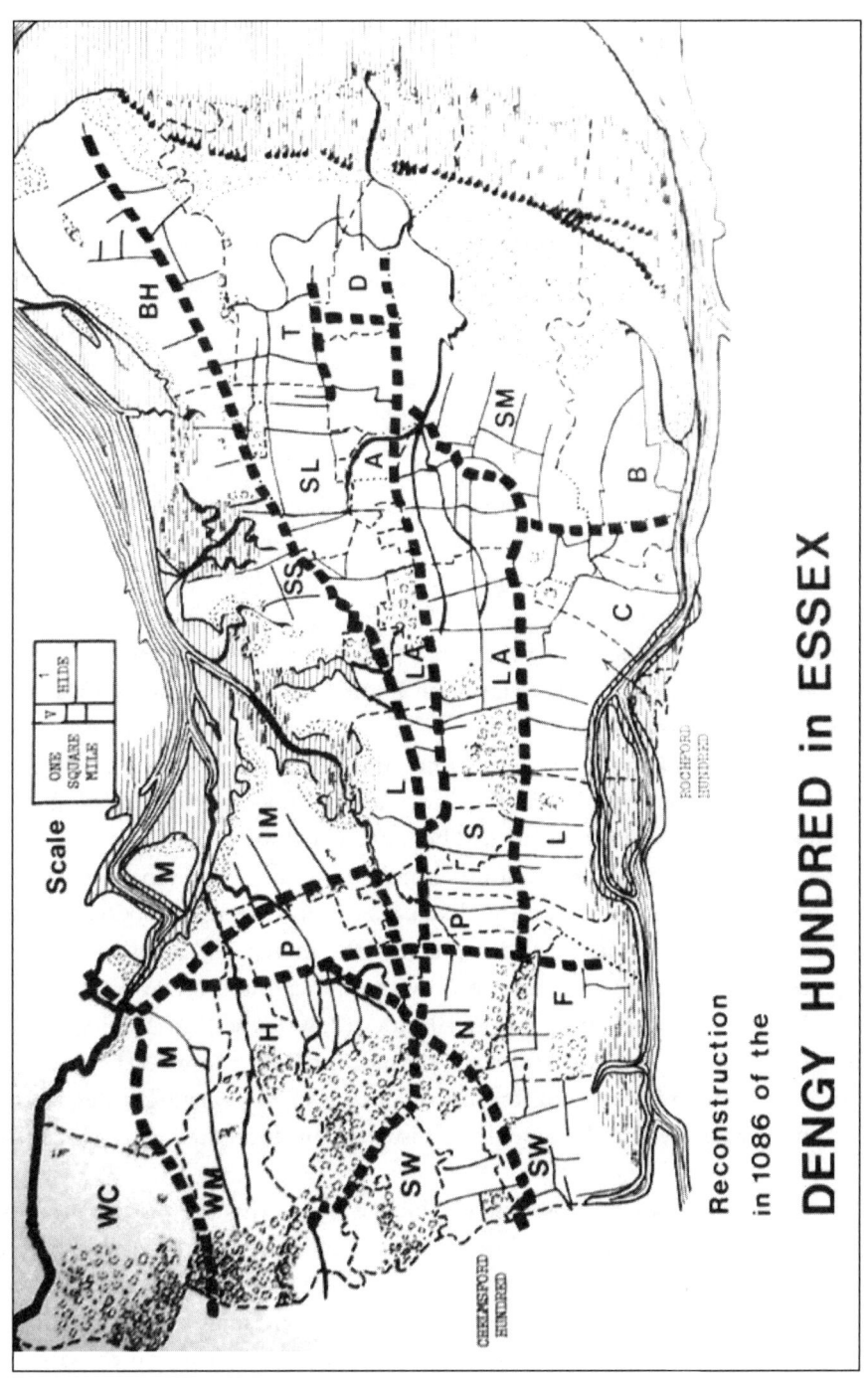

Scale

| ONE SQUARE MILE | V | 1 HIDE |

Reconstruction
in 1086 of the

DENGY HUNDRED in ESSEX

ROCHFORD HUNDRED

CHELMSFORD HUNDRED

ESSEX – COLCHESTER

At Colchester, outside the town in 1086, the Bishop of London held two hides, one acre and 6½ acres of meadow, some 487 ½ acres. In c.1900 the Bishop of London held St. Mary-at-the-Walls as 487½ acres. Round identified this estate as the Domesday entry in 1903 and the Phillimore edition of 'Essex' confirmed it[19]. It provides a remarkable example of continuity but it was ignored in 1903 because the indemonstrable hypothesis had already been adopted and acclaimed.

ESSEX – SOUTHCHURCH

In 1086 the Holy Trinity (Canterbury) manor of Southchurch, like its neighbour Milton, had no mesne lordship but the 14 villeins there had 6 ploughs of their own and 2 with which they supplied the convent (viz 720+240 acres of tillage) while the monks answered for 4 hides (960 acres); there were also 200 acres of sheep pasture and 2 fisheries on the shore (still recorded in the 16th century) as well as 80 acres of woods. Her neighbour, Thorpe Hall, had a mesne lord and 4 villeins with 240+360 acres of tillage and the lordship answered for 600 acres. There were also 100 acres of sheep pasture and 120 acres of woods: in all 2,060 acres in the two estates. The 1851 Directory listed 1,800 acres of land 'and some land on Canvey Island' (which last had been recorded since the 13th century and was at 'Leigh Beck'). Adjacent to Southchurch and Thorpe were three entries for the Shoeburys, where lordship tillage had varied a little between 1066 and 1086: in total the 1086 demesnes had 630 acres and the men 1,320 acres which, with sheep pastures, woods and a small meadow, came to a grand total of 2,057 acres. Altogether these estates paid geld on 10 hides (2,400 acres). In 1845 and 1851 Kelly's Directory recorded 2,500 acres though by 1933 the recorded area was 2,133 acres with 4,621 acres of foreshore. We thus have a very tight description and confirmation by which to begin to visualise this local area in 1086, can we do better?

Southchurch is one of those rare localities where early documents *can* supply a picture intermediate between Domesday and today. The Tithe Award map of 1839 supplies us with a detailed landscape, each field and pightel measured and named, and from this we can produce a 12" to the mile survey valid for the late 18th and early 19th centuries. However, in 1687, consequent upon the division of the manor of Southchurch Hall (a 12th century mesne lordship whose eponymous family became extinct at the Black Death) c.1660 to form 'Hall' and

'Wick' estates, an estate map of the new 'Southchurch Hall' division of lands had also been produced. This excluded Thorpe and the centre of the village but gave the names and measures of the parcels of land recorded, enabling us to fix part of the older vill and its southern field systems and then compare them with the Tithe map in order to verify that when field names changed, their areas usually did not. It shows us that the newly formed 'Southchurch Wick' farm was *originally* situated in the village (though the structural evidence of the building erected half a mile away in the middle of its new estate confirmed, prior to its demolition in 1980, a date at the very end of the 17th century) and that field names sometimes changed in order to exaggerate their areas when they were sold. By a further stroke of good fortune the Cathedral records at Canterbury include a 1508 deed where properties are fixed by a terrier which partly overlaps and also infills the central, or village, area shown in 1687. From all these records we can tentatively discern the tofts of the 14 medieval villeins as well as the common fields, roads, fresh marshes and woods of the vill and so gain an impression of the Domesday landscape, even before the establishment of the 12th century manor house. Sadly, recent researchers have chosen to ignore these details and documents, which do not support their 'accepted view' of local history based on the indemonstrable hypothesis. It is a common response and that is why archaeological reports rarely include Domesday or analyse early documents. Why, even ensuring that the cover of the report is not a mirror image may prove to be too demanding!

KENT – EASTRY LATHE

The lathes of Kent were equivalent to the hundreds of other shires while her hundreds were mere sub-divisions. As we have seen, for good ethnic reasons, Kent used her own units, not the hide but the sulung, though arable estimates, meadows, woods and pastures were recorded much as they were in other shires. The sulungation (= hidation) of Eastry totalled some 60,053 acres of which 48,600 acres were under tillage (that is were arable) with a little wood or pasture. In modern times this lathe has been surveyed at 63,500 acres.

Now that Occam's razor has cut through the mumbo-jumbo of this subject we have been able to map parts of one shire at least. We have taken our helicopter across central and south-eastern Essex and looked down upon Normans and Saxons, we have even spoken to the minds of hundredmen who died 900 years ago. We are the first to ever achieve so much, an achievement unthinkable in academia. Even in specifics we have opened up a chapter for the Selden Society in the operation of local (admiralty) courts, "flotson, jetson, lagon and all other strays" and "treasure found *in* the sea", even the application of "mos patrius" (mos patriae) in our elucidation of local definitions for the littoral. But does academia want such knowledge? As I was told thirty years ago, 'just because it works in one place, it won't work in another'. When it worked in several places I was told, 'just because it works in general, doesn't mean it works in particular'. Well we have done a few particulars and something in general, now we will open Pandora's box by looking right across England. It was at this stage thirty years ago that I was told, 'we can't possibly publish anything so lengthy, make it much shorter'. Such is the quality of scholastic debate and peer group review: if it *does* work we can always make sure that it isn't published.

CHAPTER FOUR

PANDORA'S BOX

Are we ready (like Beowulf) to take on the dragons who guard the hoard? Do we feel like the heroes of old? Well having disposed of the details *and* the particulars we will now put "harness on our backs" and go for the general view – maybe not such a pretty picture but a very satisfying set of statistics, as the accountant said of the profits graph on his office wall. I hope that by now the thrill of the chase will help you sustain a rapid fire of statistics, especially those of you familiar with Information Technology, you who pride yourselves on your facility with data? Even if you hate numbers, try to see yourself as a sort of Indiana Jones hacking a way through the statistical jungle to find hidden temples and lost treasures, hard work but ultimately rewarding and always under threat of attack. Yes we will certainly come under attack!

In 1086 the hidation of Essex was equivalent (we can say) to 957,330 acres. In 1156 her hidation was equivalent to 960,000 acres. In between they might even have found a few stray and secret holdings? By 1848 Essex was surveyed at 961,800 acres, displaying a rate of progress of only 2.6 acres per annum in the succeeding 700 years. So sad, the Norman kings had at least averaged another 38 acres per annum! So was 961,800 acres the final total? No, by 1900 it was 985,550 acres. Then, somehow, in the twentieth century we managed to lose ground because by 1955 Essex was only 959,500 acres in extent, back where she began[20]. No, it didn't sink beneath the waves, it was bureaucrats tinkering with boundaries and definitions.

The agricultural acreage (uses for all forms of agriculture) was, of course, less than the total area of the shire and is always a good guide to economic aspirations: 644,040 acres in 1086 and 696,770 acres in 1955. Thus we had a modest increase over 900 years, due (no doubt) entirely to reclamation, technical improvements, 'agrarian revolution' and a splendid war effort? Such is progress. So what do we deduce from these figures? Well, in the first place the actual area of a county comes down to civil servants and administrators fiddling with legal documents, or it does in recent times, because (obviously) landscapes don't actually grow and shrink. So when we look for comparisons we are looking for orders of value and if we can obtain coincidences over, say, 800 years of 75% or thereabouts we are not going to complain, let's be realistic. If we make 98% we will be astonished. In the second place it would appear that our more recent ancestors weren't half so clever as we have been told. Someone, in 1086, was doing very well and if the population was as low as demographers claim, how on earth did they manage it? Something is seriously wrong with the structure of all our history books if these coincidences continue to occur.

Now we will pass to Gloucestershire, which in 1086 was equivalent to 576,720 acres and in 1955 was surveyed at 600,840 acres. Next to Bedfordshire which had 287,430 acres under all agricultural uses in 1086 and yet only 239,910 in 1953. In Dorset in 1086 they made agricultural use of 553,00 acres but by 1955 this had fallen to 429,000 acres. Yes, I said *fallen*, so did boundaries change, did demographic pressures relax, or was the economic incentive much less? Isn't it worrying? Derbyshire is a county with much marginal land, poor soils and moor land, the lovely Peak District is not the best farmland. In 1086 she had 109,000 acres of arable which by 1955 had risen to 153,000 acres, which is a little more reassuring. In 1086 Hampshire with Wight had 356,000 arable acres in spite of extensive royal forests but in 1955, long after agriculture had triumphed over royal prerogative, the total was still only 408,000 acres. Kent may once have been a 'garden' to some gourmets but she has always had some areas of remarkably sour clay soil. Her arable acreage rose from 378,290 acres in 1086 to 437,590 acres by 1955, hooray!

Note how all these figures coincide so remarkably one with another. 'No', say the experts, 'it cannot be, it *must* be wrong', if only because it does not support the fantasy world of early Medieval England so reassuringly invented by historians. Such denials are the syncretism of the historical paraclete. Huntingdonshire rose from 134,400 acres of arable in 1086 to 154,410 by 1955; Oxfordshire rose from 312,960 to 383,030; Sussex *declined* from 375,600 to 328,700 in spite of the supposed reclamation of Romney Marshes. Buckinghamshire's total county area dwindled from 510,230 acres in 1086 to 492,000 in 1150 and to only 479,020 in 1955. Embarrassing as these reflections on agriculture may be (and we could discuss their alternative meanings at some length) the salient feature, or starting point, is that time and again we seem to hit the later reality almost *on the button*. Again and again our Domesday conversions are the orders of magnitude recorded by unimpeachable methodology in relatively recent times. Sooner or later the penny has to drop, even with historians. By Jove, *they* did it! On horse and on foot, as near as we can tell in something like half a year, these people who live inside our wardrobe did it. *They surveyed the lot.* What is more, 'clever people' can't do such a survey even today, ask the BBC how well Michael Wood's school's survey did in 1986? What is more *we can do it*, all by ourselves, we can now read Domesday Book without doctors or professors to tell us anything! We have embarked on a voyage over a sea of figures and *our* ship is sound, whereas the ships of fools always sink.

Bad as these figures are for the pride of agronomists, they are poison to demographers. It is so much easier to rubbish and dismiss such figures than to follow the path I cleared in 1978. Hard evidence takes time and effort, chopping through the jungle. To be fair, there *was* a researcher (someone with friends in the right places who got into print) who suggested that the 1086 arable acreage was 93% of the area under the plough in 1914. Then, realising he had gone too far, he shut up and went no further. *He is still silent.* Now with the evidence of Domesday Book finally deciphered we can no longer argue for a skeleton population in the 11th century. Take Cornwall in 1086, her arable totalled 294,780 acres in theory but her actual ploughed area, her tillage, was only 142,920 acres. Meadows were relatively few, 'pastures' were extensive (344,812 acres) and may have included moor land, yet she also distinguished 37,068 acres of 'woodlands', whatever the actual difference between woods and pastures may have been? And we must remember that whole areas of her northern coast were probably depopulated through fear of Irish pirates and slavers. You know, at 142,920 acres her tillage was even a little greater than the area under tillage in 1954 (139,222 acres); the area under crops *and* grass was 639,592 acres in 1086 and 624,114 acres in 1954. The area of the shire (less its truly barren uplands, presumably) was stated in 1086 to be 676,803 acres but by 1954 it was only 652,000 acres. It seems that men were working hard to use every scrap of cultivable land in 1086, wherever it was safe to live, so the economy *and* the population were booming. In some parts of Suffolk it was also difficult to subsist but where it was fertile men were ploughing up to the limits, as we shall see later (in chapter 7). Why did they do this, when 'primitive' agronomists are supposed to have neither skill nor incentive?

So far I have commended Domesday for its sustainable agriculture and its hidden maps, but history is (essentially) about chaps. For those who want a literal interpretation (and it is 'the bible' to some people) it is embarrassing to see how few women are mentioned. Demographers want us to believe that each villein, bordar, serf (and all the rest) mentioned represents also a wife and some children. Fair enough, but how many? If this *is* the case, are the few women mentioned the only single and 'available' ones? Out of 283,242 people entered[21] only 56 were women (including a 'female jester') a bit rough on the men maybe? No, maybe it was rough on the women? Either way, it isn't likely to be accurate. The problem is that (barring accidental inclusions) the women had to be of some economic value in order to be entered? Men owned property, few women did, so we can say that men had economic value even if they didn't pay geld. On the other hand not all businessmen owned property, especially land, but that *did not* make them poor. Only one man in every 1,600 was a 'pauper' (whatever that meant) but it is doubtful it was a richer society than ours and there were no state benefits. We have to accept that very many people were not entered, not entered because (like the rocky uplands or even, in some places, the mud flats and marshes) *they had no economic value*, or no such value for the purposes of the survey. Domesday is not a convenient modern document compiled by bureaucrats for the sake of spinning out a cushy number under the justification of surveillance paranoia, it was a 'paper' with a purpose directed by a despot and its end was finance not theory, certainly it claimed neither demography nor welfare. Even its topographic value was subservient to financial scrutiny, because the origins of its method had focussed on money. We shall come to all this again in due course and dwell more deeply on it, for it means that we cannot expect consistent definitions (however consistent the units) *or* the inclusion of every detail we would *like* to see. There was little checking for duplicates, *none* for definitions; the Domesday circuit surveys were, primarily, exercises in gathering.

So instead of saying a population didn't exist, or that it should be a modern nuclear family of 2.6 or 3 per 'household' (meaning per man entry, not per mansus!) perhaps we should be seeking some more sensible multiplier? In the 18th century, even in rural areas, houses could regularly contain 10 members of a family over three generations, bigger houses had more because anyone who could afford them had servants, houses in towns were generally overcrowded. If we multiply our 283,242 by 10 we have almost three million people and an average of fifteen would give us 4.25 millions. Even so they would be living very well on the produce of the agricultural areas; even if the population was smaller and yields were low, where was all the excess produce going to in 1086? We will come back to it all near the end of our book (chapter 9), for the present we have to review things simply, in order to open our minds rather than overloading them. One step at a time, if that is possible and maybe it is not and it might be that historians are not entirely to blame for fictions?

Professor Cantor's view of historians creating historical models to suit the politics of their age is imperfect. People also create the history they desire: Bolshevism's heroic Slavs resisting Teutonic Knights, National Socialism's parades of heroic Arians, were not unwelcome inventions of political aspiration. In our own age the Afro-American slavery issue has entirely erased the Barbary Corsairs, English and French penal slavery, slavery in the ancient world and the Church's proscription of it, so that modern translators are now rendering 'serf' as 'slave' and the popular imagination conceives black corvees harvesting sugar cane in

Hampshire! Distortions of this sort are not unwelcome to politicians and to the press, but they are sanctioned and enshrined by private individuals, for gain or out of fear, but often for convenience. Whether historians mostly create or reflect popular aspirations is open to debate but we can at least say that they should know better and should consequently try to set a better example, one that does not promote racism or erase history.

Guesstimates and economic confabulations clog our histories, all of them designed to prove that we now live in the *best of all* possible, industrial, political, material, worlds. *We have been told* that we can laugh at the Victorian social reformers and advocates of handwork or traditional self-sufficiency, the Morrises and the Ruskins, because they have been proved wrong by the rampant success of global materialism. Have they? The man who created the indemonstrable hypothesis of Domesday, by which a century of bootless theorising and speculation has been sustained, would have liked that, he apparently had no time for the politics which he deemed socialist. Were they socialist, I don't think so because I perceive that our ancestors had wisdom and experience to impart. If we honoured our fathers and our mothers, we would not belittle the achievements of the past in order to inflate or magnify our own abilities. The men who constructed Domesday Book and who made its compilation possible, they certainly made accuracy *and* breathtaking speed to function concurrently and might (thereby) even be the envy of modern administrators, but these savants were, themselves and even in 1086, deeply indebted to the past, as *we* shall now discover. Quite apart from those satellite surveys which now accompany Domesday as a muniment (though they were not made at the same time), there are much older documents of similar type.

We have been taught to believe that our ancestors of nine hundred years ago were incapable of measuring or counting, or organising, information. Clearly this is a misapprehension, largely fostered by our refusal to take Domesday Book seriously, our refusal to credit it with consistent methodology and ability, our insistence that they 'must' have been less capable than us, that the great survey was *always* an anachronism or anomaly. Confronted with evidence to the contrary we do not *want* to believe it, indoctrination sustains such myths. In addition we have been taught to conceive 'maps' as landscape pictures seen from the air; 'maps' are, to us, picture books with pictogram images and maybe this is why we find numbers so baffling? We have learned to use a different part of the brain, yet there is no reason why human beings should not think *in numbers instead*, they convey landscapes equally well. Our ancestors, nine hundred years ago, were hampered by their system of arithmetic yet clearly handled numbers with some facility. For us it seems amazing that the Domesday statistics can now be plotted onto pictographs yet to our ancestors such statistical surveys and terriers (land descriptions) *were* their 'maps', records of landscapes set down in numerical and descriptive terms. Thus the noun 'descriptio' (a drawing, diagram *or* description), applied to Domesday Book around 1100, was not inapt.

Cartographers have taught us that modern maps slowly evolved their technical content and accuracy as need arose, which in a sense, a limited sense, is true. Yet even Saxton's Maps of England published in 1579 were nothing more than a collection of pretty, coloured pictures. They were toys for the rich, for their amusement, 'oh look, I have a place there!' He included no roads or measured distances, no fields or accurately placed features, no economic information, no true coastlines or marshes. It was the Dutch cartographer Wagenhaar who (in 1588, note!) published the seamarks and landmarks, sandbanks and soundings. The eleventh century Exchequer had a better view of the statistical evidence than did Saxton whose 'maps' were a continuation of the Mappa Mundi tradition of traveller's tales, told in pictures for storytellers to adapt, visions (in fact) of faith and not of this world. John Norden's 'Survey of Barley' (1593 and 1603) in Hertfordshire[22] was a new type of document or map, a composite of description and pictograph, so it was a 'true' map and a departure from the picture book tradition of conceits; his was an attempt to make maps reconcile with arithmetic. But, by now, educated men were using algorism, which made arithmetic much easier.

Speaking of arithmetic, how shall we excuse the refusal of scholars to read Domesday Book accurately in our supposedly mathematical age? Let us consider our principal thesis, our Domesday hoax, for we can perhaps (with a little charity) excuse this failure? Consider that a successful academic hoax must, of course, be convenient. It may also be said to require five things in order to go undetected: these things are expediency, facility, vanity, mythology and sustainability.

1. Expediency: it must be expedient in that it provides a solution to a difficult and embarrassing, academic, problem.

2. Facility: it must offer a simple and undemanding answer or theory to its acolytes, for facility (not industry) is the most beguiling of inducements when we wish a thing to be widely adopted. We are all naturally lazy.

3. Vanity: obviously it must flatter someone's ego and, in theory at least, 'set them up' for ridicule (even when it fails and is accepted as genuine).

4. Mythology: it works best when it encourages the construction, or

invention, of many layers of mythology, if only because these create new and esoteric realms of knowledge for acolytes.

5.   Sustainability: is derived from mythology, for mythology provides self perpetuation, each succeeding generation of acolytes adding to the arcane accumulation (or lexicon) of 'knowledge'. Without this quality a hoax cannot continue to delude, so it follows that undetected and successful hoaxes are those which offer the widest scope to contributors.

The indemonstrable hypothesis of an infinitely variable and arbitrarily fixed hide is probably one of the finest inventions of this genre for, like a religion, it relies on faith not proof. We might say it has become a religion. Superficially it is beguilingly attractive in its simplicity and it may also be used to explain *all* other units and systems in a similar way, which is even better. For a century, generations of students have hypothecated why none of these systems appear to work, which is to say they have spawned other shoals of indemonstrable hypotheses to swim alongside. Not only do such additional possibilities appear conformable and limitless, *reinforcement* of the lexicon makes the original hypothesis unassailable, revision becomes unthinkable. Why, a century of inventions cannot possibly be wrong! Without labouring this point we will now look at one or two of these mythological additions as we journey on through Domesday England.

The rock upon which it has been possible to build all this 'study' is aniconic authority and the refusal to permit review, the proscription of return to first principles, the destruction of any demands for proof and insistence on an induction into the arcana itself prior to academic acceptance. Indeed, demands for proof are unlikely to arise when students are forbidden to ask for evidence and are instead required to possess the estoppel of a foundation knowledge of this mythology before they can commence study. I was told that to use arithmetic to analyse a statistical survey was "to interpret the survey (Domesday Book) anachronistically" and asked (by way of an animadversion) "what *is* the purpose of your arithmetical method?" These qualities in academia, and the lack of such longstop physiological evidence as the artefacts of Piltdown provided, have guaranteed the sustainability of the Domesday hoax. It is not without a twinge of conscience that I have intruded a demonstrable hypothesis into this happy picture; in calling for a rational and scientific reappraisal I do accept that the religious element will inevitably repullulate. Yet for those of us who have serious doubts about the present system of education and who adduce its political dimensions, there must be an anarchic pleasure in the destruction of the spurious and the pompous. *If* we believe in the value of the study of history we must enable others to believe. History cannot be said to serve a purpose if the only one it serves is quasi religious and, of course, ours *is* the delight of discovery. In this modern world there are few new lands left to discover, all but Domesday England are already on the tourist's map.

So, what is this Pandora's Box we have opened, releasing all sorts of things that historians would rather not know? The name means, 'all gifted' but the story is that Zeus created her, as the first woman, not as a gift but to bring misery to the world of men through her perfection. Legend says that Pandora opened a jar or a chest which contained all the human ills, but then shut it again so quickly that she imprisoned hope. At a later period the legend said that, instead, the box had contained all the blessings of the gods, so that in opening it she let them escape from mankind. Perhaps we can view Domesday Book in the same way, maybe it can still be a blessing to mankind if we can put the genie back into the jar, who can say? We will then need to open it intelligently and understand it perfectly, so let us try to discover more about this amazing and ancient archive before making a final decision.

The archive, the box, in fact contained more than the Domesday muniments, as we have said, for assuredly Domesday Book's methodology did not arise spontaneously in 1086, at best it only contained some novel features. In its broad concept it was not new, so let us now try to trace its origins back into the mists of antiquity, into what used to be called 'The Dark Ages', to see which dark lords first generated such expertise?

CHAPTER FIVE

THE BONES OF A KINGDOM

Where did the units come from and, in particular, when did the areal hide or mansus come into being, and why? We will find that the answers take us back (in more ways than one) into the bones of a kingdom, to the formation of England and further into that congeries of the 'gens anglorum' which conglomerated to form both the language and the people. Later we will go even further but today this is our journey.

The English have always been reticent about, even ashamed of, their own ethnicity so it is not, perhaps, surprising that the Normans should generally be credited with Domesday Book? Yet this is not the truth for we know of no comparable European document. Its antecedents and exemplars were Saxon and its formation was only possible in an English context. That is why the terms used have a Saxon lineage. What happened around 1900 (when our hoax was devised) was that political affinities changed, French associations were becoming 'a good thing', German associations 'bad' (as in all the best histories), France was acknowledged as the nation of culture, cuisine and polite society. They never tired of telling us so. Late Victorian and Edwardian historians began to characterise our Saxon ancestors (naturally by ignoring the linguistic debt) as lazy, drunken and ignorant while they saw the French and Normans, who formed the aristocracy after 1066, as vigorous, martial and intuitive. This socially sycophantic view of history was able to point to such dramatic achievements as the Bayeux Tapestry and Domesday Book, even to motte and bailey castles, as chronologically part of a 'new order', essentially Norman (though now we know otherwise), thereby ignoring both their context and their evolution. The truth actually was that all these things flowered at a point in time where a previous culture, nay previous cultures, had reached a peak and so the bulbs were already in the flower-beds when the Normans purchased the garden in the figurative early spring, just as the fields, hedgerows, mills, meadows, swine, kine and kindreds had already been established on the ancient topography of England.

The Northamptonshire Geld Roll[23] is a document which, all agree, pre-dates the Domesday survey: it was produced at least ten years earlier, maybe more? Let us commence, therefore, with this incontestable survey. It gave Northamptonshire 28 hundreds and 2,664 hides (639,360 acres) and using the other statistics we can account for 2,648.5 hides of this gross figure, so its total area ante-1076 was 99.8% of the recent, surveyed area of the shire. However, by 1086 it only answered for 283,680 acres, or 44.4%, in spite of the other statistics enrolling 316,920 acres of arable land! Who says tax evasion is a recent phenomenon? Incidentally in recent times Northamptonshire has had between 215,000 and 292,000 acres of arable land under cultivation out of a total agricultural acreage of 532,995 acres. So the 1086 hidation may actually have been the *arable acreage* at the time? Nor is this all for circa 1010 a document now called the County Hidage[24] gave Oxfordshire, Cambridgeshire, Huntingdonshire, Northamptonshire and Bedfordshire together, in a block (we shall see later that this included Buckinghamshire), a total of 10,150 hides, some 2.436 million acres. In modern times this same overall area has been surveyed at 2.24 million acres, including the Isle of Ely and the Fens, which being drained and surveyed with modern instruments must now be easier to deal with than was a watery wilderness? In other words, the area defined by the stated hidation of a series of documents *steadily contracted* from the gross of 1010 to that of 1070, and then even further to 1086.

This coterminous palimpsest of periods is beguiling, but it does mask changes. Well, we should expect changes should we not? While England's topography is not likely to expand or contract significantly, *we should* expect county borders to flex just a little over hundreds of years. In fact, in the County Hidage, Northamptonshire encompassed the equivalent of 0.876 million acres (3,200 hides) when recently it has only been 0.58 million acres, but then Warwickshire was only 0.288 million acres as against 0.56 millions recently. County boundaries and areas changed in the 19th century, for administrative reasons, we should indeed expect them to change with changes of ownership as well as administrations over an interval of eight or nine hundred years. We can see that only four shires (Worcestershire, Herefordshire, Warwickshire and Staffordshire) were selectively hidated in c.1010, though by 1086 the number had *risen* to ten out of the thirteen listed in the County Hidage. Things had been changing in the mid-11th century.

It would appear that the process of revising, of deliberately selecting, hidation was only just beginning in c.1010 and that it was happening in the heart of Mercia, where traditionally hidated England met the selective or revised hidations, the carucations, of the Danelaw? This is hardly surprising, nor should we be surprised if this 'good idea' gradually extended over the next seventy years, though the real impetus may have come from the 'new lords' of 1066? What of the document itself, the County Hidage, what was its purpose? Maybe it is just a fragment of a more extensive geld roll, but maybe it was intended as a form of map, produced orally, to record and broker a political settlement? Do not be alarmed. In an age of oral tradition and nuncupative evidence it should not surprise us to find our earliest maps in this form.

The County Hidage and the Northamptonshire Geld Roll are not the only Saxon documents to adumbrate the Domesday Survey. Perhaps the earliest evidence we have is a survival now called the Tribal Hidage,[25] in recognition of its listing of many peoples, all of them Saxon, Angle or Jute, a veritable congeries of the 'gens anglorum'. Space does not permit the exposition I once offered, but though its analysis is complicated I must try to make as short a work of it as may be possible in this place. Bear with me. The Tribal Hidage (suffice it to say, without an extensive exposition) is a composite document containing three lists of information that were, apparently, originally separate products; at very best we have two separate charters which have been drawn together for some special purpose. For the convenience of those with some prior knowledge and for general reference I have used numbers in order to relate the evidence to the analyses made by Cyril Hart in 1971 and by Vierk and Davies in 1974, even though the numeration does not proceed seriatim (apparently because the scribe who eventually engrossed the surviving copy from older sources had no real understanding of the component parts).

The first, or oldest, list concerns the majority of the minor hidations entered and these probably represented an historic picture when the list was first drawn up? The map shows how these peoples covered the body of England. Absent from it are the foci of the succeeding lists (viz. Mercia, Anglia, Essex, Kent and Sussex). However the total absence of the first of these foci (Mercia) *can be supplied* with a total of 12,000 hides or mansi (2.88 million acres for north and south Mercia together), thanks to the Venerable Bede[26]. The other absentees can be reconstructed, syllogistically, in order to add more foci to the aggregation of minor tribal areas, resulting in an area equivalent to 18.52 million acres. To this we can compare a recent area of surveyed totals, once we have placed these tribal entries on the map, which comes to 18.75 million acres. Coextensive coincidence of 98.8% is not bad at all, is it? "Mere coincidence", the conversi will sneer. So, let's see *you* do the arithmetic even *half* so well! (Even when I made you a 'gift 'of it you failed, Dr. B-.) .

The second (and third?) list(s) are headed by Mercia, or according to the author of list two that 'area first called Mercia', for Mercia was a kingdom which grew inordinately and became a super power. The map shows this consolidated picture with Mercia allied to the Hwicce (XXI). Next we see Anglia (XXXI) claiming Essex (XXXII), just as Kent (XXXIII) claims 'Suth Sexena' or Sussex (XXXIV) until, finally, Wessex (XXXV) is presented as the overlord, laying claim to all these lands. This listing, therefore, appears to present us with both a history of the emergence of several overlords and also of their subsequent absorption of all tributary and minor tribes and peoples, accomplished in two stages. Who were these overlords? I suggest the Bretwaldas or 'High Kings' of whom Raedwald, buried (as we believe) at Sutton Hoo, was the unifier of Anglia and Essex (East Saxony), high king of Norfolk, Suffolk, Essex and Middlesex. Finally this documentary claim (or pedigree) promotes overlordship of *every kingdom* in southern and midland England, 'Rex totius Anglorum', a nation of Anglo-Saxons. Who was this over-great king?

First let us explore a byway, just to be sure that we understand the reciprocity of Bede's work and of the Tribal Hidage. The Venerable Bede gave the people of the kingdom of Wight credit for doubling their area since the days of the Wihtgara (XVIII), that is from 600 hides (144,000 acres) their kingdom expanded to 1,200 hides (288,000 acres) by his day, which was before c.730 A.D. Clearly this kingdom was, as Bede said, separated by the Solent from South Saxony (presumably the Spithead side) for that kingdom measured 7,000 hides in both documents. As Bede put it, 'it stretches west and south from Kent as far as Wessex and covers an area of 7,000 hides'. Ethelwalh of South Saxony received the Isle of Wight and the Province of Meanware (in Hampshire) from King Wulfhere of Mercia. Bede said this expansion of Wight was about the time that Cadwalla of the Gewissae captured the kingdom and exterminated its heathen inhabitants (c.686). If so, an amputation by him of these western-most South Saxon lands, under a pretext of restoring Christianity, was not censured by Bede, who actually condoned the massacre! Today the island is a mere 94,144 acres but another 50,000 acres on the mainland opposite would have granted a strategic toe-hold, subsequently enlarged by another 600 hides from Meanware? If so, western Hampshire of the first list can probably be amputate from the area of the 'Suth Sexena' (XXXIV) of the second list? And so another riddle is laid to rest.

Now, in order to answer the question, 'who could lay claim to be king of *all* the English peoples' we will need to travel forwards from the Tribal Hidage to another document, one called the Burghal Hidage[27], itself (still) much older than Domesday. In it we have not only a series of hidage assessments and a form of mapping, but also a specific defensive and administrative application of hides

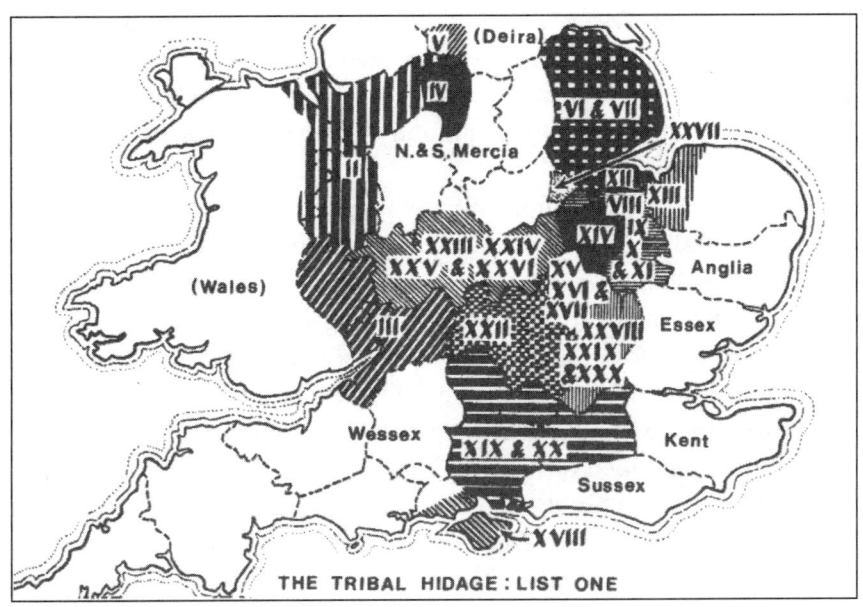

THE TRIBAL HIDAGE : LIST ONE

to demonstrate that such cartae were, indeed, sophisticated and working documents. It is generally dated c.910 – 920 A.D and it tells us how many hides 'belong' to the men of Wessex in a circuit running from Sussex and Kent to Wessex, South Mercia and the environs of London by what had been Anglia,

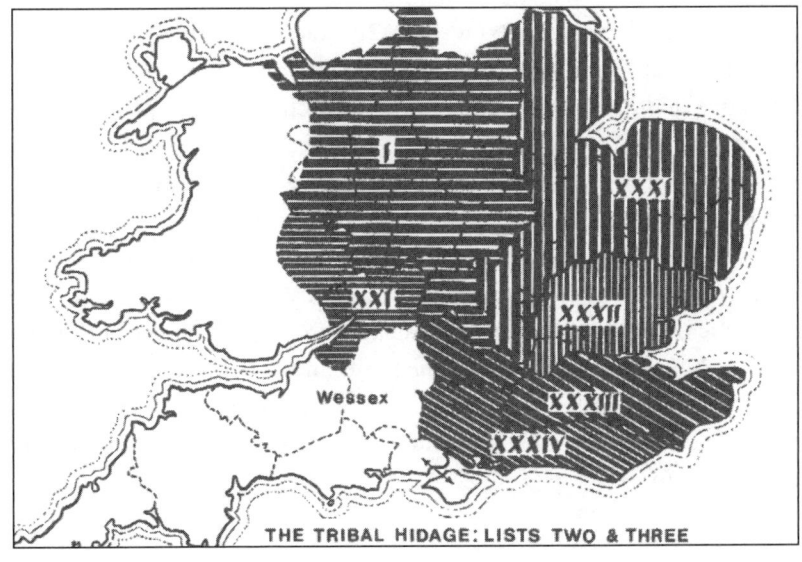

THE TRIBAL HIDAGE: LISTS TWO & THREE

encompassing all the Wessex sphere of influence. It tells us of burghs (forts and fortresses) and of the hides required for their support or maintenance: the equivalent of 2.9266 million acres in Kent and Sussex, 2.9945 million acres in Wessex, 0.6240 million acres in Anglia and 0.3360 million acres in Mercia, by our calculation of the hide.

From other sources we can identify two super fortresses, Winchester, capital of Wessex, and Wallingford, a vital strategic strongpoint covering the Mercian border and controlling an east to west chain of burghs or forts. Far away in the West we see a few minor strong points covering what may have been the last Dumnonian tribal lands of Cornwall and the scattering of burghs of less than about five acres in size may themselves be older sites, while those of less than one acre (Southampton, Lydford and Lyng) may have been towers? One burgh alone did not belong to the men of Wessex.

Now, how do we know the actual areas of these burghs? Well the key is in the colophon to the document. First of all it tells us how many hides are required for the maintenance and defence of 'an acres' breadth of wall' and then it says that if a hide is represented by one man, then every pole of wall can be manned by four men. There follows a ready reckoner to calculate the hides required by any given length of wall from twenty poles to twelve furlongs in length. Well, these are all antique units and so we must grasp them like the proverbial nettle! The pole (we will assume) is a rod of 5.5 yards, so this calculation is easy: each man represents 1.375 yards of wall and covers a field of fire of one furlong (viz. 220 yards). The ancient standard of a 'bow-shot' was 200 to 240 yards (10-12 score yards), so 220 is its average. Fair enough. Now hold on to the loops in the figures, it's a rough ride. Thus 16 men cover a linear perimeter of 22 yards (O.K?) with a field of fire out to 200-240 yards, making 'an acre's breadth of wall' ('anes aecres braede'). Do you follow me, 22x(average)220 yards=1 acre. So, 16 men to every acre's breadth, that's simple enough. Using this formula we may calculate the circumference *and* the (hypothetical) area of each of the burghs listed! Yes, it is true, we can do this: listen.

I concede that few forts will have identical entrances, even identical plans, such is the art of defence, but the form and the fact of an entrance dictate the number of defenders required. Have a look at the tabulation below, it won't bite. In fact, most wild or angry creatures don't bite if you stay cool and in command, so pick up the columns of figures and whack 'em round the ears. Don't you feel good? Ain't they attentive now, sitting there and waiting for your perusal? So sorry, this really isn't politically correct but you must not let them frighten you. Maybe statistics have feelings too and maybe they don't, but we must retain control over them?

THE BURGHAL HIDAGE

Burgh	Hides	Million Acres	Yards of Nominal Permieter	Acres of Nominal Area	Kingdom
Eorpeburnan	324	0.078	445½	2.56	Kent
Hastings	500	0.120	687½	6.1	" "
Lewes	1,300	0.312	1,787½	41.26	" "
Burpham	720	0.173	990	12.65	" "
Chichester	1,500	0.360	2,062½	54.9	" "
Portchester	500	0.120	687½	6.1	" "
Southampton	150	0.036	206¼	0.55	" "
Winchester	2,400	0.576	3,300	140.6	" "
Wilton	1,400	0.336	1,925	47.85	Wessex
Chisbury	700	0.168	962½	11.96	" "
Shaftsbury	700	0.168	962½	11.96	" "
Twyneham	470	0.113	646¼	5.4	" "
Wareham	1,600	0.384	2,200	62.5	" "
Bredy	760	0.182	1,045	14.1	" "
Exeter	734	0.176	1,009¼	13.15	" "
Halwell	300	0.072	412½	2.2	" "
Lydford	140	0.034	192½	0.48	" "
Pilton	360	0.086	495	3.16	" "
Watchet	513	0.123	705	6.4	" "
Axbridge	400	0.096	550	3.9	" "
Lyng	100	0.024	137½	0.24	" "
Langport	600	0.144	825	8.78	" "
Bath	1,000	0.240	1,375	24.4	" "
Malmesbury	1,200	0.288	1,650	35.15	" "
Cricklade	1,500	0.360	2,062½	54.9	" "
Oxford	1,400	0.336	1,925	47.85	Mercia
Wallingford	2,400	0.576	3,300	140.6	Kent
Buckingham	1,600	0.384	2,200	62.5	Anglia
Sashes	1.000	0.240	1,375	24.4	" "
Eashing	600	0.144	825	8.78	Kent
Southwark	1,800	0.432	2,475	79.1	" "
	28,671	6.881	"All but one belong to the men of Wessex"		

Winchester, a super fortress, had 'belonging to it', some 2,400 hides (576,000 acres). Multiply by 1.375 and it makes *3,300 yards* nominal perimeter and this (hypothetically mind you) produces a square of 825 yards (each way) = 140.5 acres. Then we also have an extramural field of fire averaging 220 yards in depth, so add that on if you wish, but we will concentrate on the intramural area. A site this size, containing 2,400 fighting men would average (taking into account roads and administrative structures) perhaps 50.5 feet square per man, enough for a dwelling each but not a proper curtilage, 283.5 square yards, adequate in a camp behind earthworks even if roadways stables and livestock pens had to be included. Loyn[28] says that the excavated and traced perimeter was actually in the region of *3,280 yards*. Not a bad working formula for a nation of drunken punchies and certainly worth the roughhousing of a few statistics? We are flying over a fortification garrisoned by King Alfred and if we cannot see all the layout for mist and wood smoke, it is still the best reconstruction yet of such an earthwork. Now let us look at others.

Not all the burghs were of a standard plan or allocation, we can hardly expect them to be if they were working bulwarks. Chichester was given only 55 acres for its 1,500 men (188.5 acres if we include the extramural field of fire) making an allocation of only 40 feet each way (177.7 square yards) per man. Archaeology has proposed (but not proved) a site of about 100 acres. Bath, at 1,000 hides, should be 24.5 acres in area and has been archaeologically estimated at 23.5 acres. Here every man would have a theoretic allocation of 32.6 feet each way (118 square yards). Wareham, at 1,600 men, should be 62.5 acres or less and its 2,200 yard (hypothecated) perimeter accords well with the 2,180 yards given by Professor Loyn. It has been archaeologically estimated at under 90 acres and our formula gives it 62.5 acres, or 202.5 when including the field of fire.

Southampton, perhaps the site of Roman Clausentum itself, had only 150 men on 0.55 acres internally, an allocation of 4x13 feet living space per man. Lyng had only 100 men on 0.24 acres, a mere 5x7 feet per man, very much a 'castle' rather than a township. Defences would have been manned in watches, so each off-duty man would have rather more space, but the circumference has to determine the area enclosed and our estimates are just that, they cannot take account of duplicate lines of defence or multiple entrances. We are flying too high to make a tactical appraisal of what lies below. The three acre Pilton Camp with its nominal circumference of 1,485 feet may today be measured as 1,520 feet, with possible water obstacles abbreviating the actual vallum of the camp in the past.

Portchester is an interesting example as it certainly involved no earthworks but a mainly intact Roman fortress, which still stands today. The allocation of a mere 500 hides to such a substantial structure therefore seems convincing and we will draw in closer. Today the Roman fortress is 700 feet along each face, or 600 exclusive of internal 'towers', the difference in area being 11 or 8 acres. Let us elect 8 acres. According to the Burghal Hidage it was assessed as 515.625 feet along each face making an area of 6 acres. If we allow for the site of the church inside the fort, there in Saxon times, we reduce our 8 acres to 6.5. Thus the presence of the church restricted the garrison but the high masonry walls would require fewer defenders and less maintenance than an earth and timber camp, being (at that time) impregnable. A religious community around a minster-church could be accommodated within such a fortress, it could even survive. The allocation per soldier would be between 31 and 23 feet (each way) per man, depending on the area given over to the convent. Now we can see that maybe all three of the burghs listed as under 200 hides, or 300 yard circuits, could have involved strong points and maybe even masonry structures, for what else could defend itself and accommodate 100 men on a quarter of an acre? We may even have answered the question of where did castles come from, not the mottes but the stone or timber towers? (Now will you listen to the howls of horror from historians!)

What were the origins and possible purposes of this survey? Historians have long debated this – in total ignorance of the statistics presented above. I suggest it was a logistic statement compiled for Wessex, collating old and new sites (and maybe older documents) inherited from an older hegemony? Something much like the Tribal Hidage. Superficially we appear to be looking at a simple mathematical formula, but we must remember that these people were not even working with Arab numeration, according to all the authorities. For them arithmetic was laborious, practical and, in application, manual. It used counters in a system like an abacus and Roman numerals were used to express products. Under such conditions formulations of formulae are remarkable and all the more so if conceived in abstract. When examined more closely the Burghal Hidage bears signs of a series of physical inspections, but it was also a stroke of genius and the ready reckoner presenting both the scale and scope of Wessex' overlordship defences cannot have been a diploma intended for general circulation. Its possession by an enemy would be disastrous. These defences were egregiously strong along the Wessex-Mercia border and might even have operated as a form of limes? A contumelious morsel? Well, like Domesday Book itself, this was apparently a state secret of the utmost importance as well as being a working document.

Learned palaeographers, ignorant alike of the content and the importance of the Burghal and the Tribal Hidages, have speculated widely on their dates. Neither source is an early copy, both are fortuitous survivals and we should not assume that more extensive archives did not once exist. On balance, when we recall Edward the Elder's strategy against the Danes of the Five Boroughs, Essex and Anglia, we are disposed to predate the succession of Aethelflaed in Mercia and to view that as our terminus anti quem for the Burghal Hidage: either a strategic review of Alfred's methods commissioned by his son or even a personal bequest from that great unifier of Wessex to his successor? In either case it is written large, 'Aelfred mec heht gewrycan' and we can see that 9th-century kingship was no hit or miss process but a sophisticated compound artefact of ways and means, including education, tradition and innovation. We can also perceive the basic sub-structure of a nascent Domesday Book, as it was ultimately re-christened.

Our supposedly peregrine 11th-century bureaucracy has been debunked. The best claim the Normans can make is that they became numerate of necessity and literate through the combined influences of apothegms and evangelism, for the origins of the Domesday surveys are certainly English. Yet the foreign lord who could recognise and harness this administrative tradition in order to found an exigible institution was himself a worthy successor to a long line of English monarchs. So, shall we say that the Tribal Hidage may have roots as far back as Raedwald (c.620 A.D) and thence to Offa (d.796 A.D), it may even have sub-served the political ambitions of Egberht, the last of the Bretwaldas? After him came a crepuscular age of rapine and terror which destroyed all other sources but, nevertheless, the great divide between Egberht and Alfred was apparently crossed by this document in some form. True, the scribe who finally brought all the sources together *was* confused, his picture was faulty and *his* sum of addition (using counters) actually came adrift by 1,400 hides, yet the composite charter survived. I think that Alfred at least saw it and appreciated its legal and administrative values, and its form today may even be due to his direction? OK, he did not have this invented, but he did put it to work, he had it wrought.

The Tribal Hidage allows a retrospective view of the many divisions and separate groups of peoples who finally came together to form pre-Danish England. The County Hidage tells us of the effect which Danish and then Viking pressures had upon this unified nation, even after racial integration of some sort. Yet the Tribal Hidage also shows us from whence later phenomena sprang. The peoples of the first list were tribal but also topographic realities and it is reasonable to assume that their individualities persisted. Indeed, the continued currency of their individual identities at the time of Domesday Book, perhaps 500 years later, appears to be evidenced by the logical affinities (and the logic-patterned differences) displayed in region to region and shire to shire comparisons. We shall return many times to this encapsulated logic before we reach the end of our journies. Space does not permit a deeper analysis now, but it would seem that some logic which underlay both land usage and definitions in 1066 and 1086 linked Gloucestershire and Herefordshire to the Hwicca, Worcestershire and Warwickshire to the Hendrican group and Shropshire and Cheshire to the Woecansaetna, thus (we might propose) that some of the solidarities we see (either pre- or post-Conquest) were residual affinities, ones which we can even trace back to the Tribal Hidage? As Kipling put it, 'and so was England born'. What we cannot yet say, but hopefully may one day know, is whether these affinities were organic, ethnic, or authoritarian: it opens an interesting area for debate, whether the Anglo- Saxon occupiers imposed these patterns from their own logic and practice bases or whether they inherited them with the workforce? Did they, perhaps, arise *long* before from some natural synergy? Could the exploitation of landscapes through agricultural practices possibly be subject to some form of syssarcosis dependant on localised phenomena but capable of grouped formations, whereby skeletal economies are spontaneously generated?

It is difficult, I know, to absorb such a shock of statistics. This chapter has been overlong but (I hope) not tedious? In distilling all the surprises which of them will amaze us most I wonder, the use of formulae by our distant and traduced ancestors or the survival of regional, even ethnic differences for hundreds of years? No, perhaps the most mind-numbing revelation is this, that somewhere between 600 and 700 A.D. men on horse and on foot, without even modern numerals, could collect together areas of land totalling 11.544 million acres. Today, with computers, surveying instruments and universal and higher education we think the same area of England would total perhaps 11.776 million acres. By c.900 they could take in an area of 24 million acres, though we would think ourselves more precise at 23.396 million acres. We, of course, have the technology. What price modern education? In our search for a new god of change and 'progress' we have substituted faith for science in the study of history, so that scholars revile any suggestion of 'scientific history'. Perhaps we should not so readily condemn science and neither should we dismiss the intuitive genius of peasant and artisan. Constructed alternatives, taught (but not learned) through contrived tuition, the artificial insemination of learning, may even bring forth unwanted progeny when we ignore the wisdom and the prudence of our ancestors?

> "...it is in my power
> To o'erthrow law, and in one self-born hour
> To plant and o'erwhelm custom. Let me pass.
> The same I am, ere ancient'st order was,
> Or what is now received ..."
> (Time as chorus in Act IV of "A Winters' Tale".)

CHAPTER SIX:

'IN EACH HIDE ARE FOURTEEN AND A HALF CARUCATES'

As Professor Maitland observed over 100 years ago[29], the geld lay as an obligation upon the land, that is upon the land's lord, not upon its cultivator. Succeeding generations have ignored his subtlety. When there is no system of taxation, as one might say no system of extortion by the crown, a man is proud to say what he owns. The measurement, even the rudimentary mapping, of lands was important in several respects, as we have seen, but *initially it was not part of a system of taxation.* Instead there were 'food renders' to be delivered to kings and to great lords and a rigid hierarchy based on personal obligation to be observed, even to be observed unto death on the field of battle, but there was no *system* by which to raise money. In fact, the money economy grew only slowly as wealth, culture and education (we are assured) increased and accumulated. It is accumulation of wealth which awakes jealousy and 'cupiditas', in thief or in ruler.

Not until there was a money economy and an accumulation of wealth under an established and unified hierarchy was taxation, linked to land and to areal measurement, possible. The invention of geld, 'dane-geld', as protection money made this juncture with land holding desirable and from it came many evils, not the least the encouragement to further extortion. When the new lords arrived from Normandy their leader grasped that such an impost might equally be paid to the protector as to the demander or demandant, for anyone with sufficient power can become the protector. Having deduced as much it was a simple step for the protector to become the extortioner, a system which took several centuries to perfect, for compliance does, indeed, require the payer to be the absolute pawn of the payee. The gradual replacement of professional militias, such as the 'select fyrd', by professional mercenaries was an inevitable concomitant. Ultimately and eventually the removal of great lords and their power brokerage system also became inevitable. However, we have gone too far. Our need here is merely to understand that while Alfred had no need to link land and taxes

Ethelraed ('the unraed' or ill-advised) and his successors did, and thanks to them evasions, confusion, injustices and jealousies sprang to life to divide the anciently reconciled social and ethnic groups. We may even suspect that it was knowledge of this new system of taxation which brought William to England: did Harold supply him with the secret, I wonder? (We will return to this later and more widely.) We are accustomed to accepting taxation as essential for our social welfare and individual security and this was also an article of faith to our Victorian ancestors whose preferential system, based on a limited franchise, required historical support. Although both taxation and representation have evolved since then, modern historians are locked in a time warp devised by their predecessors, one devised for social and economic engineering, serving political ends. Whether this was and is a conscious or unconscious manipulation of the facts I cannot say.

The very name 'Domesday Book' tells us of the irrevocable changes which it presaged; that this was not its official or original name tells us that popular perceptions had an awful apprehension of the truth. Antiquarians, puzzled by the title, had to wait for Arthur Agarde in the reign of Elizabeth I to make an instinctive answer[30], one which was not a bad guess, indeed it has served modern historians well. We have advanced nothing on his anodyne response that a list of what men owned was like the final account of the Last Judgement. I think this partly misses the point but that is not surprising if the meaning of the document was unknown and its real impact on 11th century society undreamt of by antiquarians or by modern scholars.

By way of an advance on Agarde, let us consider that when men christen a significant creative effort it is not unusual for them to simultaneously invoke literary and/or religious affinities. The 'Angel of the North' has both biblical and apocalyptic affirmation whereas 'Winged Figure' would have been much more ambiguous, neither beneficent nor malevolent. From the name we derive a vicarious thrill of speculation, even of anticipation. In the case of Domesday Book this frisson was created at a subsequent date; it was a sinister and later name, but was it a quip, an ironic interlude, or did it mirror what we know to be the full weight and impact of those folios which had originally been titled, 'The Book of the Lord King'?

Both Agarde and the earlier (12th century) 'Dialogue of the Exchequer'[31] tell us that *as on the dreadful day of judgement*, so in Domesday Book nothing may be hidden from the lord the king. In the hands of modern scholars it sounds like a piece of political spin rather than a sober reflection and Agarde, indeed, insisted that it was most feared by 'the poor'. Social historians will not find it difficult to reconcile such a comment by a Tudor public servant with the application of the First Poor Law! Well, if the name was no more than a quip it devalued the effort expended; no, it was *not* an aggregation of worthless statistics gathered for their own sake and the highly structured and careful editing of what we call the 'Greater Domesday' declares a work of more than common diligence. True, the 'Lesser Domesday' (Essex, Suffolk and Norfolk) is less tightly controlled and emended, *as we are told* because King William's death brought editing to a sudden halt. It was an enormous undertaking diligently carried out, it *was* a purposeful record, so we may measure the weight of the soubriquet subsequently applied by the reception it received not from the poor but from those *whose assets were recorded*. The poor did not have a voice.

This roundabout approach is no pseudo dialectic or artifice of debate seeking to obsequiously validate ancient critics in an esoteric field, it is instead an assay of any contemporary Saxon sources offering comparison with the day of judgement. England was a deeply religious society with distinct cultural, religious and philosophical authorities whose writings carried ancient weight, so we do not have to look far for a canon whose words would be familiar *to all* educated men, especially those belonging to an incipient, amorphous and clerical 'civil service' in 1086. The 'De Domes Daege' of the Venerable Bede contains some highly pertinent passages illuminated with particular force, enough to make any borrowed title terrifying. His English words would not be familiar to Frenchmen and Normans, but *all* Englishmen knew their weight and King William was (if we are to believe the posthumous sketch given by the Anglo Saxon chronicler) a stern man of inflexible purpose and the very embodiment of Bede's Old Testament, avenging God.

In his work Bede says he fears for himself and for his sinful deeds, but he also fears, 'how the mighty Lord will sever and doom *all men's kin* through his secret might.... It will be daylight clear everything *that was secret, all laid bare* in open words'. Brought before their Lord, from all directions, to his presence in order to hear their doom, 'then before everyone will everything be made manifest, things long hidden by men.... *Poor and rich alike* will be affrighted: all will be afraid because *poor or wealthy* they will have BUT ONE LAW'.

In other words, Domesday Book *like Domesday itself* was to be the means of establishing *an act of legal retribution*, also a standard applicable to *all* degrees of men, no-one could set themselves above its authority. This is of peculiar relevance, as we shall see, to the recent history of William's governance. By the authority of Domesday Book the King, God's representative on earth, could discern everything, secret or no, in every part of his kingdom and, by implication, throughout men's lives. As we have now discovered, whoever held the Book certainly *could* obtain a comprehensive view of all men's possessions and we are *now* going to see how it also gave the King a 'divine' insight into men's loyalties. And in 1086 loyalty was not optional, treason was the only alternative. The

English understood loyalty to their lord, the Normans did not. Even though 'freyndscip' and 'feondscip' were but an inflection apart the English had a long tradition of loyalty whereas the French had, as yet, no real concepts of chivalry or feudal loyalty to guide them.

So, I submit, Bede's ancient and esoteric vision of divine omniscience had actually come to pass by 1087 thanks to a superb administrative effort and a stroke of genius. For the French it was perhaps less of a miracle than a black art for the King to elevate himself to the status of God *and* possess his omniscience, but by an accident of fate, obesity and conies, King William died whilst pursuing his choler and it was upon his son Rufus that the unholy mantle fell. *He* was the first monarch to have an opportunity to apply the results of the Domesday inquests and so *he* acquired an evil reputation, but before we come to that let us examine how the King (and his secret inner circle of 'camerarii') *could* divine men's thoughts and loyalties from a Book which we already know functions as a land book, tax return and national map. As I have said already, it was a most versatile and sophisticated piece of machinery.

King William's mercenary soldiers put him on the throne for money, not for a cause. Naturally there were estates to hand out, land for grabs, but by 1067 his pressing need was for money with which to reward them. Of course he knew where this would come from, he could impose a heavy geld and use the product to pay off his most pressing and dangerous creditors, but he miscalculated. The Northumbrians, who had revolted in 1065 over the same abuse, now did so again, killing the newly appointed Earl who was gathering the geld. The next year King William imposed a second geld and sold the Earldom to a ruthless half-Scot half-Englishman, so that when Edwin and Morcar raised a revolt in 1068 the thegns of the north also joined them. A vicious spiral had commenced. By a coup-de-main King William took York without a pitched battle, seized estates, appointed a governor and allowed his men to murder and plunder the peasants. In January 1069 the Norman field force at Durham was trapped and massacred in retaliation.

Others have written up William's ruthless and capable response to these troubles[32]. He set about systematically destroying all support through murder, rape and arson so that those peasants who escaped into the moorlands of Yorkshire ultimately starved or froze to death. Their homes, livestock and grain were destroyed and without seed corn, or stotts to pull the ploughs, this self-sufficient community quickly succumbed. The retribution meted out on Yorkshire was terrifying but it gave some warning to Durham and further south. In the consequent famine those who survived did so either by selling their families into serfdom or, probably in their thousands, they fled southwards. Those who survived this migration left evidence of their flight on the pages of

Domesday Book, truly a record of a Domesday retribution, a doom visited on 'all men's kin'.

From our tabulations and conversions we can obtain measurements of agricultural efficiency (comparing ploughs with ploughlands), estimates of available workers, changes and concentrations of social status and, so, estimates of county populations by which to inform a notional expression of demographic and socio-economic changes. Central to this analysis are the logic patterns that are otherwise often individual to shires or regions in 1066, so that shifts into serfdom and increases in arable cultivation can also be seen to be mirrored by changes in expressed thoughts. Converting all these things to a simple density map we may see the wretched refugees pouring across the Humber and Lindsey into Nottinghamshire, crossing (and often stopping to resettle as serfs in) Rutland, Leicestershire and Huntingdonshire, while a significant number appear to have crossed the Fens of the Wash via Crowland and King's Lynn to enter Norfolk and Suffolk. This human wave finally lapped the northern hundreds of Essex and even perhaps Oxfordshire? Such a dramatic picture amply justifies the description of 'harrying': they ran for as long as their resources permitted and stopped when they could go no further, as though the devil himself was behind them. Back in Yorkshire, we are told, rotting and emaciated corpses spread pestilence while the wolves moved down from the hills and moors to feast on cadavers.

Turning from this apocalyptic overview we can also draw conclusions from particulars. In Derbyshire the 'wasta' (laid waste or abandoned) entries can be seen in the north and west of the shire. Domesday itself says, 'all Langendale is wasted' and says of some 72 square miles that it was reduced to, 'woodland, unpastured, fit (only) for hunting'. Woodland, as we have discussed, did not necessarily mean trees, just heath, common or moor land. These parts of this shire are naturally the least hospitable, Peak Forest, Goyt's Moss, Dovedale, East Moor and so on. However, being 'wasted' meant that they had *once been* fruitful, but a suspension of law and order combined with Peveril's Castle at Peak's Arse would make the hard living unendurable. Where marshal law ran (if that is not a euphemism) cultivation would be highly precarious. We can see areas which decreased in valuation between 1066 and 1086 and which join up the 'wasted' areas on the map, but there were other places which followed the pattern of southern England and which even had increased valuations by 1086. There is no evidence that *some* places ever felt the hand of fear or retribution. Despite surrounding troubles the 'terra regis' (the King's own estates) belt in Scarsdale and Wirksworth Wapentakes (the Danelaw name for hundreds) showed little sign of disturbance, arguing for effective royal protection. In the borough of Derby only 58% of the former 243 burgher's households survived to 1086 but 71% of the mills were operating and the dues paid by them represented an exact 25% increase on 1066. Obviously the whole town was not destroyed.

Some 30% or so of Derbyshire was not enrolled at all in 1086, but there is little to enrol on the moors you will say and I will respond that in the Tribal Hidage Derbyshire (Pecsaetna) was *traditionally hidated* at 1,200 hides or 450 square miles. In recent times Wirksworth and High Peak have been surveyed at about 440 square miles and a comparison is tempting. It seems that maybe half of the urban population of Derbyshire joined a loyal, rural minority in 1068 and though large numbers of estates were wasted and then regranted to Norman lords they did begin to recover within a few years, either because retribution was not indiscriminate or because subsistence farming is remarkably resilient? Yet, as with a living organism, there may be evidence of trauma to adduce to the case? The entry for Morleystone Wapentake was preceded by a 'Sawley Hundred' title, as though the shire had, long ago, been hidated and English, while Appletree Wapentake was simply said to be in the Sheriff's hands. Of course, he would take seisin of the ferme of all estates on the Crown's behalf, but the legati may have been commenting on a reluctance to release them? Otherwise Appletree had no entries. By 1086 Derbyshire was a long way from the royal presence.

Derbyshire was a carucated (Danelaw) shire in 1086, her neighbour Staffordshire was hidated but entered arable ploughlands as well. Derbyshire's meadows were expressed in acres, ranging from 0.5 to 120 and 200 acres; in a few cases they were said to be 'a little'. In Staffordshire small amounts were expressed as 1 – 50 acres, otherwise double-linear units were employed. In Derbyshire 'wood pastures' probably meant rough grazings and were given in double-linear units ranging from the equivalent of 10 acres right up to 21,600 acres in one case (though otherwise not over 12,960 acres). Yet these pastures or grazings strongly suggest former measurement in hides with equivalents of 1.5, 3, 6 and 12 hides being popular. The few cases of woodland pasture stated as a fraction of the pasturage of the vill may have been deliberate evasions by holders of demesne (lordship) warelands? In Staffordshire they had woodland pastures but much of their 'woodland' appears to have been rough grazing as well. At Rolleston in Offlow Hundred (Staffs.) Henry de Ferrer's wood pasture was being ploughed, so clearly he saw it as wareland (permanent fallows) to be used as he thought fit? Double-linear units were used here as well but only three out of the five hundreds recorded wood pasture as separate from woodlands and in the other two these uses were confused together. Derbyshire expressed woodland or under-wood infrequently, sometimes as 'a little' but elsewhere from 5 acres to the equivalent of 12 hides (in double-linear units) with 0.5, 1, 1.5 and 2 hide equivalents being most popular. Staffordshire expressed woodland in double-linear terms for larger areas but 10 acre and 6 hide equivalents are frequent. In

Pirehill Hundred they included copses and alder groves (or slades) and used acres for *difficult* expressions, such as 2, 3 and 4 acres when 0.5 x 0.5 furlongs (2.5 acres) was apparently inadequate: one furlong and two furlong single-linear units (Cuttlestone and Totsmanlow Hundreds) would possibly be one and two acres. In both shires waters were only sporadically expressed and in a variety of ways, but both of them referred to arable *in addition* to the established area of arable cultivation. At Rolleston in Offlow Hundred (Staffs.) the villagers used a device to explain the wareland they had taken-in which, if it was repeated across the shire, would make the 11th century arable acreage of the county equivalent to 90% or 91% of the recent (surveyed) arable acreage!

Such are the patterns of logic, the thoughts of men in 1086, maybe not imaginative but in shire after shire, hundred and wapentake, for 13,418 place names essential. The entries may seem superficially tedious but they are not so when analysed. As in Derbyshire and Staffordshire we see confusion at times, as systems were superimposed by incomers, while at others we see the court of a whole hundred, the basic unit of legal practice and of law and order (meeting, 'three week to three week'), deciding amongst themselves which unit or expression to use for their problem and, because the Domesday survey used these tenants of vills (villages) appearing in their own hundred courts to depose or depone what *they* knew, the whole record is a massive jigsaw *of retrievable information*, of thought processes and *local* practices. We can thus retrieve the bones of a peasant world by patient excavation of documents, but someone in King William's inner administration also realised – and told the King – that such details can be linked and used to detect men's innermost secrets. This is how it worked.

There are many entries in every county where the scribes simply noted that the crown was not receiving its dues from geld assessments anyway. These required no particular sophistication. In the bishopric of Hereford, they noted, there were 300 hides yet the Bishop's men gave no account of 33 of them. At Duntisbourne in Gloucestershire Ralph paid geld, but kept back the geld on 3 hides and at Lower Slaughter (in the same shire) the clerks noted that 'before 1066 the sheriff paid *what he wished* from this manor, so they (the testators) *do not know* at what it is assessed'. 'Do not know' is always a useful phrase in a tight corner and we shall see it used many times. Just how far such simple evasions were occasioned by dishonesty it is difficult to say, the law generally seeks facts not opinions. At Lechlade in Gloucestershire Siward Bairn had 6 of his 15 hides exempted the geld by the (late) King Edward, *for which he could show the King's seal!* Not many landowners could produce such evidence, but Edward, we should remember, was a Norman by breeding and probably had no concept of English law, much less of hidation. How should he have known that geld cannot be remitted to favourites without damaging the common weal? Certainly in Kent, as we will soon see, the landowners were attempting much more subtle and obviously intentional evasions and no one there could produce a King's seal.

We have already observed that the geld lay upon the land's lord, that it is the owner of an asset who pays its tax burden. How else could a tax be applied? While it might be that, in practise, one landlord would agree to pay another's obligations this is unlikely to be a common practise. Assuredly the Norman conquerors invaded under the lure of unlimited wealth and all of them received rich rewards, but the inducement of the geld was an ignis fatuus for the conquerors (and maybe even the Conqueror himself) forgot that *someone has to pay it*. In removing the Saxon tax payers the Norman adventurers eliminated the tributaries and in making themselves recipients of Saxon assets they acquired an unforeseen liability. Moreover the King, as the recipient of the geld, made himself the tyrant of his coterie and cadre. Why even historians have forgotten that in order to raise taxes *someone must pay them*, otherwise an administration's entire resources will be absorbed by the need to extort revenues. Very many things about England were unknown to the new arrivals: actually *gathering* the geld must have been hell during the first decade or so of the Norman Conquest! The word is from the Old West German for "contribution", but it was neither voluntary nor optional by 1066.

It also seems unlikely that the 'new lords' would have known the meaning of 'hide', even those who *could* read and write. Churchmen could read and write, but did they know, for after the Conquest Saxon monks were replaced by Norman convents and abbots? As we shall see, by c.1150 the actual value of a hide was a closely guarded secret which written exemplars glossed, and it has remained so ever since, through ignorance. But *the stroke of genius* within the Domesday records is the addition of one, apparently redundant statistic, a statistic (as we have seen) not employed before in similar documents. The commissioners (legati), who probably knew nothing about agriculture anyway, were required to enter the plough totals, how many were held by the 'men' and how many 'in demesne' (in the lord's personal hands or on his lands). In all innocence the peasants replied, in open court, as honestly as they could, and in all ignorance the commissioners (legati) heard them and someone among the royal camerarii (civil servants) smiled and wrote them down. Now let us see what this statistic (together with knowledge of the hide) did for detection

Leicestershire lay at the junction of north and south in Saxon England. North and east stretched the Danelaw from which she protruded, south and west the English midlands and she was a carucated shire. Her arable enrolments only came to 192,840 acres while her tillage, the area under the ploughs was 224,310 acres. In recent times she has been surveyed at 445,000 – 446,000 acres of tillage and pastures combined. So a Domesday area in the order of 400,000 acres of tilth (50 %) and wareland is possible? Domesday also tells us of 23,010 acres of woodlands and 8,940.5 acres of meadows so, altogether, we can propose that about 60% of the area of modern Leicestershire was there in 1086. Areas of 50% tilth and 40% pastures, fallow and rough grazings would compare with other shires, e.g. Essex 56% tilth, Suffolk 57% tilth, Oxfordshire 50% tilth. In a few areas of Leicestershire we encounter intrusive pockets of hidation mingling with the carucations and grouping together in contiguous vills. Whether they are survivors of an older order, or reintroductions, it is hard to say but apparently even the local hundred-men were a little confused at times. Thus when hides *are* mentioned they are sub-divided into quarters and halves, *not* into virgates: they do not mix easily with the carucations in Leicestershire by 1086, which is suggestive.

When we encounter such ethnic mixtures as "9 carucates less 1 virgate" it might be easily explained but in other cases we suspect scribal litotes underlying apparently simple statements involving mixed units. In such cases we find the scribe using a 'footnote' in order to warn us of a disguised evasion, a sort of code decipherable by another scribe but not obvious to the superficial reader or even to the ignorant listener. Such a thing is a perfect code in that it is hidden among the obvious instead of relying purely on cipher integrity. At Bruntingthorpe we are told that 2 parts of a hide *are* 12 carucates! So, 2 moieties of a unit of taxation (hide) are actually 12 x 120 acres. *This is what it means.* It also means that ethnicities have been mixed. Never mind, we can now make this estate conform to the normal averaged values of this shire in both 1066 *and* in 1086 if we read the entry as '1,440 acres' (12 carucates) but, as the scribe is noting, *paying only* 240 acres of geld. At Saltby in Framland wapentake some 28 carucates of land with 26 ploughs (plough teams) were passed off as '2 hides and 3 carucates'. The inclusion of the plough totals as well as the 'declaration' enabled anyone 'in the know' (and there were not many) to read '26 carucates (or more) tillage' at a glance, 'gotcha'! The device was beautiful in its simplicity.

Nowhere was evasion more blatant than on Geoffrey de la Guerche's estate at Melton Mowbray. In 1086 the vill deposed 7 hides, 1 carucate and 1 bovate, in all 1,830 acres rendering geld. Suavely the Domesday circuit scribe noted, 'in each hide are fourteen and a half carucates', proving that certain talents abide from age to age in the civil service. We must doff our caps to this anonymous 'Bernard' and marvel at his accomplished mental arithmetic. Remember he had no Arab numerals with which to reckon. You see, nine other places were then listed as dependencies of Melton Mowbray, the aggregated total of all assets (including meadows and a mere 10 acres of woodland) came to almost *12,300 acres* but, warned by the scribal apothegm, we can multiply the hidation by 14.5

in order to verify this and the product of the 'adjusted', declared hidation (for geld) then becomes *12,315 acres* rather than '7 hides+ 1 carucate and 1 bovate' (1,830 acres), in all 19 square miles of land! Now, if we place these square miles on a map we discover a large block of contiguous place names to the east of Melton Mowbray together with a berewick (detachment) to the north and the recent surveyed area of all these places also adds up to 19 square miles! Moreover we learn that 58.5 teams (ploughs) worked 63.5 carucates of arable, this tillage of 7,020 acres being 57% of the total (aggregated) area under discussion. So a man might crop *more* than 120 acres per plough if he chose and if the soil was favourable. What else have we said all along?

In the tendency of seigneurial power to undermine the institution of monarchy, in favour of seigneurial anarchy, we can discern an important detail of the Leicestershire survey, a detail (as we shall see) just as relevant elsewhere. Not only would Geoffrey have been baffled to understand how his legerdemain had been exposed (no doubt with fearful consequences for him, had King William lived a little longer) but in Leicestershire (and elsewhere) there was another ingredient also helping patrocinium to promote feudal anarchy against the central power of the kingship. It was land hunger and serfdom, the consequences of 'the harrying of the North'. In entry after entry we discern a demand for tilth of any quality, even arable which had reverted to rough pasture. In places there *is not a single acre of woodland* recorded, so all manorial needs (buildings, tools, ploughs, firewood) would have to come from hedgerows alone: in part of Framland the area under tillage rose from 66% in 1066 to 77% by 1086. It seems foolhardy but men may have been desperate and Norman lords were not farmers, they were instead greedy and could let, or till, what they chose. This Medieval prairie is supported by a large population of serfs by 1086, men who brought with them distinctively different Danelaw units and definitions of meadows. The result may have been a 1086 landscape (in some places) not so different from that of recent times? The 'new lords', who included the Bishop of Lincoln, the Count of Meulan and Hugh de Grandmesnil, were taking advantage of circumstances to improve their personal demesnes and positions at the expense of both the Commons and the Crown and their activities (and those of their fellows) were not confined to Leicestershire.

Lancashire was about as far away as one could get from the king's general ambit in 1086 and in the West Derby Hundred Roger of Poitou's tenants aggregated a miserable total of 8 hides and 3½ carucates (note, once again, the mixed ethnicity of the units) covering 28 ploughs, 111 sub-tenants and 7,980 acres of 'woodland' (which included moorland with 3 eyries of peregrine falcons). Suavely the scribe reconciled what these tenants had deposed by adding, 'in each hide are 6 carucates of land': 6,180 acres of land of which 3,360 acres were tilled (54%) making an average of 52 acres for each of 119 households. The *total estate* came to 14,160 acres. Yet such royal scribes were obviously very sure of themselves, despite the remote and insecure locus, and perhaps this was because they already knew what the King suspected and the evidence he required? After all, there were magnates and vast estates much closer to London who were accounting just as creatively by 1086 and logic suggests that these more obvious estates may have come to the King's attention first. Feudalism aimed to minimize centralisation by dispersing any magnate's estates, for this weakened their individual power bases, yet if they chose to direct their own finances and to override local practises, malpractice could spread like an epizootic – undetected until it was too late to remedy the situation. Did the King's advisors in the exchequer comprehend *this* danger as well as the other and obvious problems of post-Conquest tax collection, did some discovery in southern England sound an alarum for elsewhere? Let us see.

CHAPTER SEVEN

'AU TENS PLAIN DE FELONNIE...'

Kent has always been a law unto herself and quite aside from her unique system of measurement (the sulung and jugum) she was displaying a serious and individual set of symptoms by the time of the Domesday Survey. She had had the misfortune to be in the Conqueror's way *and* the misfortune to be the principal fief of his half-brother, Bishop Odo of Bayeux, what a brace of miseries! When the survey of Kent commenced it started badly: feudal protocol (not that it really existed) broke down and the Canons of St Martin's *took precedence* over the King and his terra regis. This did not happen elsewhere (it was foolhardy as well as 'bad manners') and we will return to the implications in a while. The Kent folios themselves are sketchy and inconsistent, they show sweeping changes in recent ownership, general decreases in valuations and demands for high fermes (rents). Values decreased when the new lords took possession (post et quando recepit) but there are also many which started low in 1066 and continued down that path (modo). There are at least *seven* different formulae used to express woodland (mainly pig pastures) and many unquantifiable 'denes' (a local name for a clearing). The county was clearly in structural failure by 1086 with gaps in all sorts of records and almost every place. There was also a very low ratio of ploughs to the men (villeins) by 1086, suggestive of little incentive. If Middlesex had recovered from the immediate conquest period (as the next chapter will show us) what on earth was wrong with Kent in 1086?

Most remarkable, even diagnostic, were those cases where the hundred men, when called to testify, suddenly found they did not know the name of their vill! This was not because of some general renaming either, for even Hamo the Sheriff, who had $10\frac{5}{8}$ ploughlands worth £14-6s-6d 'in chief' (held directly from the King) in Wye Hundred, could not remember the name of the place. Some chief tenants could not (or would not) remember who was subinfeuded to them, even though the revenues from their tenants were certainly recorded. Why should this be, why because *one did not pay geld on rents*, only on land. They

71

knew their mesne lords, of course they did, they simply did not want to name them and this, in itself, tells us *that they knew* they were liable to pay geld on all their lands. Now the brief, as set out by the King himself, required sworn depositions from sheriffs, barons, Frenchmen, priests, reeves and English men, so such 'lapses of memory' or 'senior moments' were and are quite incredible. Still, it was the job of the clerks to set it all on record, faithfully, as deponed, *they were not the judges* and if some person or persons had suborned the system upon which the Crown's consuetudines (privileges) were levied it was up to the King to question why? Are we able to propose evasions on a massive scale? Well, a deposition of so many solins (sulungs, 240 acre units) was regularly followed by the formula, 'and for this it defends itself', presumably meaning that this was all the geld the chief-tenants thought it ought to pay? Not quite the spirit of the law.

The footnotes are, again, instructive. One missing estate fraction eventually surfaced under the 'modo' declaration of another tenant; Hugh de Montefort's holdings in Romney Marsh were attested by sworn statements from the lathe, two hundreds, his own men and the sub-tenants of other lords, but as his evidence could not be shaken the commissioner's clerks contented themselves with noting precisely how thorough they had been in their duty of enquiry. At Tintern in Blackburn (Lympney Lathe) Hugh claimed he only paid half a solin/sulung and not the former one sulung, though nine ploughs were at work and five ploughlands of arable were enrolled! Clearly his predecessor had not been honest either, but this *was* pushing things to the limit. When asked *why he claimed this*, he said that the estate was 'outside the division' of his lands. Thus he was claiming that he should only pay taxes if the land was conveniently placed, probably meaning held in his own demesne: dominium without the penalties of proprietas? This philosophy was attractive to others as well and we may doubt that it was ever an innocent mistake. We can be sure that the King would not see it as such.

The most successful of these exercises 'de ferma' or 'firma' (letting out at rent, done in order to minish tax liability) was run as the vast 'Lowy' (lordship) of Richard de Tonbridge, whose consummate fiscal skills require our special notice. Commutation was one form of remising the liability for realty (the geld lay upon the land, remember?) and much of Richard's revenue could only be estimated in terms of old valuations, so he deponed liability for twelve sulungs (2,880 acres) although he certainly had 3,960 acres of arable alone (and in fact 4,860 under tillage), 644 acres of woodland, 21 acres of meadow and other appurtenances, a minimum area of 5,525 acres valued at £70-15-0d per annum (revised, modo, to £60-15s-0d, this man did not miss a trick). The rack rent was probably much more as the remaining moiety (supposedly, minor part) of his estates was (he finally divulged) 'outside the division' of *his* lands: another £45–12s–5d of assets were only recorded as specie and, oh yes, there were another 220 acres of woodland and dene of woodland, but they slipped into the record without declaring a value or any rent! Well, he was worth *at least* £116–7s–5d in Aylesford Lathe, with other holdings in Sutton and Lympney, probably the largest administrative unit in Kent? What he actually possessed would, one feels, be of no importance however once the King had read his returns. Neither is it without significance that the same Richard had holdings in Surrey which answered there for rather less than any reality we can calculate. Wotton was half what it had been, Tondridge fell from 40 to 10, Chelsham from 20 to 4, Tooting Bec from 11 to 1 hides of geld, and so one rotten apple can infect a barrel. But Kent was his barrel.

The Domesday enrolment of Eastry Lathe was the one which came closest to a recent surveyed area, with Milton (half) Lathe second (as we would say) in the honesty stakes. The regular incidence of marshlands and weald (in Kent) do not really excuse all the lightweight answers given to the commissioners and the lapses of memory have already warned us of the dishonesty of many chief tenants. Some three years before this great survey had been conducted, Odo of Bayeux had been arrested and imprisoned by the King (his brother), so in 1083 his fief had escheated (returned) to the Crown, as did that of Bishop Symeon. Escheats were always useful, they gave the king's men a chance to audit up to date accounts from the sub-infeudations and so to identify sub-infeudations with mesne lords. No one has told us why Odo was arrested, all we know is that no one dared to do it, even when the King commanded it and so the King arrested him in person! Such was William's fury at his brother that even when he lay dying and had freed all other prisoners (for the good of his immortal soul) he cursed Odo again and declared that he should never be set free! Blatant and extensive defalcations would help to account for this anger, especially as the King could hardly execute his own brother for treason? He would, however, suspect that any magnate seeking to destabilise the royal treasury was probably intending to challenge his authority? Defalcations might also account for the commissioning of the Domesday Survey at Christmas 1085 at Gloucester: 'tha to tham midwinter waes cy cyng aet Glowcestir & hold thaer his hired fif dagas…' and afterwards had very deep speech and much council with his Witan about this land, how it was founded and with what sort of men it was peopled….[33]. So began the most thorough (and novel) of all the surveys undertaken by the English administration, a survey to remain unique in Europe for centuries to come and a national secret whose key has remained encoded until today. It has been so well kept that surely it has become the ultimate state secret?

From the slipshod nature of the Kent survey is it possible to argue that this was the first shire of the first circuit undertaken in 1086? Its general lack of discipline sits badly with the rest of the main text, even though it was edited for inclusion in the greater Domesday. Of course, as the pilot it need not have been conducted during the six months of 1086, which period (we suspect) encompassed all the other circuits *and* twice over (with the precaution of sending commissioners on the second circuit into shires where they were *not* known and which they did not know!), it may even be that Kent was a pilot run in 1085 and that its findings framed the protocol for all subsequent enquiries? As if a charge (if such was possible) had been thrown in an arc across a gap they came together for King William, the realisation that even his brother was open to the highest bidder (and *all* kings are paranoid) and the suggestion of some anonymous, senior, camerarius that a protocol of a particular type (as we discussed before) could prise from men, without their knowing it, their innermost secrets. Yes, the ways of Providence are inscrutable for had King William lived longer than 1087 there would indeed have been a Domesday of the type envisaged by Bede.

As it was there were two surprises in store. Quite predictably Odo was freed after William's death and then laid claim to the English throne, but the English fyrdmen turned out in support of the loyal forces and he was ousted. That King William II, 'Rufus', owed his throne to his English subjects is often overlooked by historians. Then, according to the chronicler Orderic Vitalis, King William Rufus initiated a 'new survey of the hidation of England' which, Vitalis makes clear, was *not* a post-Domesday survey (as some historians have claimed) but *the first reassessment after the Conquest*[34]. Quite clearly the central department of finance, whether we should call it the 'Exchequer', 'Hordere' or 'Gerefa', and its camerarii (men of the king's own chamber)[35] had had no time in which to implement Domesday between its editing and the Conqueror's death, so that when we are told that the 'revised description (descriptio) of all the English' was Rufus' invention Orderic was clearly mistaken. It had fallen to Rufus to *employ* this most valuable of all bequests and it seems that it was the Domesday Survey(s) or Book which has been largely responsible for the evil reputation given to this king by historians. Well, the 'Book' and some important miscreants who could influence the history writers – for "there is no new thing under the sun"! Vitalis and Eadmer were Rufus' particular detractors as *they* spoke for the privileged few in society.

The arable, Vitalis pleaded was seriously affected: well, *what have we been looking at* in our analysis of ploughs and ploughlands? Great poverty was caused (to whom, only to the land's lords!) and faithful men were borne down because the king listened to "false information". This is not specific enough, of course, and he clearly did not know the difference between hide and carucate but what he says *substantiates what we have discovered*. The surveys very much discomforted the dissimulating magnates. Of course, it is amusing to think that historians have chosen to represent these words, *from a member of the privileged class*, as a plea on behalf of a downtrodden peasantry, but then historiography is full of political perversions. The hoax that is Domesday studies today could never have happened had historians been objective, let alone apolitical, analytical and critical of chroniclers.

Orderic Vitalis knew enough to have had *some* access to official sources. He did not know the secrets of the Book but he knew that the revisions bore down on freemen, not bondsmen, upon the tilth or arable rather than income or profits and he hints very strongly that these reassessments were *laid out or rebuilt in the Exchequer*. What else have we been studying, yet why has it all been rubbished for the last thirty years? The camerarii were under the King's especial protection and even the mightiest in the land could not suborn or threaten them. As Professor Tout pointed out, they were creatures of the king's, created by him, rewarded by him, marked for retribution should he withdraw his protection, men who had sons to follow them but, by the King's favour, men who nevertheless retired as bishops. They were, in all but name, index linked civil servants. There can surely be little doubt that they were the 'evil advisors' who gave 'false information', to the king (viz. told him the truth) and that such detective devices as the Inquisitio Comitatus Cantabrigiensis were constructed by them? This document not only required juries to depone, it recorded the names of the jurors, as a means of punishing any found to be foresworn. The effect of this may be gauged from South Fambridge (in Essex) where the jurors suddenly found another 500 acres to add to the 1,060 declared in 1086! Of particular notoriety, says Vitalis, was one Ranulph Flambard[36].

For a start this clerk, who possibly rose to prominence under the Conqueror as Keeper of the Royal Seal and a Chancery Clerk (camerarius), was low born, always a crime. He became Rufus' chaplain, a Justiciar and head of the King's administration and was quite a reputed 'lawyer' of feudalism but, most significantly, he was described as a 'fiscal agent' and probably concerned with the judicial aspects of royal finance. It has been said that he extended royal authority, increased interference in local affairs, complicated administrative offices and 'helped' to found the Exchequer. His promotion of royal finances was, it appears, often at the expense of the Church in particular, though given their perdurable pleas for privileged treatment he may only have been even-handed in his treatment of *all* men and tenures? In 1099 he became Bishop of Durham, without relinquishing his position as, if you will pardon the phrase, 'head of the civil service'. Indeed, there can be little doubt that he was the father of our modern civil service as well as an architect of the revenue service. No one else had a better C.V. to be the secret architect of the Domesday Surveys and Vitalis actually credits him with *re-measuring England* and regularising the *variable carucate* "by the use of a little rope". Of course, Vitalis was as ignorant as any chief tenant of the purposes and mechanisms of the Domesday surveys, he even attributed them to William Rufus! The rope or stick which Vitalis had by the wrong end was the hide rather than the carucate, though mendacity was tinkering with anything that looked like a (tax) break and continued so to do long after 1100. And is it not curious that a Norman, descendant of Norsemen (we are told) should speak of 'variable carucates' rather than variable hides? Not at all, don't go to sleep on me, please, Saxons used hides, Danes and Norsemen *only understood* carucates, what have I been telling you! Vitalis, like all Normans, knew nothing of hides. Professor Darby[37] was also adamant on this point, whether in England or in Normandy, Normans only measured in carucates. The ethnic divide came in very useful for state secrets and the area of the hide remained a secret.

The 'Domesday Monachorum' of Christ Church, Canterbury, and the 'Excerpta' of Saint Augustine's may have been drawn from older, pre-Domesday documents or, instead, be entirely new and post-Domesday, but (significantly) neither source includes the tell-tale plough totals. The 'Inquisitio Eliensis' (1093) and maybe the 'Black Book of Bury St Edmunds' appear to be demands by the Crown for new and honest account rolls ('breves') to be submitted, on pain of forfeiture by escheat (seizure and reversion to the Crown), instructions which presuppose a means of *validating* both past and prospective breves! They were not, as historians have trivially attempted to claim, imitations of a 'new fashion' set by Domesday Book! Vitalis rails against Flambard and the King's officers for intruding themselves into the affairs of deceased prelates, seizing money from their treasuries and presumably taking the opportunity to make a first hand audit from the muniments in their thesauri?. The revenues of bishoprics and abbatial demesnes were seized, he complains, against the receipt of large amounts of money, but then the church is evidenced in Domesday Book as not the least among the black sheep, or should it be goats? We may cite cases where scribal footnotes declared that a Domesday estate had been obtained by the Church 'ad falsam brevum' (by means of a forged document) even, at times, to the King's despite! At Thorney Abbey Rufus' writ *ordered the royal officers to make the same extent of land everywhere pay the same dues*, as Southern noted[38]. The Church was in need of correction, maybe even of humility?

It was not difficult for *anyone* to claim that they held land or had some privilege as a result of some (dead) king's favour. By the thirteenth century the crown was issuing writs QUO WARRANTO which demanded evidence to support any such claims, written, sealed and irrefutable evidence. Because men in the eleventh century claimed acceptance of nuncupative proofs we must not imagine that the crown believed them. At Tewkesbury, it was claimed in 1086, 45 hides held in demesne 'were quit from all royal service and tax' – indeed, then why and who would vouch for this? By what superior power to the king's was the Crown to be deprived of revenue? Much Wenlock in Shropshire claimed the dead authority of King Cnut as their exemption. Such claims were preposterous, as was the claim at Painswick (Gloucestershire) that its 53 ploughs only owed one hide's worth of geld! The commissioner's clerks dutifully set it all down, it was not their place to pass judgement and, besides, the commissioners (legatii) might become suspicious if some clerk questioned such practices. After all, the commissioners were magnates themselves and had most to gain from trawling other men's fertile imaginations.

A substantial number, maybe a majority, of the new lords, both the lords temporal and the lords spiritual, were therefore traitors by fiscal evasion and being in the King's despite. Not surprisingly Vitalis complains that the new King spent his ill-gotten gains on armaments and on enriching foreigners, that is on mercenaries whom he *could* trust. Mercenaries were in much the same position as the exchequer clerks. Even before Magna Carta, great lords would appeal to their peers if punished by the king, their 'blood' demanded consideration, but lowly clerks were creatures of the king's will, friendless and powerless. Their only protection from the great lords was absolute loyalty to the Crown and vengeful peasantry as well as great lords showed no respect for deserted mercenaries. My guess is that Rufus decided to fine the miscreants heavily (whereas his father would probably have made a few stern examples as well) and thereby gained a reputation for being the richest King in Europe? But then, as Flambard would probably have told him, to use Domesday as evidence in a court would be to betray its power and maybe to risk revealing its secret mechanisms? Rufus was not as brave (or reckless) as his father: as he once said in reply to one of Archbishop Anselm's calumnies, "your predecessor would never have dared to say that to my father!"[39] He was right. Probably only Lanfranc ever dared to argue with the Conqueror, but not often.

When Anselm succeeded Lanfranc in 1093 the Crown would have known of both the Archbishop's temporalities and spiritualities (personal and Church wealth) and it must have been very difficult for Rufus to balance a Coronation oath of equity and justice to all against the *now conflicting* promise to support the Church and Archbishop! As he remarked to Lanfranc at this time, 'who among men can fulfil all his promises?' Professor du Boulay[40] calculated the value of the See of Canterbury to be £1,500 per year and not the £500 claimed by the Archbishop. To take but one indictment provided by Domesday Book, we can now see that Otford in Kent 'defended' itself in 1086 for eight sulungs (1,920 acres) yet the Archbishop had there 42 ploughlands (5,040 acres), 51 ploughs

(6,120 acres) and a great many appurtenances! Anselm, even without the use of usury, would have had 27 years of fraud open to a claim for restitution and it is not surprising that on the day of his investiture Flambard presented the Crown's case against the Archbishopric – note, not against the Archbishop – 'inflicting upon men of the Church of Canterbury a .... cruel blow', according to Anselm's panegyrist Eadmer. As we can now perceive it was not just 'the men' who were discomfited by a claim against the Archbishopric but especially the Archbishop. Just think of the money owed by the See and think of the shame of detection!

At Christmas the Archbishop offered Rufus £500 under the colour of a gift, 'at the instigation of his friends', to, 'secure for good the King's favour'. The good natured Rufus was pleased with this until, 'certain ill disposed persons' persuaded him that double or quadruple the amount might be more appropriate. Well, £1,500 might be affordable if one could never hope to recover the £27,000 *actually owed*, such a revision would be in line with du Boulay's research. So began a bitter argument, one which did not end until the Reformation. The Archbishop retaliated by preaching against long hair and effete manners at court, raised a complaint against sodomy (which the King scotched) and claimed that Christianity in England was virtually dead![41] Next he tried again for a synod during the King's absence in France, knowing that (as metropolitan) whatever he proposed in the King's absence the bishops would have to agree; when Rufus refused him again Anselm threatened him with eternal damnation! The King, however, had a grasp of the disguised reality and replied, 'do as you like with *your* manors, then, and shall I not do as I like with *my* abbeys', a reference to the legal nicety that as Edgar had refounded all the English convents, so they were actually the Crown's property and *not* the Church's, and *he was therefore* free to treat them as royal property and take them into his own hands, pending any succession. Anselm was arguing for the persona ficta, otherwise later understood as the 'dead hand' of the Church and that her resources should not be under the king's jurisdiction, whilst Rufus was arguing that the Crown not only had a right to tax an Archbishop's personal holding from the Crown but, in default of co-operation, a right to do *as the King pleased* with all revenues from abbeys and vacant sees. Of course, at every vacancy one could take *a fresh audit and update the Exchequer's records*, just like any escheat of lay estates. The importance of this dispute can hardly be underestimated for Thomas Becket raised *exactly* the same arguments seventy years later: when asked to pay a tax of two shillings on each hide of land owned by him (rather than by the church, note, the temporalities not the spiritualities), with the same response from Henry II[42]. This difference of opinion was perpetuated and indeed formed the cornerstone for the Dissolution of the Monasteries, chantries and chapels from 1536 to 1545. Once again we have Domesday Book at the very heart of English history and the nub of the

Reformation was struck when Rufus observed to Anselm that he could not be *simultaneously* loyal to both his King and to the Apostolic See (the Pope). Finally, Henry II when disputing with Becket famously said, 'the impost *shall* be given and *it is set down in the King's own document.....*' Domesday Book was still in use, even though by 1160 the king's men were searching for more subtle ways of mulcting income. We shall come to this. As a footnote we will add that Flambard's elevation to the bishopric of Durham in 1099, whilst continuing to serve as a royal administrator, can be seen as a royal safeguard against Anselm's manipulations. Flambard always remained in England when the king went abroad (styled 'capitalis justiciarius') and sometimes acted on his own (delegated) authority, so no one could suborn the bishops when he was present. Having a base-born clerk acting in the King's place in temporal matters but under the protection and security of spiritual office would have provoked the fury of any frustrated magnate!

The 'Dialogue of the Exchequer', a comprehensive document set down for Henry II said, 'it is not permissible to contradict its decisions', when referring to Domesday Book. The 'Discriptio Angliae' and the 'Totius Angliae Reviserit Descriptio' were the same thing, they were both references to 'Domesday Book' (as the vulgar had it), the most precious artefact in the Norman Royal treasury (in Archivis Wintoniae, for the seat of government was still at Winchester). Though there was a separate Winchester Domesday compiled for that city somewhere around 1110 it is likely that references to the 'Liber de Wintonia' are references to the 'Domesday (Book) of the Lord King', or 'Liber de Thesauro In Castello Wincestre'. When a crossbow bolt cut short the life of William Rufus his brother Henry wasted no time on recovering the body. Instead, being warned immediately (if not before) he galloped for Winchester and the treasury and what Rufus had called 'meis brevibus......in thesauro mea Wyntoniae', the king's own little (!) book. Ranulf Flambard was almost certainly at Winchester as well. Incidentally, the killer of Rufus was never apprehended or punished, but that is another mystery. And, as a footnote, it seems that Henry was responsible for commissioning the 'Winchester Domesday' soon after his accession. They say that this was in order to supply one of the missing blanks in the original Domesday surveys, but we will come to it in due course. It is more likely that Henry, afraid of offending his magnates, decided to extend taxation to new areas and in order to be able to remit some of the liabilities of his supporters. Of course, there was no reason for these favourable remissions to be permanent, the Exchequer could soon rebuild such requirements once the 'emergency' had passed, but remission of their fiscal sins was what the great lords wanted most and they did not know of the archive's flexibility. Domesday Book was not (as *we* now know) an arbitrary list of imposts but a reusable database capable of almost infinite revisions and this requires a further exposition.

Traditionally what we call 'Domesday Book' has actually been divided into two volumes. The 'greater Domesday' is that collection of folios which encompass the majority of English shires in 1086 and it has clearly been edited in order to arrive at its surviving form. The 'lesser Domesday' on the other hand contains *only* the entries for Essex, Suffolk and Norfolk, and these have not been edited and therefore include a mass of detail and description not to be found elsewhere, though it makes them as large as their sister volume. The reason for this division is not clear but it is usually attributed to the premature death of the Conqueror, which subtends that there was then no further reason to continue the process of editing. As we have seen, this was not the case, the Domesday folios continued to be the most important of all the Crown's muniments, indeed they only came into use *after* the Conqueror's death. Essex, Suffolk and Norfolk were, therefore, actually accorded *special status* by their deliberate exclusion from the other circuits.

The answer to the question of 'why were these three accorded some special treatment' may indeed lie in the unique nature of the information provided by East Anglia, especially with reference to the geld and its collections, for here the linkage of measurements of area and of geld appears to be peculiar. Historians and scholars have instinctively acclaimed the lesser Domesday as the key by which to decipher its more comprehensive sister, though in spite of this no one has, in fact, succeeded. 'The relationship between measurement and geld liability', said Professor Darby, 'seems to be an unfathomable mystery', and there it stands.[43] I think it would be a good idea for us to untangle this ancient mystery before proceeding to suggest reasons for the individual treatment of the 'lesser Domesday'.

We have already examined Essex in some detail and its Domesday records *are* rather different from those of Suffolk and Norfolk. Essex is English and (largely) hidated and has already provided us with the key required to unlock the ancient hide unit and its transformations. Norfolk and Suffolk, by comparison, are carucated shires belonging to that group which contemporaries had begun to perceive as tax privileged, the former Danelaw. Here the device of the ploughs would serve the Crown as well as it did in a hidated area but the proliferation of small, but free, holders of land, apparently exacerbated by refugees from the more northerly Danelaw shires, was confusing the picture and a clearer perception of the special practices of carucated shires was required if the Exchequer clerks were to understand precisely what was happening. In these two counties alone we find a regular and proximate combination of stated areas and geld payments *in addition* to the information supplied in other former Danelaw shires. So, if such records had ever existed elsewhere this is the only remaining, unexpurgated version, or might it be that another palimpsest had been created by planting Danelaw practices onto an earlier Anglian logic? Let us continue and all should eventually become clear.

At first view the statistics, although daunting in their profusion, are not unfamiliar. Norfolk enrolled between 2,422 and 2,428 carucates, equivalent to some 291,000 acres, while her arable (plough totals) recorded about 604,000 acres.[44] In 1066 she had 19,000 acres of swinewoods, 46,458 sheep on pastures and 3,020 goats, so she was grazing perhaps another 68,000 acres? Today Norfolk has over 600,000 acres of arable and 50,000 acres of grazings (to compare with the 672,000 aggregate of 1066) and the general agricultural estimate is in the region of one million acres, her gross being 1.326 million acres. Of course, although three entries in 1086 mentioned marsh there are no regular records of turbaries at the broads, fenland, marshlands, or breckland. By now we find nothing remarkable in such agricultural coincidences, they are true to the pattern we have recovered from elsewhere, from the 'greater Domesday' and from Essex. A discrepancy of 10% over 900 years would cause us no alarm on a like for like basis. We seek consistency rather than absolute coincidence.

Turning to Suffolk we find, once again, that modern authorities are not absolutely consistent when it comes to Domesday statistics. Her carucation is given in one source as 2,404 and in another as 2,779, depending on formulistic nuances as much as on addition. So, converting our carucations will give us between 288,480 acres and 333,520 acres. Darby counted the plough teams and came to 4,502 ploughs for Suffolk, an arable acreage of 540,290 acres, or almost a duplicate of Essex. As we have seen elsewhere, such coincidences actually provide consistency for the two shires are similar in size. Today the total of agricultural land in Suffolk is some 753,700 acres out of a county gross of 940,000 acres, but not all of it is arable by any means. So the 1086 ploughmen had 60% of the modern agricultural area down to arable though the 'carucation' was only 32% of the modern area. Well, modern agriculture has no need of fallows but in 1086 we do not expect either intensive practices or rotations, which is not to say that they did not exist. Meadows and swinewoods will give us another 46,000 acres and the three accidental inclusions of 'sheep pastures' in 1086 masked 37,522 sheep and 4,343 goats, or a further 41,865 acres of grazings. Then there were two and a half parks and odd entries of 'waste' and woodlands without looking at the curtilages of 19,130 'households'. Adding another 50 to 60,000 acres we can say that we have in 1086 enrolled 60-70% of modern Suffolk.

Of other, alternative, localised economies we have little enough evidence: there were few sheep on the Sandlings and few ploughs on the brecklands yet these have not been historically entirely valueless. Prior to the war time economy of the early 19th century Suffolk was traditionally a pastoral rather than an arable shire, yet her arable capacity in 1086 was probably equal to anything which came afterwards. Entries such as Dunham, where 900 sheep were kept on three carucates, make the case for pastoral activity *and* for the existence of other tracts of land *not entered* under a general statistical record. Such a number of sheep cannot be supported on 360 acres of inland, so some sort of wareland was also involved. Such references are confirmed elsewhere. At Stanham in Bosmere there were 28 acres which were *partly* wood and partly *cleared woodland* while at Gislingham in Hartismere Hundred Lewin held a quarter of his father's woods, *even though* his father's manor of 30 acres *had no woods enrolled*. At Bernham in Bradmere and at Mildenhall in Lackford Hundred there were (respectively) 12 and 31 'eque silvatice' or forest mares. We do not need many trees by which to define a 'woodland', as we have already discussed, and Suffolk has always been well endowed with heaths and commons. These, then, were the warelands, unlikely to be recorded for taxation because they carried no obvious crops. Swinewoods were never reckoned at less than two pigs, or four acres, which might leave us with numerous spinneys and gores? At Stanham we accidentally learn of one and a half acres of 'wood' attached to two acres of land, which minute parcel of inland-with-wareland helps explain how so many small manors of freemen and socmen could exist in this shire in 1066 and in 1086.

In Suffolk we find very different fisheries from elsewhere for we have evidence of seagoing fleets. At Blythburgh and at Dunwich, on the coast, and also in a tight grouping of vills inland (at Beccles, Worlingham and Willingham), we find herring rents or renders. By 1086 these accounted for 142,000 herrings (which had, it appears, been 112,400) and which, *if* they represent a tithing of the catch, gives us almost one and a half million herrings a year. The fleet which operated out of Wangford Hundred appears to have travelled down the River Waverley from Beccles and Shipmeadow to Oulton Broad and Lowestoft, maybe the origin of the (later) Lowestoft fishery? Dunwich and Beccles, it would appear, were both considerable settlements and they possibly acted with some reciprocity, for while the Beccles render of herrings doubled between 1066 and 1086 that of Blythburgh fell from 10,000 herrings to 3,000 with fifty shillings rent. At Dunwich there is evidence in Domesday Book of the sea encroaching already, perhaps enforcing her reliance on deep-sea fisheries, but an alternative for this increase at Beccles could be that fears of Viking raiders may have encouraged the use of a less exposed, inland, anchorage?

Now to a peculiarity of these two shires, of Norfolk and Suffolk, the apparent linking of geld amounts so consistently with extents, the latter generally expressed in leagues and furlongs, in lengths and in breadths. In the past these encouraged much speculation and Round and Lees in particular constructed a system of hypothetical 'leets', by which 20d 'ora' (coins) of geld could be assessed.[45] They saw entries for hundreds paying geld-payments and proposed arbitrary levies on 'selected' vills 'which may have been tax centres for a district' in each hundred, yet they could ultimately find no congruence between extents, 'leets', carucages or geld-payments. They quantified 'leets' of 20d at 6 carucates, 720 acres, and speculated on 12 'leets' to each hundred (a theoretic hundred of 8,640 acres) which does appear to give the 24½ hundreds of Suffolk 211,680 acres of geldable land when she apparently paid for 186,336 acres, and the 34 hundreds of Norfolk 293,760 acres to compare to the 280,200 acres for which she apparently paid, though (of course) each was underpaying, thus making *any* 'system' a fraud! Personally I do not agree that the league was 1½ miles and I think 2½ more likely but we must tread with exaggerated caution over the whited sepultures of dead demi-gods. Fortunately, we cannot differ over the furlong of 220 yards and leagues make infrequent appearances. While there appear to be similarities between extents and carucations, they actually rely on disparate and not on common logic, with only some cases of coincidence. In fact, if we plot our extents, converted to 720 acre units, onto a map of the more recent Suffolk hundreds, we can begin to perceive a picture and *we* can even do better than this for *we* can add the assay of *calculation* to their blind speculations.

All taxation is targeted and in order to identify the tax-target we need to lay aside such myths as 'beneficial hidation', arbitrary imposts and comprehensive coercions. We seek system and methodology not the machinery of the modern state. The 'leets' of Suffolk were proposed by Lees as a total of 258, or 1,548 carucates, some 185,760 acres. The extents enrol something like 324,700 acres using the 1½ mile league proposed by Round. Thus these 'leets' would, on average, represent about 57% of the extents given in 1086. Of course, the reality varied hundred to hundred and the substitution of a 2½ mile league does at times make a good deal of difference. To take but one example, the Half- Hundred of Lothingland was entered only on 'the lump' at 6 leagues by two and a half leagues and two furlongs, which would make 62,400 acres, or the whole area of the hundred and probably an extension into Blything Hundred to the south. However, the scribes were *not* recording its obligations, they were noting that *it did not pay as a hundred* in spite of its acreage, for it *only paid* the notional ten shillings of a half hundred! Where have we seen such notes by scribes before? On any map we care to construct, which will show the extents superimposed on recent hundreds, we may immediately see that those hundreds with the smallest extents are precisely those with the lowest arable potential in 1086, such as Plomesgate and Lackford, the Sandling and breckland hundreds. These had saltpans and fisheries recorded but (with one exception of a belt in Colneis) little arable. In the hundreds of Hoxne, Hartismere and Bosmere and in Babergh-Samford we observe less arable and more limited extents than elsewhere, but they do contain more woodland for swine. The extents mirror the carucations because they record the arable principal of each hundred and, no doubt, this was once a conceptual tax target; we have already discussed it at length and found confirmation in contemporary documents. The geld lay upon the land's lord, on the affluent and not on the needy, what else should we expect? 'Shareholders' in the landscape (not speculators), freemen not bondmen, were targeted through the 'mansus in dominicatus', the lord's demesne, though by 1086 changing conditions and tax evasions were rapidly destroying any ability to apply such simplistic logic. If fertility improved the lord benefited from the profits of his demesne, if the fertility of the arable declined, who was then to blame? Swings and roundabouts, as we have seen elsewhere. The bondmen simply subsisted.

The extents of Suffolk do appear to offer realistic assessments of areas, certainly when they are aggregated for entire hundreds. There is an apparent but superficial problem at Beccles for it was given *two* extents in 1086, the larger, at 62,400 acres, being well in excess of even the Wangford Hundred in which she was situated! However, the smaller extent, when added to the extents given for all the other vills in Wangford, is convincing as they jointly record (overall) 28,800 acres for an area more recently surveyed at around 35,000 acres and containing some marshy and broadland areas. The plough total (arable area) for this hundred in 1066 was 26,970 acres and the total of arable, woods, meadows and identifiable pastures altogether came to 30,283 acres on record, which confirms our suspicions: total agricultural area 30,283 acres, declared extents 28,800 acres, modern gross area 35,000 acres. It therefore seems that the 62,400 acre entry is misplaced or (in reality) ambiguously placed in a conflation of hundreds all of whom contributed to the terra regis heading and that it actually refers to the Blything Hundred, an area more recently surveyed at about 75,000 acres. Both the Blything and Wangford Hundreds contained the (two) Suffolk herring fleets of 1086 and so a possible confusion of their records is understandable.

But times were changing and the Crown needed to know how change was being effected, so all sorts of details crept into this indiscriminate gathering of data. At Well in Freebridge (Norfolk) the normal extent was supplemented with a second one of 5 x 4 furlongs (200 acres) of 'pasture belonging': adding wareland to inland again. At Marham in Clackose (Norfolk) the extent of a league and one hundred perches by half a league and a furlong (2,695 acres) was followed by 'and the marsh measurement is unknown'. At Southwold in Blything the clerks noted that its 9 x 5 furlongs (450 acres) were a 'division extending from the sea as far as Yarmouth', not the apothegm we have come to expect from Leicestershire but still an honest, if tongue in cheek, emphasis made for the attention of 'Sir Humphrey' when the folios should be delivered back at the Exchequer. But wait a moment, what did we discuss a few moments ago when we analysed Beccles, Blything and Wangford and noted the herring fleets? Why, an accurate extent, apparently *intended to supplement Blything's records*, just what 'Sir Humphrey' *will* need! Yes, the information is all there, if only we bother to look for it. Lackford Hundred (Suffolk) had 126½ carucates and notionally gelded at 127½, Blackbourne and Bradmere had 193 carucates and notionally gelded at 195, Lothing with Lothingland had 248½ carucates and gelded at 249. Ipswich had 9½ carucates and gelded at 9¾. At Chattisham in Samford (Suffolk) the clerks could discover no more than that it measured eight and half furlongs by six (510 acres) and paid only 6½d to the geld, though elsewhere much smaller areas paid high values: 15 acres at 24d, 10 acres at 16d or even 20d. Everywhere (as we have seen in Kent) new lords and new opportunities were corrupting the established order but the Crown was not always sharing in these new valuations, just as it was not always receiving its consuetudines.

Scholars in the past could find no apparent correspondence between measured extents and gelds, they found them 'an unfathomable mystery', and this was precisely because there was *no* arithmetical connection. On the one hand the geld amounts tell us what the historic picture of 1086 revealed about tax evasions, but on the ground realities, even solidarities were changing, so the clerks noted against these *actual payments* such fixed and immutable realities (as they thought) as they could discover, their object being *to draw attention to the differences.* The tax system (and system there must be, in order to justify taxation) was in chaos by 1086 and multiple layers of ethnicities, imposed solutions, duplicities and exploitations did not help. Indeed, unless someone could restore order there was likely to be no legal foundation for the exercise of power, yet power ultimately depends on loyalty in order to establish legal consensus and loyalties are better established through system and fear than by financially brokered 'friendships'. It has always been the case that whoever controls the revenues controls the power brokerage, power finances fear and fear secures loyalty. Even in a democracy this is true for the citizen cannot be trusted to be honest. In this sense, we might say, Domesday is still with us, for taxation justifies all forms of tyranny.

Using the three parishes study published in East Anglian Archaeology 49[46] we can demonstrate how these extents worked (at least in south east Norfolk) for the exchequer. The hundreds of Loddon and Clavering contain these three (selected) parishes whose total area in recent times has been 5,127 acres; in 1066/86 Loddon, Heckingham and Hales also included Chedgrove, Kirby Cane and Sisland, which altogether, according to their combined extents in 1086, totalled 5,008 acres. The joint carucation of these holdings was 1,571 acres though their arable capacity was considerably higher at 3,420 acres (1066) and

3,120 acres (1086), with the demesne ploughs ploughing much *more* than the carucation! Overall 3,863 acres, or 77% of the recent gross area, was recorded in 1066 as agricultural land, falling to 71% in 1086, in which the arable of 1066 equalled 68% and by 1086 had fallen to 62%. These orders of value are quite familiar to us now for we have regularly seen them represented elsewhere. Demographically there was a slight increase in bordars by 1086 but the general picture was one of stability and established tax evasion though *we would not have a full picture of this were it not for the accurate extents.* Whereas in the 'greater Domesday' we must needs check carucation against the ploughs, in Norfolk and Suffolk we have the more accurate, *additional*, picture provided by the extents, viz. 5,008 acres (though only declaring 1,571 acres in demesne) with over 3,000 acres of arable, the majority of which was certainly liable for the geld because it *was* retained in the lord's hands. And if we can do this, so could the camerarii of 1086. Once again, coincidence of 98% between Domesday and a modern surveyed area is more than persuasive and it certainly puts paid to Round's notional 'leets' and to Darby's 'unfathomable mystery'.

Anyone who has investigated Medieval account rolls knows that the real problem was not numeracy but the system by which it functioned, the need to check and recheck sums obtained from accounts cast without the benefit of algorism. In any age genius may function independent of the limiting factors of knowledge, but then it inevitably finds achievement hampered by lack of facility. Lincolnshire allows us to demonstrate the inability of Medieval arithmetical tools to serve the potential of the methodology of the Domesday process but, in that demonstration, it would also appear to illustrate the subtlety of intellectual facility possessed by some contemporaries. Kirton in Lindsey (fol. 338),[47] part of the terra regis and once part of Anglia (see chapter 5), will serve our purpose well for it presents us with three sets of statistics, all of which (as we shall see) express the same physical reality though from dissimilar bases.

In 1066 Kirton *had* presented 8 carucates to the geld with 16 ploughs at work but by 1086, as part of the terra regis, there were 22 ploughs and 200 acres of meadow, in all 2,640 acres of arable or 2,840 acres of agricultural land. This, says the greater Domesday, measured 2 leagues by 20 furlongs, that is 2x1 leagues or 12.5 square miles of land, some 8,000 acres. This total is important. What follows is a list of carucates in the sokeland and *then* a longer list of tenants and their holdings of ploughs, meadows and (in two cases) rough pasture, a form of exegesis or exemplification of the summary entry already made by the extent. Of course, scholars in the past have been baffled by the relevance of these three statements and did not make them confirmatory simply because they had no tools by which to convert the figures to statistics. We have been freed from such shackles and *can* make the necessary comparisons, now behold!

'To this manor', therefore, 'belong(ed)' a total of 54 carucates and 49 bovates, with 'two parts of a bovate'; if we accept the latter as two fractions which, together, did not quite equal a bovate we can say we have 66¼ carucates plus almost a bovate, let us say 67 carucates. The scribes made their own summation here and called it '59 carucates of land for geld … land for 69 ploughs'. They were juggling both liability for tax *and* physical area and both sums were hampered by Roman numeration. The addition we have made from the entries, 67 carucates, comes to 8,040 acres; the 69 carucates of the scribes would be 8,280 acres. Let us look at it again and in another way.

The list of tenants (with their holdings) can be aggregated to 53½ ploughs and 14 oxen, with 1,255 acres of 'meadow' and 132 acres of rough pasture: the plough potential, therefore, will be 53½ plus 1¾ ploughs, some 55¼ ploughs, which equals 6,630 acres. Adding the meadows and rough pastures to this we have 8,017 acres in all. The scribes did their sums and concluded that there were only '50 ploughs'. They also counted the 229 sokemen at '223', the 18 bordars at '16' and the 31 villeins at '15': clearly they missed one group of 16 villeins and 2 bordars at Hibaldstow (who had 3 ploughs) but they may also have perceived a need to make 'the books balance'. You see, 50 ploughs is equivalent to 6,000 acres and the terra regis had another 2,640 acres of arable (as well as 200 acres of meadow), which would make 8,640 (or 8,840 with meadows) acres in all. Of course, the King did not tax (geld) himself or his bondsmen at Kirton, but all the outlying (soke) lands we see detailed here, tenant-by-tenant, are largely held by sokemen, that is by nominally free men, men *liable to pay* the geld. So, the extent says '8,000' acres; well the geldable area (acreage) came to 7,080 acres out of 8,040 acres (which the scribes added up to be 8,280), and that is *very* close to the extent. Finally, the analysis of the tenancies came to 8,017 acres but the scribes missed out one entry (a single place) in their summation and seem to have found that a broad '50 ploughs' would help them reconcile the terra regis as well. Now let us summarise.

So there was and is some confusion, but it is not complete confusion, the statistics are not irrecoverable. We have *three separate calculations* and they say 8,000 ≈ 8,040 ≈ 8,017 acres with the emphasis on arable and on the tax liability of those who claim to be 'freemen': it offers a maximum of half a percent of error! Moreover a footnote tells us that the scribes *then* had to cope with supplementary depositions about what was a berewick (Hibaldstow) and that there were 'inland' moieties at Graylingham and Springthorpe, though all the rest was 'sokeland' (land held by freemen). If we give credence to these we may reduce the 69 carucates of the scribes by 3 carucates to 66 (we counted 67) and we can take 2½ ploughs (300 acres) from the tenant's list. No wonder they were confused, and the root of it seems to have been that Earl Edwin's lands, *formerly* liable for tax, had subsequently been *appropriated to the terra regis* and it was becoming impossible to sort out the exact area of land involved because tax liability had also shifted in the more distant past from the (ancient and comprehensive) English model (hidation) to the (politically correct) Danish model! We can also see the complications provided by a multitude of little freemen all holding outside a manorial structure. No wonder the bureaucracy wanted to simplify matters!

The extent (we can see) in 1086 is the extent of the arable land attached to Kirton, rather than any 'taxable leet' and the additional meadows and pastures tell us that there was *more* than 8,000 acres involved at this place in 1086 and in this it differs significantly from Norfolk. We know this is repeated on other Lincolnshire estates where extents are given for 'woodland pasture' *and* then for the whole estate (e.g. Fiskerton: 10 furlongs long and 9 broad; 20 furlongs long and 9 broad), though 'rough pasture', 'meadow' and 'woodland pasture' would *all* appear to refer to wareland in Lincolnshire. At Langtoft we find 'marsh' 2 leagues long and 2 broad with 'arable' 15 furlongs long and 9 broad, at Baston 'marsh' 16 furlongs by 8 and arable 8 furlongs by 8. None of these are 'leets' specifically for taxation, they are instead appreciations of areas set aside by topography for certain uses and (when we look at the map) apparently aggregated: that is, they were not single, blanket areas, valleys or plains, instead they were pieces from here and there placed together, *recast and simplified* into extents. Let us pause and reflect on the skill required by this. Someone took the figures for each estate on this patchwork landscape and *converted each* to the accountant's checkerboard, cast the counters and arrived at a record expressed in Roman numerals. Such subtlety of thought and facility in manipulation commands our admiration just as surely as does the speed with which these surveys were apparently conducted. And woven in among the mass of figures requiring reconciliation were palimpsests of logic with some counties, or hundreds, believing that they should present whole landscapes, others only the arable, others only the demesnes and some (maybe *many* tenants) claiming to present whatever they wished to the geld! No wonder if at times the scribes found that the woof of this cloth made for a difficult design, no wonder if some circuits found it easier than others and some scribes were more advertent than their fellows, just as some historians may be today? Beresford and St. Joseph[48] drew attention to the Giddings (Huntingdonshire) which in 1279 cultivated 3,620 acres (excluding curtilages) over an area later ascribed some 3,854 acres. What they could not know was that the 1086 enrolment of 17 hides, which they identified, was equivalent to 4,080 acres, so we may assume that 'not a hide nor a yardland', in the chronicler's words, was missed in those places where (as in Essex) a hidation was used to state the gross! Here we also see reference to 138 'households' in 1279 and 58 in 1086, but only

90 taxpayers in 1327 with no more than 544 people in all by 1801, startling statistics to which we will return in chapter 9.

And so we may circle in the philosophical air and slowly, thoughtfully, return exemplified to the astringer's hand, like a disciplined spar-hawk; we will alight once more upon the problem of 'why were Essex, Suffolk and Norfolk accorded some special treatment'? It is not (as the leet was not) an 'unfathomable mystery', no, for the answer is now and in general aspect always was, obvious. The 'lesser Domesday' was not (as we have already said) abandoned on the Conqueror's death, no, instead it was employed. Now, had its employment depended on editing we can be sure that it would have been as thoroughly edited as the 'greater Domesday', so we conclude that there were good reasons for it *not* to be edited. Moreover, editing of the greater Domesday is not as thorough as some authorities have claimed for no attempt was made to restructure the Kent folios or put them in order (with the terra regis entries first) and there are countless other entries which should have been expunged or reordered if the object really was to produce a standardised or uniform text. The fact is it was merely simplified, though not to the degree where serious mistakes could have spontaneously arisen and, this being the case, there was *nothing to prevent* the lesser Domesday from being *similarly simplified*, not unless its elaboration of detail was thought to be essential to some purpose? Well, clearly it was. Two possibilities, two reasons for the lack of editing, present themselves and they are bound in with the problem of governance and with the colophon to the 'lesser Domesday'.

The most obvious alternative is that the systems and regional practices which the 'lesser Domesday' recorded were as baffling to contemporaries as they have been to recent scholars. However, *we know that this is not true* for we have seen how Essex may be dissected and reconstructed, may serve as a key to other shires. We have seen how the apparent complexities of Norfolk and Suffolk may be resolved provided we *do not make the assumption* that order and system were being recorded in perfect operation as though they were fossils, if we rather choose (instead) to see the mass of detail as a data collection process which, in common with Essex and other shires, could be processed later, once the entire database (Domesday Book) had been compiled. We are, therefore, left with *only one reason* for the unexpurgated nature of the 'lesser Domesday': it was intended to be the exemplar and to provide the keys by which to unlock all the other shires. This is how we have used it, this is what we have now done. The 'lesser Domesday' divides neatly into English and Danelaw systems of land use and of taxation because it presents the ethnicities side by side. Ultimately the *exact* amounts paid to the geld (ad geldam) were irrelevant for the object was *not* to reduce or even to maintain payments, it was to increase them – "and if more could be had?" The supplementary details, or evidences, were included *because* they exampled evasions and provided the Conqueror with irrefutable evidence of treachery *by his own people*. Domesday Book was not designed as a fossil but as a living organism or functioning machine. The three important points to be established, in 1086, were the rationale behind previous gelds, also who had been guilty of evasions (treachery) and how the system could be extended? There may also have been a corollary, to see how far the rot had spread, tracing a chief tenant's evasions from his caput (principal residence) outwards? In so doing one might at least prove his intentions? If future generations of clerks were to be trained in this new method of data analysis it was essential that some record should survive of worst practice, but it would have been tiresome indeed to fight through the minute details in *every shire* with *every* succeeding generation of bureaucrats, winnowing relevant and durable data from the evidence of ancient malpractice. It was important to record the malpractice in order to ensure that it was not repeated in the future (especially when it had been punished), it was hardly essential to emphasise it once the geld records had been set straight. Even a King finds it politic to draw a line somewhere, in the interests of justice and magnanimity!

We can hardly doubt that the lesser Domesday was the tool or exegesis by which the epitome was drawn down and exemplified, the colophon tells us as much. It does not appear at the end of the 'greater Domesday' but at the end of the 'lesser Domesday' and after telling us the year in which the survey was made (1086) it goes on to say 'thus was made this DESCRIPTIO, not only through these three counties here, but also *throughout those elsewhere'*. The importance of DESCRIPTIO, apart from its duality of meaning as either a map or a written description, is in its legal status, for it implies 'measured evidence'. When we look at the extents of Suffolk and Norfolk, which possibly originated in some old, established Anglian system not found elsewhere in the Danelaw, we are struck by the use of those fixed units by which contemporaries coped with the very real problem of *square measurement*. Acres and hides are one thing, the acres being encompassed by the furlong of 220 yards and hides being their aggregation, but large tracts of land *outside hidation* are very different. The furlong (derived from the acres' length) was the standard unit, the perch was the sub-division, and much ingenuity is evident for we invariably discover that the acres they described comprised *exact totals*. It took considerable skill and initiative to create some of the unitary combinations we have encountered *by which to express exact quantities*. Maybe Vitalis was not altogether fanciful when he ascribed a 'little rope' standard of measurement to Flambard's work? It amazes us, it must have amazed contemporaries.

Finally, we must needs acknowledge the problems of governance. The Conqueror found himself in a unique position, ruler of two realms separated by water. Whichever way he turned, wherever he stood, there was no protection for his back. To retain Normandy he needed to be constantly campaigning along a broad front, so it made sense to ensure that that realm which was surrounded by water and difficult to access (England) was as secure from revolt as it was from invasion. To do this he needed to identify his enemies at home, secure his friends and ensure that governance was in independent and dependable hands. He *needed* a civil service by which to dilute the power of any noble justiciar or regent. It may also be that he, like Henry II, realised the potential of a secure and fecund source of revenues with which to finance warfare in someone else's backyard. This, after all, remained a guiding principle of the English civil service in its advice to governments for many centuries to come.

CHAPTER EIGHT:

'ON EITHER SIDE THE RIVER LIE....'

The devil, they always claim, is in the detail. So, if we have overcome our fear of statistics (and they are, at best, an acquired taste, like olives or anchovies of historiography) let us move from the dramatic opera of history to its essential labour, without which daily round by millions of people, generation to generation, there would be no structure to which dramatic events such as revolts, regicide and religious reformations could cling. History is about people but only the places and a few things remain for any period of time to remind us of their generality, of the canvas upon which a few vivid characters splashed a little colour now and again. Domesday was established to serve one particular purpose, taxation, but we can recover *far more* of a picture than this, thanks to the detail it contains and to its wider design.

At first view one might suppose that in 1066 and 1086 the people who lived on either side of the River Thames, who shared common problems and a common ethnicity as well as an important asset in common, would think in identical ways, but this was not the case. As for us, we no longer require a helicopter for our 'shallop flitteth silken sailed' as we look down the reedy margins to the Camelot that was Saxon and Norman London, a square mile enclosed by mighty walls built by weirds and, by 1086, with an awesome, impregnable, white-towered donjon among earthworks at its eastern end. On the Middlesex bank our great survey traced the suburbs of the City from Bishopsgate and Holborn to Nomansland (west of Holborn) while at Tottenham Court, St Pancras, Tyburn, Ebery (Victoria) and 'Westminster Village' we can discern some prosperous agricultural ventures. The City, we may say, lay between Bishopsgate and Soho and was not entirely intra-mural while Westminster (even at this early date) was barely detached. Most of the north shore, the City, lies blank in our folios – for some reason its profits and assets (which were not based on land holding) were, in common with Winchester, not encompassed in 1086. If the King had lived longer, who knows? That is what they say and we shall explore an alternative in the final chapter. But on the south bank of the Thames we have a much better picture based on property and this too may be said to be a part of London's environs.

The Surrey folios recorded 124 properties in Southwark and London ranging from 2d to 40d each in annual value, a large number of the rents being in the range 6d, 7d and 9d. We can say that the (later) 'cit.'s country seat' may have had an ancient pedigree? The focus was clearly on Southwark where the king took tolls from the 'vicus aquae', Southwark roads and the town's 'Strande'. It was, therefore, the port of London where ships could ride or be careened, whereas opposite (on the north bank) under the City walls, it was possible to unload but not to strand. At Southwark, Domesday Book records, Bishop Odo of Bayeux had attempted to usurp the revenues. What a surprise. The 1160 'Tristan of Thomas' suggested that seagoing vessels anchored here in a haven before trans-shipping their wares to small boats which could then pass up river under London Bridge, and so Putney forwarded 240d annually to the Archbishop of Canterbury's estate at Mortlake from cargo tolls levied on the Thames on the Surrey shore. On the Middlesex side there were probably too many weirs and eel-bucks for navigation, quite apart from the shallower draft of the river? That there were few quays on the north bank seems to be confirmed by the scarcity of 'hythe' place names adjacent to the City (as noted by Dyson).[49] What we see is a picture very like Hogenburg's (1570) map of London, though we have had to piece it together, entry by entry, maybe even a picture like that in Camden's 'Speculum Britanniae' (1594)?[50] As we have seen, things may not have changed so much in between, maybe not even the population? We shall look at them in our next chapter. Since I first dared to suggest it, thirty years ago, the estimated 1086 population of London has increased dramatically in the imaginations of historians.

At Bermondsey the Count of Mortain had no less than a hide for his 'domum' (house), worth 96d, and although almost 31% of Bermondsey was assessed as arable only 19.25% was tilled in 1086, albeit at high values. When Stoke-by-Guildford could only average 1.875d per acre and a good average in the shire was 2d Bermondsey averaged 3.75d the acre with 13 London burgesses paying an average of 3.4d each. These London references seem to refer to transpontine properties physically situated on the Surrey shore. This was a desirable place for those who could afford to escape the confines of the City and it even had 'a new and beautiful church', a most unusual flight of fancy for the commissioners and their clerks. Fitz Stephen's picture of London a century later fleshes out the dry statistics, such as they are, of 1086.

Of course, the cispontine shore was not composed of the City alone, for

Middlesex was still a rural shire. The hidation she enrolled in 1086 was traditional, 212,054.5 acres, or 95% of the recent surveyed area (223,500 acres). She made no revised hidations, but then, in the past, we believe that she had been part of Essex (Kingdom of the East Saxons) and that both were once, therefore, English heartlands. Her arable assessment was 38% (81,150 acres) and 32% (68,040 acres) was actually tilled. It would appear that of her tilth some 85% might have been established arable cultivation and the rest newly broken? Remember, Middlesex had also suffered at the Conqueror's hands twenty years before. The aggregate of all recorded assets made up 72.5% of the hidation, with 41,870 acres of 'woodlands' and 30,690 acres of 'meadows' (20% and 14.5%). Moreover, Middlesex included individual sub-tenant holdings, but why? The simple answer is that in so doing we do not need 'revisions' to distinguish what a lord (someone holding in capite) held 'in demesne' (for his own use) from what his men (sub-tenants) held for their own sustenance, for we know exactly who owned what. So we may see that demesnes were a particular 'tax target' and *in their absence* the declared hidation could (if honest, a few were not) be a good indicator of wealth, while a traditional hidation was (as we have always maintained) a declaration of area.

For example, Stepney in Ossulstone had a hidation equivalent to 13,500 acres (excluding any appurtenant navigable waters) when all entries are extracted and collated. This makes 21 square miles for an area from Bishopsgate (the Thames) to Haggerstone, Hoxton, Islington, Stoke Newington, the boundary of Ossulstone Hundred and the River Lea. In recent times the same area has been estimated at 23 square miles including the Isle of Dogs, but as we suspect that this 'isle' was 1.6 −1.8 square miles of marshland in 1086, it may have escaped inclusion? Within our 13,500 acres were 10,300 acres of 'meadows', 'woodlands' and arable (5,040 acres). The ox-ploughs had a motive-power capacity equal to 4,680 acres so that this, or more, was ploughed in 1086. In demesne the capacity was 1,560 acres, while the men held 3,120 acres of capacity: two-thirds was in the hands of the sub-tenants. The demesne holdings overall were 3,840 acres (though only 1,560 were ploughed) and 5,791.5 acres were held by the sub-tenants (ploughing 3,120 acres) = 40.6% as opposed to 53.9%. These sub-tenants had some incentive. If 71.5% of Stepney was agricultural land some 28.5% was farmed directly in demesne and 43% of it was farmed by the sub-tenants, for themselves, with only one-third of the ploughs tilling the demesne lands. Incidentally, those estates nearest to the City were the most valuable, but what else would we expect? Not only was there incentive, five hundred years later Thomas Tusser[51] was commending the good practices of Middlesex husbandmen (farmers) in triple-cropping their 'several' (enclosed) country by putting barley before bread corn, usually with peas between, then laying on more manure and a fallow, working the soil to its natural limits without exhausting it. It makes us wonder just how far back such good practice went?

We will not labour this point, but two examples more are instructive for our fiscal case. In Stepney one Ranulf Flambard made a *totally honest* and simple declaration. We know him and will remember him for later. However, at Tottenham in Edmonton, where 240 acres had been added to 3,400 acres, only 1,000 acres were declared (deponed) by another landowner. Of course we might claim that a deposition of only 35.25% of its hidation was accurate, or that it was in the same practice as Surrey, for it looks as though we are dealing with a demesne alone, that is a lord avoiding responsibility for his tenant's holdings? Westminster was 3,240 acres in area containing 1,320 acres of arable and while the 2,220 acres of demesne only tilled 480 acres the 1,055 acres held by the men tilled 720 acres out of a possible 840 acres. These sub-tenants also held 41 market gardens, but then we might expect an even greater output right on the City's doorstep. Such figures at least show us how it was that clerks in the exchequer could subsequently distinguish areas worthy of further investigation and where more ploughs might be employed, a device and solution (I might add) not previously available to Domesday scholars? Some 19 other London burgesses held plots at Lambeth on the Surrey shore (worth 22.75d on average), surely an Arcadian reflection of our Westminster market gardeners who paid half this average value each year for plots worth twice as much per annum? And if 41 represented the City side and 19 Southwark, then we may have some indication of the development of the south bank?

The hidation of Surrey enrolled in 1086 was equivalent to 485,850 acres, or 104% of the county in the late 19th century (it is slightly smaller today, so 107% of the recent) but she also offered a selective or revised hidation of only 36%. The arable was assessed at 121,845 acres (25.5%) though 31% was actually tilled, presumably because of incentive provided by London? The subordinate assets or land uses were precisely defined and together totalled 57.5% of the traditional hidation and, of course, there must have been dwellings, curtilages, royal forest (mentioned but not quantified, the King did not tax himself), chases, rough-grazings or wareland as well. Woods and pastures suitable for swine grazing, made 2.5% of the traditional hidation (11,540 acres); meadows, probably (as we shall see) mostly water meadows, just over 0.3% (1,722 acres); waters, ponds and marshes 3.75% (18,040 acres). A very particular set of accounts and we can probably argue for a reconstruction of 80 or 90% of her true area as being detectable in 1086. But, for the present, let us examine the details further for they have something very important to tell us.

For a start, if we table all the swine-woods together we find there are 'preferred' sizes, viz. blocks of 6, 40 and 60 acres, which *is* a surprise. Less popular but numerous are blocks of 10, 12, 50, 80 and 200 acres. The overall range was from 2 – 200 acres, by the way, so that the line defining gores and hedgerows from the swine-woods must have been drawn at 2 acres. Well, it had to be drawn somewhere. In Middlesex, however, the line was drawn at 30 not at 2! The swine pastures of Surrey in 1086 showed a range from 2 – 301 acres and a clear preference for 100 acre blocks. Larger areas appear to have been covered by those pastures that rendered one pig in seven or in ten as a due, up to 1,000 acres at a time it would appear? Maybe Londoners liked bacon? Thus ordinary grazings, the swine renders, were a matter of opportunity while swine-woods and wood pastures were discrete areas of woodland management. Oh yes, and before we forget the pigs, a little humorous aside. Many years ago Professor Maitland[52] drew attention to that 'monstrous progeny' the 'Bedfordshire semi-bos' (viz. land for half a beef and 'ibi est semi-bos'!) to warn us against literal interpretations. Well, in Essex we can find 'homo dimidius' and in Cambridgeshire 'dimidii villani', but here in Surrey we also find the 'Surrey semi-sus' ('silva de CL porca et dimidia')! What a place to get lost.

Water meadows have to be carefully situated, drained, flooded artificially and properly managed, but they *are* profitable and are likely to be jealously guarded. In Surrey three of the meadow entries actually included half acres whilst most were under 20 acres, certainly under 40 acres (despite a range up to 200 acres). The 'preferred size' was 4 acres, then came 1, 3, 5, 6 and 8 acre blocks. Less frequent were 2, 10, 16 and 20, preferences encountered in other counties as well. Middlesex was nowhere near as fussy and, except for Gore Hundred, used broader definitions. Thus Surrey had 1,722 acres of meadows but Middlesex apparently had 30,690 acres or, to put it another way, 0.3% as opposed to 14.5%. Here, in Middlesex, 'meadows' were measured in carucates or in oxen (viz. one-eighth of a carucate), though some might have been evasive (vide Edmonton below), the overwhelming preference being for one carucate with a range from one ox to forty carucates! Incidentally, near to London itself, we discover a rent of 60s from hay, but what else would we expect? Someone had to feed the transport for London. Pasture and 'pecunia' (rent) formulae are common: for 'meadows' the rent was usually 2, 10, 20 or 25 shillings but 'pastures' yielded a preference for 1s and a range of 3d, 13d, 20d, 24d, 40d, 60d, 84d, 180d and 240d.

In Middlesex woodlands were always swine woods though 'wood for fences' and money rents occasionally appear. The totals were 15, 20, 30, 40, 50, 60, 100, 150, 200, 300, 400, 500, 800, 1,000, 1,200, 1,500 and 2,000 swine with preferred blocks of 100 and 500 (equivalent to 200 and 1,000 acres). Separating them into hundrethal groups is also instructive for clearly in Middlesex 'woodland' was defined as wood *and* trees, maybe it included heathy common as well?

Hundred	Totals Employed In The Hundred
Hounslow	500
Edmonton	500, 2,000
Spelthorne	30, 100
Gore	200, 800. 1,000, 2,000
Ossulstone	50, 60, 100, 150, 200, 300, 500, 1,000
Elthorne	15, 20, 30, 40, 50, 200, 300, 400, 500, 1,000, 1,200, 1,500

Next we will compare the woods, meadows and arable of each hundred all together, and we will find that a hundred with only a *little* woodland had the *most* meadow while several with *much woodland* had *very little* meadow (Gore especially so), even though all of them had fairly similar totals of arable. No, differences in vegetation alone will not explain these anomalies, we are instead looking at the way men thought and expressed what was important to them, we are looking at *logic patterns* betrayed by statistical reciprocity, the everyday thoughts of our ancestors which they required for the exercise of commerce and administration.

Hundred	Wood as % of Hidation	Meadow as % of Hidation	Arable as % of Hidation
Hounslow	4	11	38
Edmonton	53	(?)	43
Spelthorne	1	35½	40
Gore	32	¼	36½
Ossulstone	15	23	43
Elthorne	22	7½	33

Then there are the waters to analyse, terraqueous appurtenances. Every landowner appreciates that he has fishing and maybe other rights over the waters and marshes on his land and in 1086 there was more pressure, probably, than today on fishing and on the movement of cargoes by water. Water also provided power for mills (we think windmills arrived a century later) and tenants would have customary rights to allow them to water both their cattle and their water meadows. Hundrethally we have weirs entered under Elthorne, Spelthorne, Edmonton, Hounslow and Ossulstone (Middlesex), the last two showing one on their common border (1.5 + 0.5), Hounslow's rated at the equivalent of 2,660 acres and Ossulstone's at 2,100 acres. The general equivalents were anything from 560 to 5,833 acres while mill ponds and fish ponds only ranged from 41.6 to 62.5 acres and 93.6 acres, as we would expect, a neat confirmation of our methodology. Edmonton boasted an aggregated total of 1,680 acres of ponds (perhaps wetlands?), Elthorne had only 250 acres. So the smallest of these ponds and races would, in theory, represent about 450 yards each way of water, though the configuration on the ground would be anything but geometric! Whilst we think with facility in square measures our ancestors probably aggregated things visually, unit by unit, small shape on small shape and acre by acre.

The limits we have set for our running waters are the Thames above Chiswick (Barnes) and below Windsor (Staines), the Lea from Cheshunt to Poplar and the Colne from the Thames to Watford. This is an area probably a little over the 5,000 acres, we have suggested. Well, quite apart from the intervening centuries making some difference to river captures and reclamations, Domesday tells us that the Lea had a weir rated at 630 acres at Edmonton: the area of the Lea from Cheshunt to Poplar today is probably a little under 600 acres? In 1086 the Thames seems to have been estimated at 5,200 acres but in recent times the same area (ut supra) has only been about half that size in surface low water. Well, might it not once have been more extensive? Then again the Colne-Thames area of Spelthorne Hundred in 1086 was apparently rated at a gross 20,400 acres though more recently waters alone have been encompassed in about 2,000 acres. Upriver Elthorne and Spelthorne returned eel-rents, but most hundreds had commuted all their rents from all kinds of fisheries, though Surrey had some large eel-rents: one and a half fisheries of 325 eels at Byfleet in Godley Hundred but 1,000 eels and 1,000 lampreys from Petersham in Kingston! Still-waters are much easier to 'measure' by hidation than are running waters, where eel-rents might be more appropriate? It is also possible that the Isle of Dogs, if marshland, was either subject to an eel-rent or, being so close to the Tower, a part of the King's (hawking) preserves?

Elsewhere men sometimes had more comprehensive ideas. For example at Wisbech (in the Fens) in 1086 was an area of 4,000 acres of farmland with 12,000 acres of waters and leased out fenland, 16,000 acres in all. In the 1930's the town itself was said to be 4,600 acres and the whole of the fenny hundred something between 16,300 and 16,700 acres. However, at Wittlesley (Cambs.) in 1086 we can propose about 3,000 acres of land and over 5,000 of water which by 1800 was returned as 3,950 to 4,050 acres of land (hidation + meadow = 2,160; arable

+ meadow =1,980 acres to which maybe 1,000acres of 'pasture' could be added).[53] Chapter 3 has shown us how differently men might define a coastline hundred-to-hundred, whether in 1086 or in 1800, so the point at which land actually ceased and water began depended on its perceived value. Continuity cannot be guaranteed in the Fens unless intermediate documents can be found to support an argument. Thus at Downham in 1086 a woodland and two fens together totalled *695* acres and in 1251 two marshes and a little park together (at the same place) made about *700* acres.[54] Names may vary, units do not.

The Fens were largely still-waters, the Thames was not. A superficial aggregation of Middlesex in 1086 suggests some 24,290 acres of water and, quite arbitrarily, we might reasonably divide this by 4 to obtain 6,072 acres of water surface, or 2.7% of the recent surveyed area of the shire. In recent times the surface area of her waters has been estimated at about 5,000 acres. So, if we now take the *known* still-waters of Middlesex in 1086 and obtain 1% of the recent area of the Shire (2,398.6 acres) and add these to the hidation we can approach very closely to the recent area of London with Middlesex. Is it not persuasive? In Berkshire fishery entries were restricted to certain entries along the Thames, which hundreds, with one exception, deponed only money rents. Wyfold Hundred entered 23 square miles of fisheries, her overall area was 23 square miles; Ganfield Hundred entered 25.5 square miles of fisheries for her 25 square miles of area: thus in Berkshire fishery entries were concerned not with waters but with *rights to fish* over given areas. In Oxfordshire, however, in 1086 only 2% of the gross area of the shire concerned fisheries; in Berkshire this was 19% at superficial view or 14.5% of the larger, traditional and unrevised hidation. Furthermore the area of Berkshire entered in 1086 was equivalent to 938.5 square miles which by 1086 had fallen to a claim of only 528.25 square miles at best and of these 938.5 square miles 137 were 'fisheries', which when subtracted leaves us 801.5 square miles to compare to the recent surveyed area of the shire at 721 square miles. On the Hampshire/Wiltshire borders no fisheries at all were returned. Whether fisheries meant fish, waters, wetlands or rights in 1086 was as much a matter of debate as it remains today.

There is a further possibility here which could explain the low Berkshire fisheries entries of 1086. Around Reading, Charlton, Beynhurst, Brey and Ripplesmere the totals become anomalous when logged as factorial changes between 1066 and 1086, all of these places being contiguous. All this area was well covered with woodlands and heaths and (unless we propose that Burnham Wood to Dunsinane had gone) were probably intercommonings and grazings, parcelled out between other hundreds maybe, but perhaps by 1086 swallowed up for the King's demesne forests? If so it suggests that King William really did put 'out of bounds' that which had once only been put to King Edward's use? It is possible that they became preserves. The King had power over the waters as well as the vert and venison and even in the 11th century the Commons may have been losing their rights? Then when we plot these factorial differences onto a map of the shire we have, if nothing else be admitted, a remarkable illustration of men's logic patterns or thought patterns in 1086, and evidence of unity in the Reading to Windsor topography. The same is true of the logic employed for several types of assets, hundred to hundred: the thoughts of our ancestors, just as Professor Maitland promised we would eventually discover them (back in 1897). What a pity it took so long to realise his vision.

Looking back to the Burghal Hidage we can see that Wallingford was among the largest fortresses recorded, comparable with Winchester and requiring 2,400 hides (576,000 acres) for maintenance while physically covering 140.5 acres of land. The 1066 hidation (2,505 hides) certainly provided for this. Domesday Book also recorded that Wallingford shared dwellings and extramural toftlands with Oxfordshire. Of 276 'hagae' (houses) and 480 acres, which had been the King's tenants, some owed riding or ferry services into hundreds within Berkshire but Benson Hundred was *in* Oxfordshire, with 85 of the 'hagae & masuras' being appurtenant to Oxfordshire. Now, if 276 'hagae' are equivalent to 721 square miles (Berkshire, see above) then 85 are equivalent to 222 square miles and by

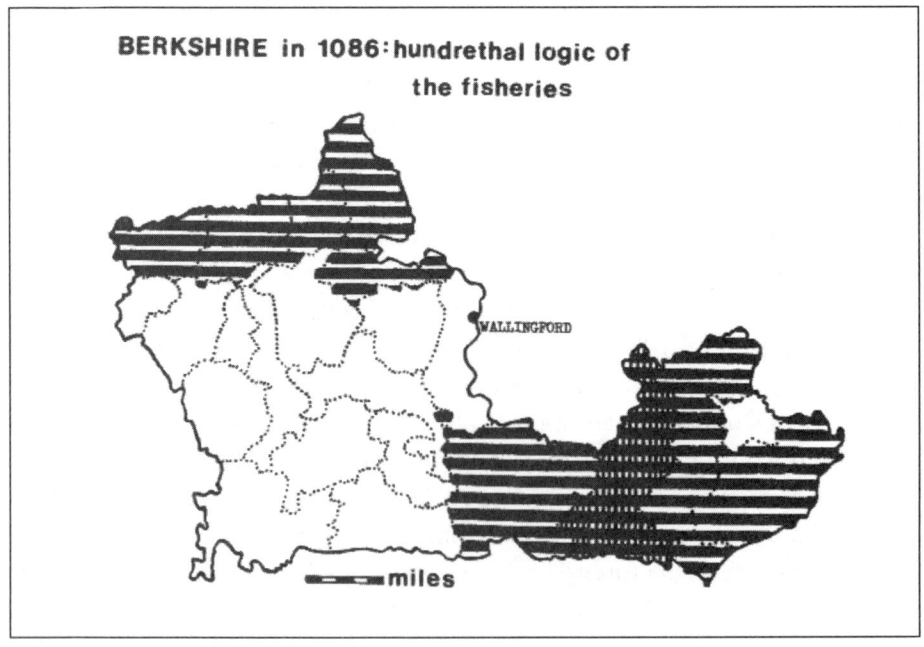

BERKSHIRE in 1086: hundrethal logic of the fisheries

subtracting the equivalent 142,000 acres from the Berkshire total we are left with 459,000 acres, *or 99.5%* of the gross area of Berkshire recorded in 1895! Coincidence, that may be so? An alternative possibility, that we are looking at superimposed systems and a palimpsest of obligations which had thoroughly confused contemporaries, is not inherently unlikely: hides of area, areas responsible for defensive works, taxation of areas to provide money for defence, the raising of taxation (on areas) for its own sake. It is just such confusion which infuriates modern tax payers and which encourages attempts at tax evasion.

It is not inconceivable that contemporaries were aware of such anomalies, after all a man must know if his tax assessment is unreasonably high when compared to his neighbour's, that is providing the impost is not just capricious?

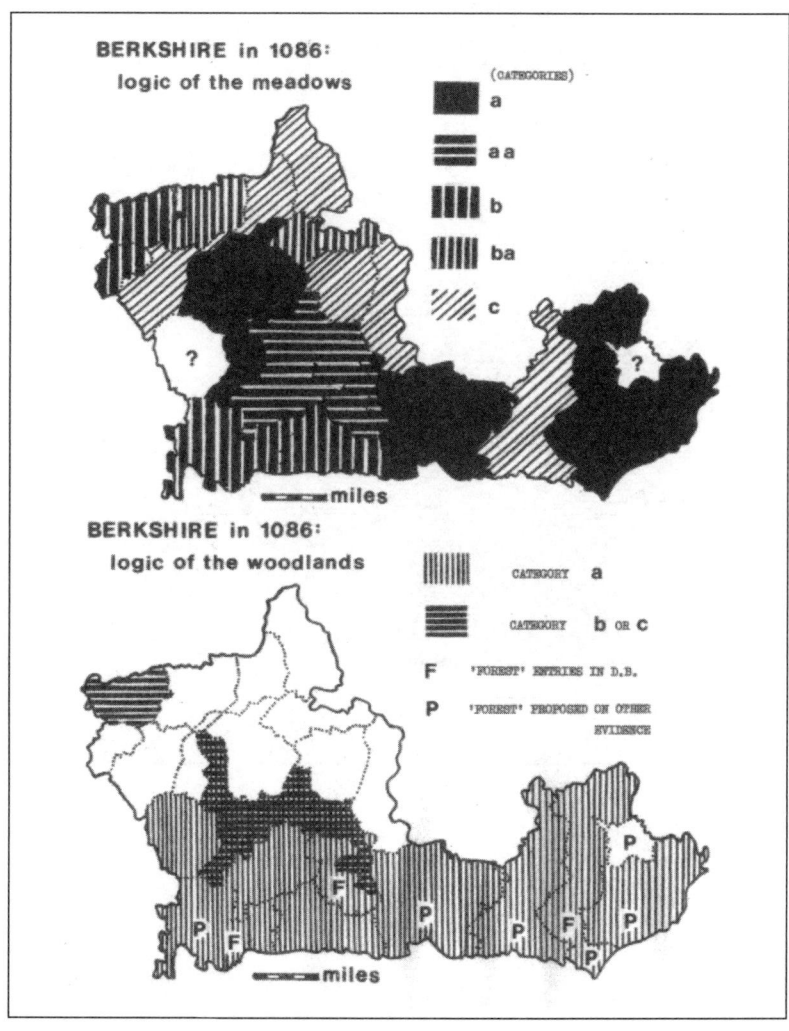

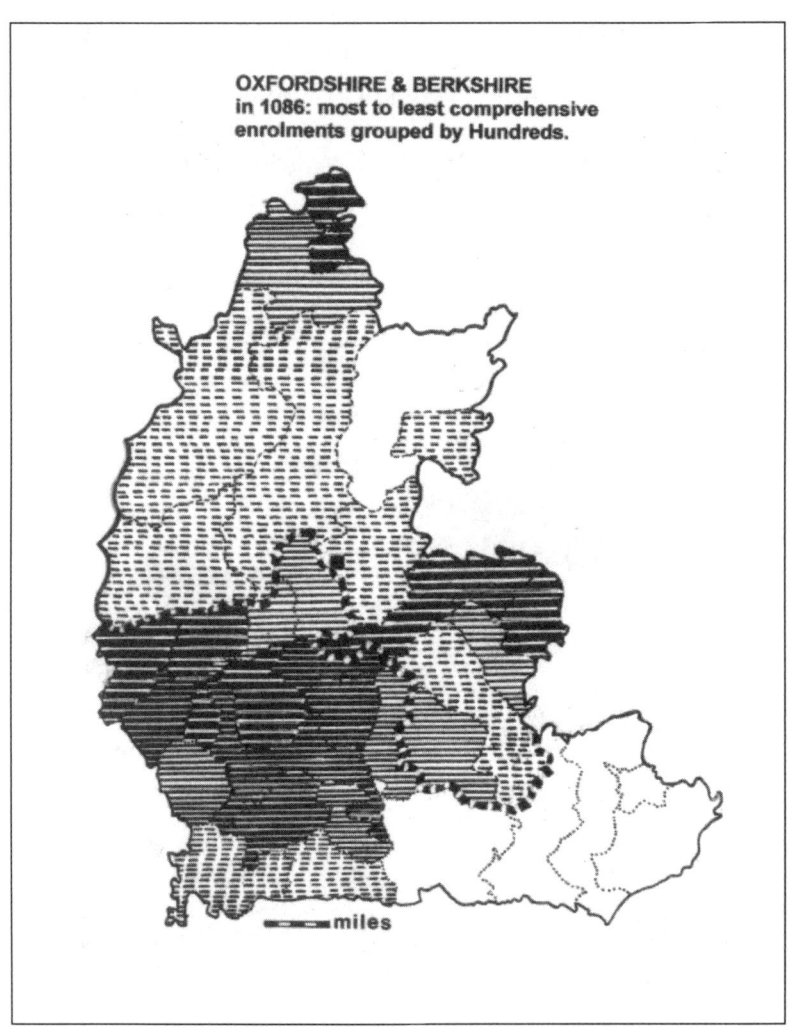

OXFORDSHIRE & BERKSHIRE
in 1086: most to least comprehensive
enrolments grouped by Hundreds.

miles

We know that Wallingford's fortress (Burghal Hidage) required a logistic hinterland of 900 square miles (0.576 million acres) and that in 1066 Berkshire was assessed at 939 square miles (0.6012 million acres). By the mid-12th century she was paying on only 756 square miles and in modern times the shire contained 725 square miles. Now, let us look at the Blewbury Hundred, by way of an example. Her hidation was given as equivalent to 30,480 acres in 1066 but only 15,540 acres in 1086 (at least 10 hides being lost to the terra regis), her tillage was 12,060 acres out of 12,240 acres of ploughlands (arable) and she had 410 acres of woods. Thus we can amass about 16,000 acres in 1086 of which 75½% were under tillage; her recent area has been about 18,500 acres. Is it not at least an interesting coincidence that our 1086 total makes 86½% of the recent? On the other hand the Thatcham Hundred was hidated at 17,040 acres in 1066 but only 7,200 in 1086 (with 10,320 acres of tilth on 11,445 acres of arable lands), yet her recent area has been 16,700 acres. The Rowbury Hundred was 29,280 acres in 1066 and only 15,480 in 1086 (with slightly more tillage than the arable could sustain), yet recently only 20,480 acres. There are hidden currents and pseudo-morphs to be charted in Berkshire.

Certainly we may suspect some subtle influences, amongst which we should not discount education any more than necessity or convenience. Which of these factors dictates the most persuasively will depend on many influences, but even hundredthal decisions must be seen as a form of education and fascinating snippets of information surface now and again. At Aynho in the Sutton Hundred of Northamptonshire we find 'one hide *and a fifth part of a hide*': who was it divided a unit of 240 so successfully, we wonder, into five times four dozen? At Wollaston in the Corby Hundred we find numbers of 48 acre meadows and elsewhere meadows of a dozen (though also, at times, ten) acres are not uncommon in this shire. Another 48 acre meadow can be found at Uffington in Lincolnshire. The enrolment of woodlands suggests some 'education', for although woods of some sort must have existed in every hundred in 1086 there is a distinct group on our map of Berkshire which made no account of them at all. Essential appurtenances for tenant's homes and tools ('ploughbot', 'hedgebot', 'firebot', 'housebot', as we have already discussed) may not have needed entries while timber resources (exploitable assets) may have been a different matter? After all, the language of woodlands and of timber trading is only used by those who make use of them, so royal demesnes and education, as well as topography, may be indicated in the logic patterns we discern among the Domesday entries for woodland?

There is also an argument to be advanced for royal demesnes. The King did not need to know what he owned, he owned the kingdom, but he did need to know *who* had carried away *what* to his despite (laisse-majestie). Parks were very popular, some 31 being recorded, but the demesne forests were the King's and perhaps had always been Crown property? Thus his demesne forests, those 'anciently' (as later jurists said) 'in' the Crown, needed no entry. Indeed they might be increased by escheat or when estates became 'wasted' and so return to the king's own estates and, thus, in the words of contemporaries, become 'fit only for hunting', a neat way of augmenting the royal demesnes. Other men's preserves might be appropriated by the Crown, as at Odiham in Hampshire where Earl Harold's "80 hides less 1½" were taken, presumably *because* they included a private forest or 'park'? How do we know this? Well, prior to 1066 this estate only paid geld for 38 hides (9,120 acres) although it had 56 ploughlands (6,720 acres of arable) and 341 acres of swinewoods and meadows, leaving 11,779 acres unaccounted for. By 1086 there were also 4 churches with 2½ ploughs on 2½ hides, so the area of preserves was probably 11,179 acres. The survey team did not need to record this but their statistics provide us with the details. At Neatham no hidation at all was given for the ancient terra regis but a similar set of statistics suggests that King Edward had enjoyed a similar area of preserves immediately to the south of Odiham?

Forest was a legal definition, it need not mean 'trees', and the king's demesne tenants might be granted assarts which they could farm, at his will, even in a forest. Thus at Ripley (Hampshire) Wulfgeat, who had paid for five hides under King Edward, now paid on only two as three hides "and all the wood are in the King's forest". We can see his dilemma. Moreover, forests not only contained hunting they were the principal resource for farming venison, the royal viand of preference, as well as a valuable source of income from mature trees and under-woods and, where few trees grew, a valuable source of rock from quarries. Only seven places are mentioned as quarries in Domesday Book, but these were almost certainly the ones in private hands and they would present a problem: how to tax a chief tenant for a valuable appurtenance which could be 'fermed' and exploited but not cropped? This is our old problem, how to mulct farm *and* ferme?

Significantly, two of these entries concerned millstone production, an essential and very lucrative trade.[55] These were the assets and appurtenances which particularly concerned the King's clerks and the treasury and they do show how an ancient principle of taxing *all* land, irrespective of its agricultural, arable or farm-produce, was an equitable principle, if a little lacking in fiscal definition and in subtlety? (Incidentally, in the centuries to come the crown was to fight a running battle over 'ancient demesne', augmenting whenever it could precisely because stone and timber were so valuable, to the great annoyance of those lords who owned 'the soil' and could not exploit it.)

Oxfordshire in 1010 (the County Hidage) had been assessed at 2,400 hides (576,000 acres) and in 1086 (after deducting those estates physically situated in

Buckinghamshire and Berkshire) at 2,399 hides and 196 acres (575,946 acres). No 'revised hidation' was entered. In 1895 the area of the shire was only 485,322 acres so her 'claims' in 1086 and in 1010 represented 139 square miles more than her recent area. Her arable represented 53% of her hidation (her tilth being 50%), her woodlands and rough grazings 28%, pastures 3%, meadows 2% and fisheries 2%. Some 12% (108 square miles) went unrecorded. As 22% or 24% of the arable or the tilth (say 69,100 acres) this might represent fallows, though the exact status of woodlands and rough grazings is uncertain and some of these could have been wareland (ancient fallows or 'manorial waste'); when necessity overrides convenience even poor soils are likely to be cleared for cultivation, but here there were (apparently) no hungry mouths to feed? Thame and Dorchester Hundreds *particularly* claimed much larger areas in 1086 than in recent times, and five or six hundreds in all claimed larger areas, so did Oxfordshire actually lay claim to part of Berkshire? It is (at least) an hypothesis. Let us see.

Banbury Hundred (composed of Banbury and Cropredy) claimed 155 hides but had only 114 ploughlands (13,680 acres of arable) and 127.5 ploughs (15,300 acres of tillage capacity), also 125 acres of meadows and woodland. Thus her agricultural area came to *24 square miles* (15,425 acres) despite her claim to 58: her recent area has been about *21 square miles*. In Thame Hundred (Thame and Great Milton) 188 hides were claimed yet only 116 ploughlands (13,920 acres) and 122.5 ploughs (14,700 acres of tillage capacity). When we add the meadows we still have only 14,929 acres, or *23.3 square miles* (not 70.5) and more recently the hundred has been estimated at *27 square miles*. Is it possible that Buckinghamshire was, therefore, the tributary for Thame and Northamptonshire for Banbury? Taking just these two hundreds we may now remove 91 from the excess of 139 square miles.

Dorchester Hundred (Dorchester and Hunesworde) claimed 145.75 hides on her arable assessment of 45 ploughlands with some 72.5 plough teams at work. The arable had increased from 5,400 to 8,700 acres and she had at least 542 acres of other assets, in all a minimum of almost *14.5 square miles* (9,242 acres). In recent times the same hundred has been surveyed as *16 square miles*. Similarly Pyrton Hundred comprised at least 17.25 square miles (11,039 acres) and was more recently assessed at 23 square miles although her 1086 claim had been 35! Lewknor Hundred was 19.5 square miles (12,571 acres) or more and has recently been 18 square miles, though in 1086 she had claimed 35.5 square miles. Could it be that our extra 139 square miles *never existed within the county in 1086*, and (if not) where were they?

In the Burghal Hidage we find the bailiwick of Oxford set at 1,400 hides and advancing to the County Hidage we note that Buckinghamshire was not listed among the Middle Anglian group of shires to which she should have belonged. Instead that group totalled the equivalent of about 2.5 million acres, much the same as the area today *when Buckinghamshire is included*! Supposing she did not exist at the time of either hidage, well, in such a case the fortress of Sashes was also likely to have 'belonged' to Oxfordshire, if Buckinghamshire was her property. Sashes was supported by a bailiwick of 1,000 hides, Oxford by one of 1,400, so in total Oxfordshire would be responsible for 2,400 hides of burghal hidage, a burden *identical* to that of Berkshire. Thus in both cases we appear to be looking at burghal fossils! Of course, none of these fortresses was necessary by 1086, so the bones of a kingdom had become veritable dinosaurs. Yet even if the original reason for the taxation (the bailiwicks) had passed into history that was no reason to discontinue the taxation itself. In the eyes of the Crown, there is *never* a good reason for abolishing taxes only for augmenting and renaming them.

Neither, it would seem, was it possible to abolish the recently discovered 'art' of 'self-assessment'. Domesday was implemented not by the Conqueror but by Rufus and, whatever his faults, the son was *not* as ruthless as his father. We hear of many people's complaints, from the time of Rufus onwards, but we hear of no memorable examples being made of miscreants and this is why the mischief continued to work (like a yeast or a poison) and why succeeding monarchs found it necessary to revisit Domesday with more up to date information. It certainly provided a terminus post quem all discrepancies must have arisen, so that it could be consulted whenever there was a dispute. The following example drawn from material already published by Dr. Sandra Raban,[56] will illustrate the method in succeeding centuries. It also tells us that evasions continued and that scribal apothegms (which we encountered in chapter 6) were now a feature of any Exchequer record: they were not the memoranda so many researchers suppose, entered because the Exchequer was trying to set a standard for the acre or the virgate (or oblige future researchers), *but highlights* within each record *marking out evasions and deceptions.*

Thus at Caldecote in Huntingdonshire in 1086 there was land for 6 ploughs which only 5 were ploughing and it declared its liability at 5 hides (*1,200 acres*). It also had 15 acres of under-wood. In 1279-80 two separate rolls, undoubtedly representing two separate surveys, just as we believe was the procedure in 1086, returned similar but not identical accounts of this same manor. The most comprehensive gave this place 3.5 hides 'each hide of which contains 5 virgates of land and each virgate contains 25 acres', according to (what we now recognise as) the scribal apopthegm. Thus, expressed in terms of virgates, this later survey gives us 4.375 hides where there had (in 1086) been 5 hides, for, of course, there never were 5 (only 4) virgates in a hide. In terms of acres, the face value claim will only be 437.5 acres (or 3.64 carucates), so we begin to perceive how the 5 hides of 1086 had reduced to 3.5 hides; presumably because 3.5 ploughs were at work and the area of the hide was still a secret? How shall we verify this supposition?

Well, 3.5 hides is 840 acres, but as in reality there were not 4x 3.5 virgates (=14) but 5x 3.5 (=17.5), there would actually be some 1,050 acres with yet *another 4 virgates* (we are told) *in demesne*: so 240acres + 1,050 acres = *1,290 acres* (but which claim only 840 acres of liability for the geld). The anonymous scribe is right , it works now (as in Leicestershire in 1086) if we appreciate his humour and his arithmetical skill. Details of the sub-tenant's own holdings then inform us (corroboratively) that 6 villeins hold 6 virgates and 9 villeins hold 4.5 virgates, in all 10.5 virgates *or* 630 acres, while the rector has another virgate (=60 acres) and various tenants have small parcels such as acres and curtillages, making up a tenancy picture of around 700 acres (as an absolute minimum) to which we may add the aforesaid demesne of 240 acres and a marsh of 20 acres. From this review of the estate made 200 years after Domesday Book we can see that not only does it reconcile very well in total area (1,290 acres in 1280:1,200 acres in 1086) but there is also an array of *supplementary detail* which would allow the Exchequer to close in very precisely on William de Brus, holder of this manor and ask him some very embarrassing questions about his liability. The more perfunctory of the two entries (the Huntingdon Roll Return) may have been taken a year apart (or mendacity could not remain consistent) for *it* claims that the demesne was then only 180 acres (1.5 carucates), not 240, and it totals all the villein holdings together at 630 acres (10.5 virgates again) while giving another person a virgate and three other tenants a virgate between them in addition to mentioning marsh, turbaries and pasture by valet alone. From this we have a minimum area of 930 acres (vide the 940 of the first Roll and the marsh of 20 acres, which was not actually measured in the second) but this time with *more emphasis on rents and cash* than on actual tenancies, landholding and geld liability. Asking so much about William's finances might seem to help him evade any geld or carucage, but it might also leave him with some difficult questions to answer when it came to paying scutage on his one-third of a knight's fee? As they say, there is more than one way of skinning a cat, or an eel! What the logic patterns were, shire-by-shire and hundred-by-hundred in 1279-80, if they are there at all and how they may have changed, I am not qualified to say. Other people will need to look into that, should academia give its permission.

The law, as opposed to its amelioration, which we style 'justice', takes no account of circumstances, certainly not of intentions. It is concerned with adherence to limits and proscriptions and where these do not apply, actions *may* be deemed to be licit. So we may think of jurisprudence (especially when it includes customary law) as a river and upon one bank lies the law and on the other justice. Sometimes the barque of state veers to one bank, sometimes to another, in the early Medieval period the current often kept it against the legal bank for that current's name was the Crown. Prior to Bracton and Glanville the concept of ownership, of property, seems to have been absolute and that is why *we* have taken the inflexible view (so far) that tax evasion could not be involuntary. Even today, especially today, we expect a citizen to have intimate knowledge of the law, even when he is not permitted to practice it? The law does not accept excuses. In Norman England there is unlikely to have been a defence called 'ignorance of the law'.

Much of the law was customary and it was of course ancient and if the King knew it (from his camerarii) it is unlikely that his liege men had been warned about it by their servants, especially not about the geld, for it has been the conclusion of our deliberations that every county, may be every hundred or wapentake, was interpreting the confusion as they saw fit with positive encouragement from magnates who felt themselves incommoded by any form of taxation or authority. But just supposing we *could* plead local perceptions as interpretations of jurisprudence, how would we concede any presumption of 'innocence' based on ignorance? The operation of tax, of the geld, had indeed become a bit of a mess, as we said when we began and the Norman world does not appear to have entertained any element of central polity. The magnates lived upon their estates and incomes, tallaging and renting as they saw fit, and no doubt expected the Crown to do likewise, feudal perceptions did not run to national concerns and collective weal. Nobles wished to exploit their servitors and the Church sought to limit secular powers as well. In the centre of these forces, the Crown must either be despotic and strong or subservient to both factions and the further the distance of the magnate from the King, the less was the power of the Crown. In general it seems that a strong King interpreted his rights with a similar implacability to the Church.

In the Danelaw we have seen that the concept of tax liability was very different from that of the English lands and other men did not see why *they* should not be equitably treated, especially if they lived where the two cultures fused, for there it was possible to make comparisons. In the light of modern experience we are tempted to perceive such differences as political correctness, but they may not have seen it so, it might just have been favouritism or incompetence to them? Elsewhere we can see even greater inequalities. In Devon and Cornwall the tax liability had at some time been generally reduced to a bare minimum. Thus at Hatherleigh, in Devon, the church of Tavistock had paid geld on only 3 hides since before 1066 but it held land for 30 ploughs (3,600 acres of arable), 100 acres of meadows, 6,000 acres of 'pastures' and 5,000 acres of 'woodland'.[57] At Liskeard, in Cornwall, the Count of Mortain gelded for

2 hides, 'yet there are 12 hides' noted the scribes, presumably in demesne as they also recorded land for 60 ploughs (7,200 acres), 400 acres of wood and 32,000 acres of 'pastures' (Bodmin Moor)![58] By what political process had these 2 shires obtained such concessions? The comprehensive hidation of Alfred's day appears to have undergone its own metamorphosis in Wessex, so that 'unprofitable' land was (by the time of Domesday) generally excluded from otherwise honest declarations. The concision of the greater Domesday enables us to detect such variations. So, in Somerset the Abbey of St. Marie of Montebourg held of the King (as the gift of Nigel the doctor) a manor of 5 hides with land for 3 ploughs, 2½ hides and 2 ploughs in demesne and 2 ploughs of the men with 20 acres of 'pasture'. Thus this manor of 1,200 acres had 360 acres of arable, tilled 480 acres, and 600 acres were held in lordship. However, there were also 1,000 acres of 'woodland', which sounds like wareland which was not, in this shire, declared for the geld. When in Dorset we learn that land had 'never divided for hides (nor) gelded'[59] we are probably looking at such 'woodland'-wareland, or at terra regis held in demesne by the King himself, but the 'never' indicates only 'living memory' (as Medieval jurists called it) of 90-100 years, not an historically recorded fact.

We have already seen many cases of deliberate evasion and cases, like the Count of Mortain's, where evasion was piled onto evasion. In parcelling out a country it was also possible to act illegally. It is impossible to say how Shoyswell Hundred (Sussex) *in its entirety* managed to evade all gelds but in two entries (f.19 and f.19v) we are told that this hundred "has never paid geld" and it seems to have been the Count of Eu's responsibility. At Carshalton (Surrey) Geoffery de Mandeville took five manors and made them into one, simultaneously *reducing* his geld assessment from 27 to three and a half hides, though the men of the shire and the men of the hundred all deponed that they had never seen the writ or the livery officer giving him seisin from the King! At Ashton Under Hill (Worcestershire, entered as Gloucestershire) Earl William made a manor of 2 vills (totalling 8 hides with 10 ploughs) which Roger de'Ivry put at ferme for £30 but, the scribes recorded, 'the men of this shire, when questioned, said that they had never seen the King's writ which said this land had been given to Earl William'.[60] And not only did magnates work to the King's despite, he did it to himself, because the terra regis couldn't pay geld to the Crown unless it was regranted! Thus in Wiltshire, 'the King holds Calne.... and it has never paid geld hence it is not known how many hides are there', though the scribes recorded 29 ploughlands with 29 ploughs, 45 burghers, 7 mills, 50 acres of meadow and 8,000 acres of 'pasture' (presumably the White Horse and North Downs?).[61] At Hitchin in Hertfordshire King William took Earl Harold's estate to himself and so lost even the 5 hides it was assessed at in 1066, yet this tax liability was a fiction for it contained 34 ploughlands, meadow equal to another 4 ploughlands, pasture and 1,200 acres of woodland for pannage.[62] Taxation, by 1085, had become a very knotty problem. There would have been no shortage of claimants for mercy had the Conqueror returned.

We are told of the Gordian knot that it was solved by force and what we hear of King William's implacable nature suggests that once having cut the knot of taxation with his surveys he might have applied the law very strictly. No wonder the terrified English called this collection of surveys 'Domesday' book! For 20 years the King had striven to secure a kingdom for his offspring, largely through atrocities, and now with the sands of his time running out he must (for the good of his soul) ensure that the end justified the means he had employed. Thus his fury with the King of France may even have had more of a root in England than in William's own corpulence? We can only speculate on what sort of a Domesday *might* have happened, but for the intervention of Divine Providence? 'Domysday de Domino Rege'.

CHAPTER NINE

PEOPLE MATTER

We have come a long way since we came out of the wardrobe. We have flown and travelled in space and time, we have come so close to the Conqueror himself that we need to tread very carefully. We have taken the indemonstrable hypothesis and skinned it, grilled it, eaten it and buried it. Now we have a demonstrable, an irrefutable hypothesis to put in its place. Now we can sit before a log fire in a comfortable inn with our stimulating cordials, sharpen our quill pens with tiny knives, crease and prick the parchment, reseal the ink (it makes a permanent stain, even into parchment in time) and we can wink at one another and joke in low voices, for we are the senior scribes, the camerarii of the King, and we can read these rolls and membranes better than any 'baby eating bishop'; we know the secrets of high and low born, rich and poor and have absolute power over them, under the King's Majesty. The barons and legati may hate us for being royal pets but they dare not touch us or deny us what we ask. It is good to be an accountant of thesaurus and exchequer. I call him 'sir', he calls me 'sir': he means it, I don't.

What of these subject people, these peoples: English, French, Norman, Breton, who had been Angles, Saxons, Jutes, Frisians, British, Welsh, Danish, Norwegian, Swedish, Baltic Slavs? Who and what are they? What of the man born into serfdom because his father, when starving, sold himself to a master for bread to give to his wife and children? 'Hlaford' means 'loaf giver', the master must feed his serf (quite apart from it being stupid to let him die), so the 'hlafeata' (loaf eater) tills the soil, ditches and carries for his lord every day until dinner, at about the canonical hour of nones (1500 hours) and after that works for himself: this is how he pays his rent for a cottage and maybe an acre or more. Then there is the bordar or cottar (cottager) who contracts to do so much work in return for his cottage and whatever curtilage he can negotiate. Sometimes he has the chance to commute his labour for rent and sometimes he would rather not. Labour rents do not inflate when prices, and money rents, rise. Some of these men have other work: 'bordars super aquam' indubitably means fishermen, but they live on or in a manor and so give services to an estate and rents, and in return they receive 'toft and croft'. Richer than them (and some may be small business men) are the villeins, the tenant farmers. Typically they hold sixty acres in return for services of all sorts, they are usually the men who have and are expert with the ploughs and the carts, so they plough and carry, at least they do this until they have a family old enough to take over. Sometimes they employ cottars or bordars, they may even have a serf themselves, but it is rare. The fortunate ones can grow relatively rich in their village. A couple of centuries from now these will be the well dressed peasants who are too proud to carry a sack or do manual work for their lord, they 'send a man' instead.[63] Strong lords will insist that from time to time the village reeve makes all such senior tenants do some publicly witnessed labour, just to prove to everyone that rents have to be paid and no-one is above service, unless he was *born* 'free'.

Freedom is a relative concept of course. Socmen or sokemen and freemen are entered in Domesday Book but everywhere the 'new lords' are bearing down on them, trying to make them into villeins or worse. It is a struggle which continues for the next three centuries as jurists do the bidding of the powerful and attempt to put all freely held land under a lord with a manor. By doing this they can create 'knight's fees', which in time become scutage (tax). Well, if it happens to you the advantage is that *you* don't pay taxes, instead the lord takes a 'tallage' from you (if he can) and otherwise receives gifts in kind. Eggs and poultry are always acceptable, so are eels (if you have fishing rights). Within a century of Domesday the socmen disappear but freemen do not.

The chief lords hold 'in capite' (from the King) but many smaller lords have sub-infeudations of manors for which they owe the chief lords all sorts of 'reliefs' (fines), rents, services and, particularly, military service – so that the chief lords can field an army for the King whenever he calls. And this 'servicium debitum' is no joke: forty days fighting when called up, forty days annual exercises, castleguard duty (someone has to be the garrison) and find your own armour, weapons, horses and servants. Oh yes, you'd better stay fit and proficient as well, there are no pensions for you or your family when you can no longer fight. You're as good as your last parade when it comes to holding on to the manor (incidentally, your wife runs it, you don't have much time to be 'at home', so she had better be competent) and you need to be a good companion to your lord when off duty. It's a competitive business being a knight or sergeant (militus) and your son will not necessarily inherit. You can also, usually, get free meals when on duty, though not always very good quality. Gradually the custom of paying money (scutage) to be exempted from the call-up grows, but it is expensive. However, money payments can be divided up, laid off, among others, if you know how (sub-infeudations).

Here and there we find little people who are specialists, though still cottagers. Men who use or make and repair crossbows (ballistarii), riding men or professional messengers, cooks, a female jester, bee keepers, an interpreter, a falconer, a huntsman, a gold embroideress. There was, apparently, only one doctor (if you believe it), 'Nigel the doctor' who (appropriately) lived at Murrell's End, Gloucestershire. All our people, of course, have families – and not just the Mrs and the kids! Great lords have many servants, grooms, huntsmen and companions. Mesne lords (holding manors in demesne) have servants and live-in labour, men at arms or soldiers, aged parents and grown up children, maybe even unmarried siblings? The villein may have a maid, maybe labourers, wife and children, eventually some useful sons. The serf, well he has the wife and kids, maybe also her widowed mother? In the monasteries are many monks, some youngsters, servants and royal pensioners (like disabled soldiers) living in, also lay-brothers. No-one has a house with 2.3 children, that's for sure and the 'people' entered in Domesday Book are, in reality, legal entities, otherwise our sympathies would certainly go to the 11 half-men and the 49 half-villains, especially the left over bits! That is why we find only 56 women among 283,242 'people' (or 1 in 5,000!); these are the women who for some unusual (but, we can be sure, legally valid) reason were included when wives, daughters, servants and nuns were not. English women are legally entitled to hold property in their own right, technically French women can't. Incidentally, one person in 1,600 was entered as a pauper, which rather upsets the view that many were starving because of poverty? Were they entered because they were *avoiding* serfdom or labour, or were they disabled?

It seems that most of our 'people' listed in Domesday Book were heads of households, subjects accountable in law for *themselves and others*, subjects responsible for the good order kept in their properties and that is why men predominate. We can also be sure that many people kept bees and that there were a lot more falconers and huntsmen working for the great lords and the King, we can be sure that half a dozen millers didn't work all 3,500 mills and that millers also had households and families. What shall we allow for a chief lord's household; there had been 4,000 men with this status in 1066 but by 1086 there were only 180? Later documents speak of establishments of 100 or 200 servants, companions and family, figures still repeated 800 years later in some large Victorian country houses! How many would the average mesne lord be responsible for, 20 or 30, or more? There were 36,900 freemen and socmen plus 109,000 villeins, what would their households look like with half a dozen (living) children at least, maids, servants, aged parents: maybe 15? Thus 51% of our 'people' (some authorities count 283,000 and others only 250,000)[64] represent perhaps 2.25 million inhabitants and then we have to ask if *all* the King's subjects were entered, or were there outlaws, monks with lay-brothers and servants in the monasteries, how many inhabitants were there in London and in Winchester? What of the royal household (at its several locations), the ordinary garrison soldiers of castles, maybe there were other citizens missed in other towns, what of burghers, journeymen, apprentices, were all those engaged in seafaring accounted for? Without any difficulty we can begin to creep towards 4 million people.

The demographers hate such proposals. Not only have they been wildly wrong in the past but when we propose a population not unlike that of the late 17th century, given in Gregory King's tables, we have a very different political picture, a picture which will not recommend the demographers to their political lords and masters. Yet the ploughlands and plough capacities, even if we *assume* very poor yields of cereals and livestock, tell us that the agricultural produce had to be going somewhere. Either there were a lot of mouths consuming it all or England was running a major export industry? The problem is that demographers would like to see a simple progression and expansion, but populations do not *have* to expand, century on century, they *can* contract. We know of one catastrophic die-off in and after the middle of the 14th century but population pressures and famines caused other major problems (which economists barely understand) before this.

One way of reviewing the evidence for population is to look at the internal evidence of the 1327 'Lay Subsidy' (a form of taxation which replaced the geld) and the 1377-81 Poll Tax returns (the statistical exercise which triggered the Peasant's Revolt).[65] There are problems with these sources also, of course there are, they were not designed to be comprehensive even if we assume that the returns made were competent, but they will give us some idea of what was happening in the 14th century. The Black Death or bubonic plague, which arrived in 1348-51, was probably the most dreadful event experienced by Europe outside a nuclear war (though the famine years of 1315-22 were also ghastly). In England we estimate that between 30% and 50% of the population died in this initial plague period – and it came back, again and again. The Lay Subsidy figures, of course, represent a post-famine but pre-plague picture, the Poll Tax figures a post-plague picture and for both of these sources we will focus on Essex. The 1377 figure *appears* to represent 65% of the 1327 figure while this pre-plague figure is not unlike the population of Essex in 1801, in spite of the famine and murrain ten years before.

In the Hinkford Hundred of Essex we find that the 1327 figures returned only 1,300 people *of taxable status* and of these only 769 were men, but in 1086 the total number of 'people', almost exclusively men, had been *2,000*! Of course, these are not poll counts, they were (as we have seen) 1086 households, or taxpayers, but it is important to remember that they were such in 1327 as well. We have proposed that only landowners paid tax in 1086 but most historians want to include every peasant, which *certainly* spoils the proposition that the population had increased by 1327! Moreover, if demographers consider comparisons between 1327 and 1377 valid, on the grounds that the heads counted were mainly (if not exclusively) male, we have every right to compare *all three* sets of figures. Certainly there were common features between all three: the exclusion of parents, children, sisters, brothers, servants, apprentices and any sub-stratum of the very poor from the totals, for the latter certainly had no liability to be taxed, even in the 14th century. Was the population in 1086 *larger* than in 1327, or was the methodology employed for recording people in 1086 superior to that of 1327? Neither proposition will fit into 'accepted' (viz. acceptable) wisdom.

Some historians have called it a 'fraud' that only householders and their wives were included in 1377 while dependants went unrecorded, but not only is this to look with a modern eye upon the past, it does not help us with the difference between 1086 and 1327 or 1377. No one recorded dependents in 1086 either. No, instead of looking at the past with modern eyes, looking to find what we have been educated to believe, we should instead consider the role of traditional and customary practices. It was an insistence on customary law which, after all, commended the insurrection of 1381 to so many people. Yet the very term 'peasant's revolt' (in 1381), is misconceived, for it was, if anything, a revolt led by lower, artisan and middle classes against the nobility and the gentry. As always the very poor were the victims because they may have been misled into thinking that they would be included in the new tax, because they became involuntary recipients of retribution and because they were numerous but it was the *villeins and virgators* (the tenant farmers) who had more to gain by destroying records than the day labourers or serfs of 1381. They were the ones who had, formerly and up to then, escaped the land tax and who were now being assessed (for the first time) on their profits (movables). Serfs *had* no property in law!

If we *only* multiply the 'people' statistics for Essex, in 1086, by three we will have 70% of her population of land workers in 1801,[66] yet *we have seen* how improbable such a small household average would be. In 1801 Essex was still a predominantly rural and agricultural shire (by 1951 her land workers were only half the 1801 figure) and in 1801 'land workers' included a high proportion of wives and families all of whom were required to work if a family of labourers was even to subsist under the prevailing system. In 1086 the wives and families were not included. This means that there were (possibly) fewer men in 1801 than in 1086; more people in 1086 than in 1801? Very many other shires demonstrate the same anomaly and though in Essex the population per square mile (by the

115

ultra-conservative estimate) was *possibly* less than in 1801, in Suffolk, Norfolk, Rutland and Lincolnshire it was about the same! In other words, if we multiply *by more than three* our 1086 populations will grow alarmingly over each square mile. But then, this list of counties represents those shires we have proposed as major recipients of wretched refugees from Yorkshire and the North after 1070. In 1086 they might have been packed very tightly into some shires? The argument advanced by historians that the Lay Subsidy of 1327 only represents those liable for taxation, so that the exemptions, exclusions and 'mistakes" together prevent us from obtaining a guide to the overall population of any county, are only half true. Such an argument is a matter of convenience by which they may dismiss an uncomfortable possibility. The position with Domesday Book is almost exactly the same as 1327, for when we look at the people statistics we are looking at those *liable to pay tax* and the households for which they were responsible, although it was (in 1086) not a 'fee fraction' or 'lay subsidy' (as in 1327) but a geld or tax upon the land and not all of those recorded were actually paying, for some men represented 'assets' rather than taxpayers! In 1086 *and* in 1327 we are looking at what we might call 'tributaries', those *liable* to pay tribute to the government *if* their means of paying can be identified. All we can say in amelioration of the figures is that some of the 'people' of Essex in 1086, the poorest serfs, might not even be included in any later list of taxpayers. However we can be certain that taxpayers at any *later* period *included* the equivalents of our villeins and many bordars (let alone the freemen) of 1086 as these were the very people who had heretofor escaped the geld and the object after 1086 was to widen the tax base, not to narrow it, by switching from a land to a property qualification.

In Essex in 1086 some 14,722 tributaries (people statistics) were recorded. In 1327 only 8,177 were recorded.[67] If we wish to remove the serf element of 1086 (obviously entered in the survey as assets rather than as potential tributaries) we will have something like 14%, so we arrive at an emended total of 12,660 and if we accept that the government's (Crown's) policy was, then as now, to augment rather than diminish the revenues with any new impost, we have to admit that the Domesday 'population' of potential tax payers/tributaries was at least as big, maybe rather larger, than a similar population base just prior to the Black Death. The real difference in the imposts raised at these two dates is that in 1086 the government was including villeins *although it could not tax them* (under a land tax) while in 1327 it *could tax* their surplus or 'movables' and indubitably included them in order so to do. If we then look at those assessed in 1327 for more than two shillings we have 2,834 and if we look at the entries for those holding freely in 1086 (as freemen or as mesne lords) we have 1,796 'upper band' payers. Those assessed at less than two shillings in 1327 were 5,347, compared here with those holding as villeins in 1086, who had numbered 4,346. This rise to 8,200 in 1327 from 6,100 in 1086 (in broad terms) seems satisfactory as taxation, but how was it achieved? Well, the villein, it must be remembered, held his land purely at the will of his lord and the geld was an obligation which fell upon the land's lord. Thus villeins in 1086 did not pay the geld. But by 1327 the tax was being levied upon movables, possessions, not on land, so all men of some substance paid and those of insubstantial merit did not, so the villein was now being taxed on his affluence. As it seems unlikely that mesne lords would have foregone their ancient right to tallage their tenants, the villein may have been hit with a double burden, hence his unrest? If a man was now paying taxes, why should he also owe services and various gifts and dues? Here is the nub of the dissatisfaction in 1381. The villein would no doubt appeal to customary practise but customary practise was not on his side for now, as a taxpayer, he was dealing directly with the government and that meant statutory law, which *may not* be emended by appeals to precedent. We believe that many mesne lords were feeling the pinch long before this date (1327) and no doubt *they* found it difficult to maintain *their* customary revenues from a peasantry who, as well as being incensed at being charged more by someone else in authority, were trying to hold on to profitable service sub-infeudations, rather than commute to rents, which could be revised upwards whenever their lord saw fit. This is the myth of commutation, for instead of benefiting the peasant such a change benefited the lord! Of course we do not *know* for villeins had no chroniclers, but what we can be certain of is that the villeins were being taxed on the profits they were making from their *advantageous service rents*! One other element needs to be added. Thanks to famines and widespread harvest failures in 1315-16 and the murrain of 1319-21 the population was already compromised in 1327. Population loss in itself would provide an incentive for re-appraisal of the tax system whatever (as some historians maintain) had happened to the old demesnes and the money economy (not subsistence) would be worst affected by want, but that is another story.

The poll tax returns of 1377-81 recorded a lay 'population' of 50,917 in Essex. Of these 6% were inhabitants of Colchester (it had been 9% in 1327, perhaps driven in by famine) while the national enrolment (of those who were 'tax liable', of course) came to 1.36 million people. If we look at the Lay Subsidy Roll for the Hinkford Hundred of Essex in 1381 we find that among some 1,300 entries only 63% were tax payers, for this exercise was counting tax payers *and* their wives. Once again there is no mention of children, siblings, servants and so on but the inclusion of wives is interesting; with 2,000 men in 1086 yet only 769 returned in 1381 there is a *considerable* discrepancy. The administrative method *may* have been imperfect but we are *not* looking at a poll count of the general population, instead it is (as we have said) a poll count *of those liable for taxation*. We should note that there is no mention at all of the very poor, those who could pay no taxes because they did not meet any qualification. The 'higher tax brackets' of 1327 and 1381 coincided, the 'lower brackets' did not, suggesting that the most profitable of those tenancies left vacant by the plague were soon retaken by survivors even though vacancies then remained among the smaller tenancies. Moreover there are artisans, though nothing like the numbers we would expect if the Roll had included those apprentices, journeymen and poor labourers who could not meet the property qualification for taxation. The hated Poll Tax, it would appear, was no concern of the really poor and peasants but it did very much concern their more substantial neighbours.

At Chesterford, in the Uttlesford Hundred of Essex, in 1086 the land use totals enrolled for the area represented 93.5% of the area of Great Chesterford in 1930 and 100% of that of Little Chesterford in 1930.[68] Their people figures in 1086 were 47 and 14 respectively, meaning of course 'people of some importance' (to the local economy) rather than the total number of inhabitants, so the terra regis (King's own land) here was a sort of small town and very intensively worked, though (surprisingly) servile tenancies were minimal. In fact the town was of great antiquity even then and we may, perhaps, be looking at an established service sector settlement? Anyway, by 1327 the 47 and 14 notables of 1086 had fallen to 32 and 12, but in 1933 the total for bailiff, farmers and commercial traders listed in the local directory was 65. So we can perhaps say 61 'notables' in 1086, 46 in 1327 and 65 in 1933? The combined population of the two parishes in 1930 was however 881, so only 65 (some 7.4%) were then deemed to be worth listing, as people of property! Littlebury, on the other side of the River Cam from the Chesterfords, had 51 in 1086 (including Strethall) but by 1327 had only 18 and in 1933, 28. Here the total population in 1933 was 556, so those worth listing in 1933 came to 5.0%. Could this be true of other places in Essex? Surely the 1.36 million people of 1327 did not represent only about 10% of the national population? Did the 283,242 recorded in 1086 represent only 5-7%, was the total population some 4 – 5.6 millions?

Consider, if you will, the possibility that the 1086 population of the English shires may have been 18-20% of the mid-20th century population of this area, or something like half the population of 1801, with perhaps 120% of the mid-20th century total of male land-workers? I say 'male' because that was what the 1951 census recorded and what Domesday Book acknowledged although in 1801 the land-workers apparently included both male and female. So, in Suffolk in 1951 the rural population was 44% of the total population and numbered just under 150,000, of whom 20% (30,215) were male land-workers. In 1801 there had been 55,744 land-workers and so 1951 may have been comparable if we add females? The 1086 total of land-workers appears to have been a little higher and the rural population perhaps approaching 200,000, so perhaps 30% were male land-workers augmented by women and children? In Norfolk and in Essex the broad picture is much the same, though Norfolk recorded a much higher percentage of 1086 male land-workers and Essex a rather smaller one than Suffolk (around 70% of 1801 rather than being over 100%). As far as one can see, many shires in 1086 fell within the range 49-74% of the 1801 total, so if the 1086 population *was*, broadly, half of that recorded in 1801 the land-workers represented the majority of the 1086 population and their economic contribution may not have been much less than that of 1801. Unless anyone can actually *prove* the inadequacies of eleventh century agriculture we are entitled to consider the output per acre much the same in 1086 and in 1801. Let us now return to the problem of 'principal inhabitants'.

An imperfect but alternative means of verification would be to try to define the 'principal inhabitants' of a vill or parish in 1086 *and* again in recent history. Domesday provides us with (resident) freeholders, villains and bordars (on the one hand) while there are also 'gentry' and 'commercial' entries (on the other hand) in Victorian directories. Obviously vets, dentists and schoolteachers are unlikely to have been found in 1086 but, mutatis mutandis, the comparison is interesting. In Essex the rural parishes of 1845 and 1848 were filled with farmers and rural businesses, though where other industries subsequently followed the opening of communications, or leisure interests, or oysters, the picture began to change and distort rapidly within 50 years. When we see that different compilers set different standards (e.g. 41 *or* 66, 34 *or* 91, in 1845 and 1848 respectively) we might expect some enormous differences between 1086 and either of these dates, but we do not find them. Moreover, although we would also expect initiatives of limited technological value to have effected changes in the intervening centuries this is rarely observable. A village might expand to take advantage of a textile boom, seigneurial investment will underwrite a market, population foci will shift for a mile or two, but nothing will be as dramatic and distorting as 19th century industrialisation and the railways; the rural rhythms remained much the same for centuries and made for only modest anomalies in localised economics. A finite 'wealth base' will only permit limited population expansion and if unseen but fixed limits of local solidarities were being approached by 1086, then there would be little room for further *major* and subsequent expansion in a strictly rural context in succeeding centuries.

At Southchurch in Essex in 1086 were 14 villain holdings, yet in 1845 there were only 9 'principal inhabitants' (mainly farmers) and in 1848 there were 12. By 1851 13 were recorded while across all three Victorian dates the number of inhabitants was constrained by a (constant) census return of 432 people. As the

ESSEX: COMPARISONS OF 'PRINCIPAL INHABITANTS'

PLACE	1086: freemen+ villains+bordars	'Principal Inhabitants'		
		1845	1848	1933
Bradwell	7+0+14 = 21	28	43	41
Tillingham	0+20+8 = 28	41	66	58
St. Lawrence	2+3+4 = 9	-	9	12
Asheldham	2+0+8 = 10	-	7	11
Dengie	7+6+14 = 27	6	13	14
Steeple	4+0+4 = 8	13	24	19
Southminster	15+11+41 = 67	53	102	
Brightlingsea	0+24+26 = 50	66	116	Leisure & Oysters
St. Osyth's	1+22+22 = 45	54	101	
Clacton(s)	5+47+95 = 147 } 190	34)50	94)121	
Holland(s)	2+25+16 = 43	16)	27)	
Frinton	2+5+0 = 7	-	4	
Sturmer	2+3+3 = 8	15	16	22
Stambourne & } Toppesfield }	24+18+25 = 67	42	68	65
Twinstead	18+0+7 = 25	10	12	10
Wethersfield	10+28+30 = 68	65	110	88
Stebbing	2+27+64 = 93 } 102	67)88	87)114	61)81
Gt. Saling	2+2+5 = 9	21)	27)	20)
Lamarsh	9+6+17 = 32	10	14	
Pentlow	19+8+8 = 35	13	19	13
Southchurch) with Thorpe)	1+18+9 = 28	9	12	Urban
Shoebury(s)	1+15+17 = 33	16	18	
Chesterford(s)	4+41+32 = 77 } 150	53)79	73)121	65)93
Littlebury } & Strethall }	2+45+26 = 73	26)	48)	28)
Ugley	1+7+10 = 18	7	13	29
Parndon(s)	3+5+17 = 25	26	29	45
Borley	1+10+10 = 21	6	8	5
AGGREGATED TOTALS -	1,074	697	1,160	N.A.

Directory of 1845 forgot to include Thorpe Hall, and we can see this in the overall acreage for as we saw (in chapter 3) this remained constant for Southchurch with Thorpe at around 2,000 acres from 1086 to 1851 (when there were 1,800 acres *and* land on Canvey Island), I will emend the villain total in 1086 to 18 farmers on the assumption that Thorpe Hall should be included at this early date, as she was to be later, in order to make a true comparison. At neighbouring North and South Shoebury there were, altogether, 2,400 acres in 1086 and 2,500 acres in 1851 and the total population across 1845 –51 numbered 366 souls. In 1086 there were 15 villains but 33 'principal inhabitants' (if we allow the inclusion of others) while in 1845 the 'principal inhabitants' numbered 16 and in 1848 19, and in 1851 only 15. Well, the villains of 1086 were not tenant farmers in the ultra-modern sense but in terms of 18th and 19th century tenancies of 60-150 acres per farm, they qualify. Were bordars of a few acres sometimes craftsmen with special skills therefore? Well, if they were not how could subsequent taxations, Lay Subsidies (fractions) based on 'movables', have been so effective?

Unfortunately we cannot apply the 1933 Directory to any of these parishes because the urban growth of Southend-on-Sea had already overtaken them, but we can make similar assessments of other places in Essex, ones which remained relatively unaffected by urban and leisure developments even in 1933. The accompanying table will make uncomfortable reading for all sorts of historians, for what if we multiplied all the Domesday 'principal inhabitants' by 24, we could then perhaps confirm 6 million people in the 34 English shires? Each time we seek to revise, confirm or deny, the guesses we have made in the field of 11th century populations, whatever we try to do to allay our suspicions that demographers have been seriously mistaken, we only seem to increase the possible population. It seems that even after a tragic century England, in 1086, still had a populous landscape on which to present her "fair field full of folk".

We have, as I said, come a long way from our wardrobe and have discovered more than any other previous researchers in this field, but the information is not really secret, not any more. *As I promised*, the formula is (or formulae are) all yours. Military intelligence is constructed from many scraps of information which, when brought together, form a pattern. Only when this pattern has been revealed by patient work can we recognise that which should, often, have been obvious from the outset. So it is with *our* story, piece by piece we have accumulated a garment with which to clothe the King; because we have now found his robes we dare to say that once upon a time he had nothing to wear. But again, the problem is not to deny what every one can see, it is not even to say what one should not see, rather (to speak in riddles) the problem was always to keep hidden away that which everyone was looking for. Consider, if you will, that once Rufus had implemented the Domesday formula many men, without doubt, sought his secret? The inner circle of the King's bureaucracy could be trusted because they depended absolutely on royal favour and protection, but then how could such a secret be revealed to a new King and *when* should it be concealed during an interregnum? The question arises as to how much King Stephen knew, or Matilda? We can observe that she had more success in raising revenues than he, but we cannot say with any certainty that one knew and the other did not. All we have is a tantalising reference to a royal clerk who in Henry I's reign suffered a dreadful punishment for some indiscretion. What seems certain however is that Richard fitz Nigel (son of Henry I's treasurer, the Bishop of Ely) passed the secret to Henry II, for even the text of the 'Dialogue of the Exchequer' is circumspect, though we are reasonably certain of his authorship. It says enough for us to know that its author knew the secrets, and that he knew that secrets cannot be written large. Let us return and look once more at the 'Dialogus de Scaccario'.

This volume makes it clear that the *villein was not required to pay geld* and his lord was not exempted from it, only the barons of the Exchequer and the sheriffs, those who accounted and those who collected the geld, were quit of its payment. This we have said already. We can only shake our heads when we think how many historians have ignored this text. And what does this source say of the hide? It says it is *an areal measure*, one which 'in its primitive form' contained 'one hundred acres', but this is preceded by a gratuitous inclusion, the phrase 'country people know (or can tell us) better than this', surely a punctuation mark or scribal apothegm of the kind we have encountered before? 'Sustine modicum' one might say 'ruricolae melius hoc norunt' for 'in each hide are fourteen and a half carucates'! And anyone using 100 acres would not only fail in their calculations (as historians have done) but also betray themselves, for the figure is a tell-tale! How else could one catch a spy? The source has more to add for it goes on to say, 'it is not by earlier accounts, such as exemplars use, but by reckoning up accounts' so that 'as sometimes arises when considering special cases, we say that these are our secret calculations which, at the right moment, we reveal and so expose them'. That few were admitted to the secret we may gauge by Roger of Hovenden's testimony, as a royal auditor to Henry II, that he understood Domesday Book to be primarily a record of the baron's lands. This is at least half of the truth,[69] presumably *as much as he needed to know?* The path through the labyrinth may have been excruciating, but we were and are dealing with the *ultimate* state secret. It has lain buried for hundreds of years and now we have discovered it, in spite of all fitz Nigel's cunning.

The Domesday section of the 'Dialogus' tells us of the thesaurus or treasure house in great detail and useful as this may be, as a picture of a secret place, it appears to be designed to parry the pupil's absorbing interest in Domesday, it resembles a digression and deflection. However, it tells us unequivocally that the Domesday and the Great Seal are of equally pre-eminent status and that the thesaurus is a whole bureaucratic *department* of records, seals and specie. Thus Domesday, ab initio, was guarded among the ultimate treasures and symbols of power in the realm. We also learn that Domesday (together with the triple laws of the English) was intended to guarantee the submission of all men to the royal will, that it recorded woods, pastures, meadows and arable lands and that the hide was equated with areal units, not imposts of fiscal units. 'In its primitive form' it (the hide) was 100 acres 'but country people know better', thus it was a defined total even though both 'county' and 'hundred' are noted to be *indefinite quantities*, as "the wise men of old" had seen fit to create them. This leaves us in no doubt that the information contained within Domesday Book was conceived and used as a series of areal overviews and not just an ad hoc gathering of arbitrary imposts. Then the 'Dialogus' goes on to say that the hundred was also called a 'centuriate' and why, because *it did not* always contain the *same* number of hides! Really? Does it point the moral that things are not always as they have been named, or is it telling us of etymological ambivalence: was the author embarking on a trivia quiz at the end of his practical treatise? Such knowledge as this last nugget is not worth imparting *unless* it serves as a reminder to the pupil (the King) that some totals or pieces of information should always remain concealed: 'when is a hundred not a hundred' we might paraphrase, why 'when it is a hide'! We have already asked how such a state secret might be transmitted across an interregnum? This is how it was done, with a handbook requiring privileged information from an unidentified individual before it could make sense. State secrets if not betrayed are inevitably lost, yet secrets may be prised from any man who can be identified as their carrier. What was required was a secure vehicle and an unknown messenger.

The closing section of the 'Dialogus' hints at more. When the pupil digressed under the discussion of 'murdrum', to ask "what is a centuriate or hundred" (a strange question to interpolate here, unless it is again one in code) he was told "wait a little, you shall know hereafter, in its place: this is under the heading of Domesday", yet the discussion did *not* answer all the pupil's questions even then. Something was reserved for a more advanced lesson. "The Exchequer which is a sort of inner sanctuary of mysteries where all is revealed when everyone's books are opened and the gates are shut…. for the present I pass over *them*, reserving them to another day's lesson….. Be content, therefore, with what has been said and that which thou hast elicited".[70] There is no evidence that this lesson was ever written, though it might have been delivered, all the same, by an author who

Professor Tout declared was, by his Latin, clearly an administrator and not a scholar.[71]

Education is usually about little packages, goods wrapped up and delivered to be weighed and stamped. Perhaps it shouldn't be, but it is. History, however, has become a series of increasingly strong boxes which one may not open, they have to be accepted at their declaration. We have been thinking the unthinkable for nine chapters now, thinking outside the boxes. Of course, the exponents of each discipline, the palaeographers, geographers, topographers, demographers, cartographers, medievalists and general historians will raise an outcry in order to dismiss and condemn this form of re-examination of principals. The scholars may well deny the primacy of our principal principle. I anticipate they will use anything they can, but figures are figures. Ultimately *their* knowledge has been founded on what we do not know *and can never know*, what *they* can invent *but not prove*, about Domesday Book. By proving what it actually says we threaten them and the integrity of their training, integrity they could have displayed a long time ago if they had had scientific methodology and a proper system of review. We clearly do not need historians to function as Douglas Adam's 'electric monks', saving us the effort of believing in *everything* we are fed by modern society, we need instead a scientific attitude to the proselytisation of those who, so far, only see history as useless entertainment, so that they may learn to think for themselves, learn to evaluate and discriminate effectively.

Finally, consider if you will the uses to which the servants of a system may apply its authorisation, consider how a body of men may conflate *their* personal interests with those of the state? English local authorities always design for a multiplicity of purposes, thus ensuring that (ab initio) nothing they build is ever fit for purpose. Such attempts at 'homologous design' never produce the apparently desired homeostasis simply because the results are predestined to be haphazard and unpredictable. Any lack of definition in a human activity will help us to avoid responsibility for failure and it matters not that it actually foredooms our endeavours. We might be forgiven for taking our present economic woes as proof that academia as a whole is suffering from scholastic dementia, whereas it may instead be that everything is due to lack of perception and to indeterminate targeting? The instability of those foundations on which we built our modern (aka 'developed') states rests on Domesday Book as one of the key components, rests on *un*defined and insubstantial definitions. Thus when we turn to administration we can see that if we collect amorphous statistics for fiscal purposes this invariable unpredictability is also reproduced and can be used (as with building design) to effect, for it similarly serves *to diminish the accountability* of the bureaucracy, removing from them any need to justify any given modality. It creates a comfortable reassurance that time wasting, heteroscedastic intrusion may be valid but, over the course of time, it reinforces this with an homoiousian elision of Crown and Crown-servants to form 'the needs of the State'. This is why I say that the genuine need of the Crown to verify the integrity of its tributaries has evolved into a justification of amassing useless information for its own sake, yet without such forces and undercurrents how would we have developed a large and efficient Civil Service?

> *"But a bold peasantry, their country's pride,*
> *When once destroyed can never be supplied.*
> *A time there was ere England's griefs began,*
> *When every rood of ground maintain'd its man......"*
> (Oliver Goldsmith, 'The Deserted Village')

CHAPTER TEN

'FROM WHENCE COMETH ALL THIS....'&
WITHER SHALL IT GO?

Systems do not just arise. They may evolve, mutate, be adapted for new purposes (as we have seen happened to the hide) or, like our old standard 'imperial' units, become confused and discarded, but *they do not* arise spontaneously. Measurements metamorphose, but they come from somewhere and by way of something. Human nature has a predilection for destruction and, so, if a system appears to fail (often because it is imperfectly applied) it is superseded by another: it is an article of faith that what is 'new' is better than the 'old', but it never is new and novel, it always comes from somewhere and often it is only a rediscovery. Thus most things are cyclical, but most people never realise this because they only believe what they are told, and they are not told, and because the language changes anyway. History is almost a study of reusage – of ideas, systems, tautologies, excuses, deceptions. To quote but one example, in the late 1960's science 'discovered' a new principle for conserving heat in buildings, only to realise that we had been looking at it for at least a century whenever we excavated a certain type of Roman hypocaust. 'Vanitas, vanitatis et omnia vanitas'. More particularly, the UK Food Animal Institute is at present conducting experiments in pig keeping under a woodland and forage regime, as a means of improving yields and reducing costs in 'conventional' pig keeping. We might have taken a hint from Domesday a century ago had we not been so arrogant and obtuse.

The idea of paying geld *only* upon an area being put to arable use, tilled or (as we say now) farmed, came from the practice of Danish immigrants in the 10th century and for them it was a natural conclusion to make and extend from the averaged capacity of one plough and its team. The hide as *a unit* of geld came from the hide as an areal unit of measurement, useful alike for describing topography and for assessing a man's status. This unit itself came from the older expression used to describe the land holding of a freeman and his household (basically a plough and its reserve of wareland) which was apparently employed in the 7th century if not before. What, we should now ask, was the source of this agricultural appreciation, itself tied to the most useful of all agricultural implements? *Who else,* before the Saxons, used the concept of a plough's potential benefit in order to define areas of production and productive land?

Traditionally the origins of Saxon husbandry have been dismissed as idle speculations, meanderings of the ignorant across a fallow landscape devoid of fruitful cultivation. Even 20 years ago many historians thought it stupidity as well as heresy to propose even a tenuous connection between Saxon and Roman societies. 'Everyone', they argued, knew that the Romano-British inhabitants had been massacred or driven into Wales. So much for the picture-history exemplars. Of course, whatever happened some remnants of the previous culture were certainly residual, some proportion became (if nothing more) the slaves of the new lords, in this case Angle, Saxon, Jute and Frisian lords. Were it not for slavery the picture would be different, but until we had machines and sources of energy slaves were essential for civilised societies. Arguably slaves still form the foundations of even modern, mechanised, civilisations. In 1066 the lords changed again (in the main) but the population remained to do the manual work.

The logic patterns embodied in the Domesday statistics clearly demonstrate just how isomorphic and multivariate changes, rather than monocausal change, are created and cannot be avoided. This being the case, it is reasonable to look to the origins of our units among the enslaved and the subjugated rather than within any educational matrix of the masters. Conquerors anyway, unlike colonialists, are never educators. Among the few works of antiquity which now survive to convey colonial agricultural practices is the 'Res Rustica' of Lucius J. M. Columella.[72] He has a great deal to say about Roman farming practices and land measurement, much that is valuable to the practical man of any age.

In Book Two Columella says that the labour of two yoke of oxen, two ploughmen and six labourers will be required in order to plough 200 'iugera'. Note that the 'jugum' of 60 acres in Kent in 1066 and 1086, is from the same noun but 'iugerum' itself is said to have come from 'to join together'. The Roman 'iugerum' measured three-fifths of a statute acre; thus 200 iugera = 120 acres, and also 120 acres = 4 oxen, 2 ploughmen and 6 labourers. Two teams of this size, or 8 oxen (our Domesday plough-team), will give us 240 acres of tillage. Even if we do not have 12 labourers it should not be difficult to average 120 acres of plough-land in a year with eight beasts, especially if harrowing had now replaced the hand-breaking of sillion, the practice apparently common amongst the ancients. Columella also tells us that it is 'inconsiderate and imprudent' to run a furrow further than 120 feet (pes Monetalis) using a yoke of 2 oxen. It seems strange for anyone, Roman or Saxon, to show consideration for beasts so the imprudence may lie in exhausting the men or beasts? Perhaps by combining yokes and working 'one up, one down' it became possible to run a longer furrow? I am convinced that Saxon ploughmen employed this technique. Moreover, the survival of relict landscapes tells us that Roman fields not only remained in continuous use, but that they were of similar dimensions to those often still being ploughed in c.1900.

Elsewhere Columella seems to suggest the origin of strips of land of simple area and so, in this, reinforces our 240 unit. The 'actus', he says, is (was in 60 A.D.) 4 x 120 feet, the 'clima', 60 x 60 feet. The 'square actus', of course, was 120 x 120 feet and *when doubled* became the 'iugerum' of *240* x 120 feet. He was, of course, referring to the pes Monetalis but this does not matter, what we are reviewing is the 240 unit. In the Roman world 'joined together' (doubled) *meant a unit 240 in length* whose components were 120 and 60 and which derived from the simple expedient of running the oxen for 120 feet, or as far as they should go without a break. Opinions as to the actual and practical distance may vary, as may the number of beasts involved, but in England we called an acre's run a 'shot' for centuries: for us, as we have already discussed, a 'shot' was an acre strip of 22 x 220 yards. I cannot say whether Saxon ploughmen took a 'breather' at every 30 or 60 yards per yoke of oxen (and 4x30 = 120 while 4x60 = 240), but I am sure they did not destroy their stotts. There is a rhythm to most agricultural practices which encourages parallel evolution, as ethnographers call it.

Columella has a great deal to say about the management of stotts, they were (after all) critical to the survival of all communities. He also gives extensive lessons in simple geometry and the measurement thereby of odd shapes of land. In the 1820's William Cobbett, on his rural rides, used to guess the exact area of a field as he rode by, whatever its shape, and then confirm it with any local he could find. He was (he tells us) invariably accurate. One feels that Columella had the same party trick by which to impress his companions but it was a product of application which can be mastered by most practical men. One does not *need* surveyors for fields.

Walter of Henley wrote of the loss of production by the interference of 'holy days and other encumbrances' and estimated that in the 13th century one could only hope for 260 days of ploughing in a year.[73] Columella made a similar estimate, presumably for slave labour, which took account of rain, holy days, rests and other things and came up with 175 days, maybe more. So the Roman slave had a quarter to a half of a year in which 'to do other things' and Walter's (or even Aelfric's) ploughmen had less than four months of rest days, which does sound hard, as Aelfric's Coloquy maintained. We must be grateful that 'trani' and tractor

128

enable us to work day or night, rain or shine and for as many days in the year as we choose.

Two further notes from Columella are enlightening. In Book Two – seventeen – he says, 'the keeping of meadows is, moreover, a matter of care rather than labour', while in Book Two – sixteen – he says, 'we take notice then of two kinds of meadow, the dry and the watered'. This is exactly what we have found in our Domesday statistics so we have no reason to believe that our Saxon farmers knew less than Columella about agriculture, even though they did not generally read Latin.

'Very well', it might be argued, 'but would the Saxons actually adopt Roman terms?' Well, the argument I have advanced is that the Saxons *practiced* agriculture rather than *learning* it and so their solutions were the practical consequences of having similar needs and similar tools. But even if this was not the case, the use of the term 'hide' is itself borrowed from the Romans (locus classicus) for it was derived in the following manner. [74] Dido, daughter of the Tyrian king, sister of Pygmalion and wife of Acerbus, fled to Cyprus and thence to North Africa. Here she negotiated as much land as might be covered by the hide of a bull and she then ordered this hide to be cut into the thinnest of continuous thongs and so encompassed enough ground to build a fort called Byrsa ('the hide of a bull'), which later became the centre of the city of Carthage. She was subsequently deified by her suicide. In a modified form this legend was repeated by Virgil in his Aeneid, which would be the most likely text for anyone in the Roman world to encounter. If such a legend survived into the 'heptarchy' (Saxon kingdoms) there is no reason why traditional measures and units derived from them should not have done the same through continued application. The noun "geld" is Saxon in origin and, equally, there is no reason why Danes or Norsemen (Normans) should know the value or use of 'a hide' if it was a peculiarly Saxon unit. "Ruricolae melius hoc norunt" may not have been an idle flourish, Saxons not Normans had cultural links with the classical world. Sutton Hoo testifies to this.

A break of ten or twenty years would obliterate the boundaries or tracks of a landscape, yet relict landscapes survived into the twentieth century (in places) to prove that such breaks did not happen everywhere, maybe happened quite rarely? Now we can also say that we have discovered 'relict units' to demonstrate that there was little or no disruption of commerce, agriculture or practical education! How much of a tax-break there was in the intervening centuries must remain a matter for conjecture. Ultimately it was the collapse of Roman administration which brought in a new aristocracy and society – whatever the mechanics of that change. In default of documentation it is difficult to know how effective either food renders or gold-giving were in early Saxon communities.

We can, however, feel sure that it was the growth of a money economy, the profitability of agriculture and more wide ranging trade, recreating conditions similar to the old imperial world, which caused a recrudescence of taxation. The conversion of grain mountains into durable and portable specie, as the Romans had found, made older forms of impost outdated. So it is with Domesday Book, even the concept of land providing specie had obviously been overtaken by new capitalistic ventures by the mid-eleventh century, but how was the government of England to encompass new concepts? More especially, how was it to cope with them, to put new taxations into effect? The inception of this process is of interest to us because it adumbrates all our later and modern taxations.

What is called the 'Winchester Domesday' is *not* a part of Domesday Book but a compilation of two rather later surveys: 'Survey I' of c.1110 and 'Survey II' of c.1148. [75] Because the real nature, scope and limitations of Domesday Book have never been appreciated (before this book was written) these Winchester surveys have not been critically examined in context and their essential role, as logical developments of the Domesday surveys, has been overlooked. We are the first to have such an opportunity. Domesday Book itself *did not* include either Winchester or the City of London, the two seats of government and two principal trading centres, and so scholars in the past have simply written down these omissions as 'lack of time', because (of course) they had no understanding of the problem which the Anglo-Norman administrators were attempting to address. Tax evasion, whether intentional or accidental, never figured in their simplistic view of arbitrary imposts of a 'primitive' administration, even though they happily accepted as 11th century a practice of gathering useless information 'for its own sake' which appears to be extremely modern! Well, 'never, never, let us doubt what nobody is sure about'. We have seen that the Domesday surveys were not administrative luxuries, that although very clever for their day they were not as sophisticated as modern surveys in point of fact, and we now know, from irrefutable evidence, that diminution of the royal revenues combined with diversification of capital-generating practices was perplexing the Crown by the 1080's. It seems obvious that someone working in one of these two great commercial centres, either in Winchester or in London, as a royal administrator, saw the need for reform of the tax system and also saw the need to first gather and analyse that body of statistics which must give form to any economy, both the land and the money systems. This same person, presumably, suggested safeguards and snares to his royal master, in order to guarantee verification of the statistics, which suggests that some powerful men at least had a good idea that due legal processes had been circumvented to the Crown's despite and wished to keep things that way. They in particular were the targets of this new and secret methodology. I like to think that the man behind all this new technology, this information technology, was Ranulf Flambard. He is important to our story. Let me come back to him in a moment.

The immediate problem faced by royal tax gatherers working on the Winchester surveys was *not hidation*, not even carucation, not land at all in the traditional sense of 'landed gentry', *it was rents*. Within the confines of this city people were sometimes densely packed into ancient divisions on plots of tenure. 'Landgable' was a low, fixed, perpetual money rent, later called 'burgage tenure' because it was derived from the division of a burgh into units housing burghers. Not surprisingly, when we look back at our 'cits'. country seats' of London in chapter 8, these tenures were often fixed at 5d or 6d per annum. However, what these men paid as landlords was nothing like the value of their property and the full rack rents, as Barlow and Biddle have informed us. Even the payment of a lump sum (gersuma) to the landlord might not avoid responsibility for an assignable annual rent to his nominee (e.g. a church) for these men could assign, devise and tallage as they saw fit, whatever their sub-tenants could stand. Whilst these special 'tenants in chief' (burghers) paid rents in pennies they were receiving incomes in pounds sterling yet often paying, in the contemporary terminology, no 'custom' at all, or even when there was 'custom' due very little or very infrequently. In other words, no one had revised the intra-mural system of tenancies in years because simplistic review was no-longer possible.

As with the geld, we see in Winchester Survey I that 'custom' fell *upon the landlord*, not upon the tenant. As he could do with his property pretty much as he pleased it was essential to discover and record *who* was responsible for these liabilities, liabilities which could then be varied as the King saw fit. Burgage tenure, however, was not quite like the simple arrangement with the tenant farmer represented by villeinage and feudal sub-enfeofment: the forms and types of sub-tenancy were so diverse and imaginative that the problem was more akin to the letting of properties 'de firma', at ferme, where (as we have seen with men like Richard de Tonbridge) the evasory claim was that the realty lay 'ex foris divisionis' and so not under his control. Disingenuous, but not satisfactory to the Crown. Thus it was that properties occupied by their owners *were not valued* but (as Biddle and Barlow observe) the properties of owners of let tenancies (however elaborate their arrangements with their tenants) *were* being valued. After all, burghers had duties and non-resident burghers could derive profits from ownership whilst avoiding their obligations. It was also critically important to record for posterity which of the city's properties lay in the 'feudum regis' (royal demesne) and which in the 'terra baronum': terra regis might not be encroached upon for laisse-majestie is treason, whether inside a city or in the countryside. We must also appreciate that physical and jurisdictional encroachments, in a feudal society, established solidarities. To usurp the King's property was to usurp men's allegiances and this led to private jurisdictions, 'commendam' and treacherous reassignments of individual loyalties. Feudalism united societies under personalities, not under abstracts. The royal promise of justice was a contract and the cement which bound consensual class divisions: we have only to recall the accession of Rufus to understand as much while the dispensation of death was the ultimate royal prerogative. In the case of Henry I we know that a dubious accession made him dependent, at first, on his supporters and chief lords. A prudent monarch would, however seek, consensus from the masses, not from ambitious magnates, and in this we may guess the Conqueror's jural purpose in apparently seeking a Domesday of justice?

Winchester Survey I is a corollary to the Domesday Inquests as well as a supplementary survey. For the first time a rigid enquiry was made by the Crown into *rented appurtenances* and it may be that it was only in a city that this could really be achieved? It is also very probable that only someone familiar with raising the geld and yet resident in a city could see both the reciprocity possible and the reciprocity practised. We are not surprised to find that Survey II, conducted after Flambard's death and at a time when Stephen was having great difficulty raising revenue with which to sustain his kingship and armies, is specifically enquiring only *into the payments made* for each tenancy. There is evidence of speculators moving in and breaking up the old burgher-household solidarity and though earlier writers have (typically) dismissed this as 'mere nostalgia for the past', it would in a fiscal world provide both a real threat to local administration and royal finances *and* an opportunity to profit from the profiteers. And this, after all, has been a guiding principle of royal and national taxation ever since. It is the principle which led, within a century, to the application of Lay Subsidies or 'fee-fractions' in place of the inefficient geld and which ultimately inspired Hundred Roll Enquiries such as that of 1279-80 which, as Dr. Raban has observed, is not overtly concerned with taxation, certainly not with its traditional manifestations. There is no reason why this Hundred Roll enquiry, or its companion of 1255, should have been intended to *fix* some arbitrary impost, rather their purpose was to extend the overview and *discover what was taxable,* including justice. The form that the tax would take could come later and once again it was best that those executing the surveys should know no more of the mechanics and methodology employed than did the Domesday legati in their day. Yet Dr Raban found one reference to a proposed levy in 1280 of 4d on the bovate, that is 4d per yoke of oxen or 32d on each hide (2s 8d), which would be 'ejusmodi quamquam sui generis' the earlier hidations and carucations, which observation makes us smile. It was, indeed, one possibility, but it was also a very old fashioned proposal by now. Moreover, there seems to be clear evidence that the Hundred Roll Enquiries were also used (see chapter

8) to verify scutage payments, yet the chronicler Vitalis also thought that Domesday itself (though he muddled things by attributing it to Rufus) was" a careful record of all the knight's fees in England". He was writing (of course) before scutage payments had been devised, when the only measure of a knight's fee was his manor, *his land,* and this may suggest to us one reason why so much emphasis was placed on manorial entities in 1086? Manors meant milites, vavassors (knights and sergeants) and so the loyalties involved needed to be secured to the crown rather than to the feoffor (though swearing fealty made this difficult). There were always paradoxes within the feudal 'system', even after the asymmetry of spoliation had balanced out. Times change, needs do not. Domesday was subtle enough to serve many purposes but 200 years later it must have needed revising and knight's fees, divided into fractions to avoid manorial responsibility for knight's service (always onerous), had already been re-affirmed by the imposition of scutage. As we have seen, the development of a money economy did not automatically work in favour of taxation. The stage was indubitably being reset for more innovative taxations in 1279-80.

It must always have been a tight-rope, this business of telling lords and knights what they owed without revealing how it was done. Yet the taxations raised, in the period between Domesday and the Hundred Roll Enquiries, *provide us with clear evidence* of Exchequer calculations at work.[76] By the mid twelfth century (whatever the upheavals caused by civil war) assessments made for the geld seem to have had some relationship to the perceived honesty of the declarations offered to the Crown in 1086: which is to say that succeeding gelds were *not* themselves arbitrary imposts but relied on method. We can see this through the correlation of 'so-much-on-the-hide', which *we* can now convert to acres of hidation, also the correlation of other statistics declared in 1086 but especially to the hidations and carucations returned therein. Those shires who had paid *less* in 1086 than any realistic area which we can calculate today (whether we use a modern survey or the Domesday aggregates) often *paid more* at a later date. *We* can now review this very simply by converting everything to acres. Thus Norfolk (recent gross area 1.3million acres) paid geld on 792,000 acres in the mid-twelfth century though in 1086 she had only declared liability for 467,000 acres; Derbyshire and Nottinghamshire (recent gross area 1.18million acres) paid geld on 264,000 acres in the twelfth century and not on the mere 160,000 acres declared in 1086; Suffolk (0.94million acres) paid on 564,000 acres and not on the 325,000 acres declared in 1086, and the extents must also have been of assistance to the Exchequer in making this last calculation. Oxford we know was paying heavily, due to historic factors (see chapter 8), but she increased from 576,000 to 581,000 acres for geld purposes and it is tempting to view this as a political 'fine'. When we plot these high paying shires onto a map, however, we see no obvious territorial relationship by which to suggest that political allegiances were generally involved. No, it seems the Exchequer was (generally) using its database in order to revise taxation to a realistic level in each shire.

Was this done equitably? Well, there were other shires who had paid *heavily* in 1086 but who, in the mid twelfth century, were reassessed on smaller areas, so we can apparently affirm this. Thus Berkshire (recent gross area 0.464million acres) *had* paid for 601,000 acres in 1086 but was now reduced to 484,000 acres; Surrey (recent gross 0.449million acres) *had* paid for 480,000 acres in 1086 but was now reduced to 425,000 acres (almost reciprocally); Buckinghamshire (recent 0.479million acres) *had* paid for 510,000 acres but reduced to 492,000; Middlesex (recent 0.224million acres) *had* paid 212,000 but was now only asked for 204,000. For the moment, make a mental note of Middlesex for, until the 'Winchester Domesdays' were made, both she and Winchester had had no urban assessments that we know about to cover the burgage tenures.

Henry II also asked for half mark 'dona' ('gifts') in 1156 and 1158 and these too can be converted to acres. Once again the Crown (or the Exchequer) offered rewards for honesty, generosity or loyalty, call it what you will. Kent (recent gross area 971,000 acres) offered 768,000 acres as her 'assessment' in 1156 and so in 1158 she paid only on 576,000; Wiltshire (recent gross 480,000 acres) offered 480,000 acres and was subsequently only required to pay on 384,000; Norfolk with Suffolk (recent, combined, gross 2.243million acres) offered 1,536,000 acres and was subsequently only required to pay on 960,000 acres; counties like Hertfordshire, Cambridgeshire and Huntingdonshire seem to have escaped altogether in 1158, unless the records are incomplete. On the other hand Somerset (recent gross 1.032million acres) paid on 480,000 acres in 1156 and was subsequently required to pay on 720,000 acres; Northamptonshire (recent 585,000 acres) paid on 576,000 acres but was subsequently required to pay on 672,000 acres, which seems harsh unless she actually was larger. Shropshire (recent gross 862,000 acres) paid on 192,000 acres in 1156 but on 336,000 acres two years later; Derbyshire with Nottinghamshire (recent combined gross of 1.180million acres) paid on 384,000, then on 672,000. Middlesex (recent 224,000 acres) actually paid on (a notional) 420,000 acres in 1156 but then only on 192,000 acres in 1158, so here we may suggest that the 'gift' to the King encompassed *not only* the area of the shire (or its agricultural output) but possibly some concept of the City of London's burgage capability? Thanks to the Winchester Domesday this may now have been possible; just possibly there was once a London Domesday, now lost, which would have made this 'gift' calculable?

Of course, the reciprocity appears simpler than the details will permit. By now the concept of the *total area* of a shire was undoubtedly old fashioned, force majeure had seen to that! Aristocratic comprehensions were limited to carucations and carucation of the demesnes may well have become the common conception, but Domesday also permits us to speculate that the principle of any gelds or dona could be agricultural aggregations, or even the arable capacities represented by the ploughs themselves. Until we can explore all the possibilities we cannot be certain though we appear to have some regional confirmation, at least, in the Dorset folios. Here, at Swyre (f.80v) William de Eu acquired land formerly seized of Toxus the priest and which had once been "in the demesne and in the farm of the King ... and he held it in the life and at the time of the death of King Edward and in the time of Harold. Formerly it was for grazing, *now it is for sowing.*" The actual knowledge of any of and of all these things was contained in the database of Domesday Book, and it was probably still valid even a century after the great survey had been made. What we can say with some certainty is that method and system were now (in the 12th century) being applied from the top down, *that there is a pattern* to those variations of post-survey assessments, county-to-county, which, at superficial view, always seemed so baffling and arbitrary to historians.

What is more the dona of 1156 and 1158 and the mid 12th century gelds enable us to estimate how effectively the Exchequer was thinking of new systems. It has been proposed that Medieval men could not cope with fractions, yet clearly the Lay Subsidies were just that and if we give credence to the value conversions which I proposed in chapter 2 these earlier payments may have been based on similar principles. The total of 12,611 half marks raised by the dona come to £4,203-13-4d which in 1980 values would be about £30,266,400.00, provided that money had not devalued greatly between 1086 and 1156? When we look at our tentative, national (gross) annual value of about £525,600,000.00 this is about one seventeenth of notional, national income. The mid 12th century geld of £5,318-0-0d (£38,289,600.00) would be a thirteenth. When we consider the sums raised by 'fractions' in the 13th century it becomes obvious that with the application of a Lay Subsidy the tax base had changed to encompass a very much greater range of assets than just land.

Nevertheless, the story of the search for fiscal perfection is not the purpose of this book, I only point to the perfection of the method, the gathering of relevant data under a 'strategy of alternative objectives', which today has become the collection of information for its own sake, the purpose and the relevance of which can then be assessed (in camera) at some later date and by an appropriate protocol. The change from collecting specific information for an immediate and specific purpose to collecting comprehensive information for subsequent specific use came about around the pivotal point of 1086 when, *for the first time,* a fiscal record collected and embodied extraneous information intended to verify (in secret) payments claimed and made. In so doing the king's clerks put the fear of God into miscreants and reinforced the structure of royal justice with a veneer of divine revelation. To do this the men at the heart of the Exchequer had to cease thinking in terms of arbitrary imposts and, instead, to think in economic and topographic structures. It is this flash of genius which I attribute to Ranulf Flambard.

What we know of Flambard is not much, but it is enough.[77] He was base enough in his birth to earn the hatred of the rich for being a loyal servant of the Crown; or rather I should say of each king, for he seems to have set the standard for personal loyalty without the usual vice of undue ambition. Before he became Bishop of Durham his 1086 holdings were not excessive: about 25 hides, a house in Oxford and two churches, in five or six different counties. He probably began his career under Maurice, later Bishop of London, who was chancellor to the Conqueror, and (we are told by the Liber Eliensis) Flambard rose to the same favour with the King as though he were his son. In Southern's view he was not part of the King's peripatetic entourage but an official with a fixed centre and more independent sphere of work and although not permanently at Winchester the district appeared to be the centre of his activities. This would certainly fit our view of him. It was, after all, the location of the Exchequer, or whatever it was officially styled at this date.

The problem for historians has been to reconcile the judicial side of finance, which we know Flambard pursued, with his being a treasurer and an accountant and, again, to reconcile 'royal justice' with 'the rights of the church', but *we* know now, from all that we have discovered, that these things would not be mutually exclusive, that just such a man *was required* to draw together these peculiar yet interdependent facets of the Domesday process. In the light of our knowledge we find it difficult to appreciate the difficulties experienced by these older historians; this is the beauty of efficient intelligence gathering, reconstructed piece by piece and fact by fact, until the picture seems self-evident. 'Wherever land, justice or finance − all inseparable − were involved, there is the possibility of finding Ranulf', said the puzzled Southern, but to us they are indistinguishable from one another *because we know that their composite formed the Domesday*. He was styled 'prince of tax gatherers' (publicanam princeps) and 'chief gatherer of the King's wealth' yet he attended both the 1095 and 1096 circuits as an itinerant (royal) justice. His subordinate 'court' stirred up and disturbed all of England, his tax collections set all England alight, we are told: can we doubt that his 'gemot' (it is not called 'curia' and there is a legal difference) was a *treasury-court or exchequer* while the link we have proposed between taxation and proceedings in camera *is now made for us by the chroniclers*! Rufus' reign was marked by the devolution onto itinerant justices and onto shire courts of those investigations

136

into royal rights formerly entrusted to commissioners, with what has been called 'vigorous administration' by royal officers often allowed to act independently, but this should occasion no surprise for the framework of the economic and feudal structure had now been set by Domesday and there was no need for the Crown to labour the process. *The important and probatory facts were a matter of record at Winchester*[78] and there was no need of further special enquiries, not until the 13th century anyway. The information did not date that quickly and the exchequer (probably already the Exchequer?) no longer required local reconnaissances or interrogations to take place. The King could simply send out his writs, leaving the administrative analysis to Flambard's 'court' of the exchequer, and the administration of justice to those delegated to hear it. That Flambard may also have been among the latter only provides what we would today term 'technical evidence'. One way of analysing the knottier problems was to require chief tenants to produce their own surveys or 'breves', resubmissions against which to compare their Domesday Book declarations, leaving comparative analyses to Flambard's exchequer 'gemot'. The Inquisitio Comitatus Cantabrigiensis[79] appears to be just such a demand and *it actually speaks* of a separate 'breve regis', as if to confirm the process of review. Loyalty had become demonstrable, no longer merely a protestation, a significant advance in social cohesion.

There can be no doubt that by the time of Rufus' murder Ranulf Flambard was *the key figure* in the royal administration, hated alike by the Archbishop of Canterbury and many magnates but hardly the 'enemy of the people' Vitalis would have us believe. When we are told that 'the people' (probably as representative as Hitler's S.A.) wanted to lynch him, and so he was put into the Tower of London, we may instead suspect that King Henry wanted him alive and in protective custody, even though he desperately needed scapegoats with which to ingratiate himself with the magnates and the Church. When we also learn that the 'prisoner' Flambard was given two shillings a day (say £1/4 million p.a. in 1980 values) with which to make merry we may reasonably surmise that *he was no prisoner*. When he 'escaped' and went to Henry's brother, Robert, the alternative claimant to the throne, in Normandy he still did not forfeit the King's favour, no. Not only was Flambard subsequently pardoned but he was restored to favour and allowed to commute regularly between Durham and his new benefice, the See of Lisieux. In this ambiguity, acting as both royal administrator *and* as a bishop (bis-bishop)he was followed (apparently in office) by Nigel, nephew of Roger of Salisbury, who himself became both royal treasurer and Bishop of Ely. Nigel, you will remember, was the father of Richard fitz Nigel, the treasurer who wrote the 'Dialogue of the Exchequer' and who undoubtedly passed the Domesday secret to Henry II.

What we have discovered is amazing and we must be careful not to read too much into the results. We have already discovered that we can decipher and completely reconstruct Domesday Book, that much is indisputable. We have also discovered that it is possible to *map the topography* of Domesday England, at least in some shires, down to a scale of 1 inch to the mile! We have discovered many things about politics and governments, especially the ancient Saxon pedigrees and roles of such surveys. We have established the problems of taxation encountered by kings in 11th and 12th century England and have had psychological insights into the minds of men, high and low, insights into the way in which *they* (not modern historians) interpreted their world. We have seen how politicisation of history has corrupted academic practise and prevented scientific progress, nay, even how it possibly created a deliberate and monumental hoax, *the biggest hoax in English history*? And if it was not deliberately constructed, the misapprehensions certainly *functioned* (at best) as an enormous hoax, leading historians (and others) astray even (in the end, I would say) discrediting academia through academia's sustained attempts to suppress the truth. Alumni of the world's most prestigious universities have done their best to hide what they could not honestly dispute for the last thirty years, because where there is a discrepancy between *their* 'guide' and reality, reality must have got it wrong! How sad that a hoax should prove to be so lambently attractive as a fraud to dedicated people.

Perhaps more speculatively, we have apparently identified the author of Domesday, the author of its novel methodology, father of our civil service, the King's 'evil genius' and we have dispelled the myth of Rufus' evil exactions. He would appear to be a king much wronged and now urgently in need of rehabilitation, and not only for some bogus accusation of Regalian right,[80] 'persuasione Flambardi', which had in fact been practised by his father and which now, thanks to the Domesday surveys, could even be equitably implemented. Well, surely it was equitable to expect the Church to share the burdens of the laity, for magnates to be treated as any of their mesne lords? Then, when we read of Louis IX investigating his officials in order to 'make amends for the sake of his soul', we remember Bede's description of Domesday (in chapter 6) and how 'they shall have but *one* law, rich and poor'. Was this the inception of a general, legal equity in England? Quite apart from the Coronation Oath the fiscal advantages of accessible justice are not difficult to distinguish. Would it also be too far fetched to suggest that the transition from Britannia to Anglia was largely a shift in aristocracies, or at least in those with social privileges? The survival of landscapes, units and practises suggests a previously unacknowledged degree of continuity, the existence of early records suggests a surprising survival of bureaucracy. I hope that others will now consider how closely late Imperial regional practises may have been carried over into the early Medieval world? Such an appreciation would tell us much about sustainability and natural rhythms and enable us to reappraise the effects of divergent practises. And if so much is assayed, then it may be that the thoughts of our ancestors, their everyday thoughts about common things, will assume new significance for us and maybe for our futures?

I have already touched on one aspect of another Domesday mystery, the emphasis placed by Domesday on 'manors', when we mentioned knight's fees and scutage payments. There is yet another aspect which links manors more directly to taxation. In 1066 there had been about 4,000 tenants holding in chief (in capite) whose liability for geld payment was indisputable. By 1086 this group had fallen to 180, no doubt an unforeseen disadvantage of the great 'land grab' permitted by the Conqueror? Sub-infeudation of mesne lords became essential, not only to ensure the provision of vavassors (knights and sergeants) for military purposes but in order to spread the tax burden! How was 'freedom' to be validated now, quite simply by commencing that re-emphasis of 'free' and 'unfree' social divisions which seems pursuivant upon Domesday and, most particularly, by the simplistic device of creating 'manors' and thereby replacing all allodial tenures. Within a given ambit 'tenants' now owed service. A man who stood alone was liable to pay geld on his land, even if he did not hold strictly in capite. Then again, the import of the new social order, created by the superimposition of 'Frenchmen' over 'Englishmen' in law, which itself had inserted a new class into the English hierarchy, was that these 'Frenchmen' who claimed superior free status *were undoubtedly* tax liable. It may have been that in many cases the surrender of relative freedom (such as was enjoyed by freemen and socmen who had become commended to the direction of some lord or other before 1086) into socage (unfree status) had its compensations when freedom came at a price? 'Nulle terre sans seigneur' meant that it was no longer possible to be allodially 'free' when a tenant paravail (free tenant) found himself at the will of some lord of a manor because his estate was restricted by customary practices and the lord's unfree tenants. This also left medieval jurists with a neat problem of banging square Saxon pegs into round Norman holes. Whether or not the Normans had invaded, the evolution of a land tax had already created the need for hierarchical definition.

I am sure that many historians give little credit to medieval jurists for their subtlety of thought. They should show more respect for their ancestors, especially when it came to tax evasion. Sub-infeudations were, to coin a Hervey, a double-edged sword of Damocles. They allowed taxation (and later scutage) to be 'laid off' on vavassors (as mesne lords) when the burden would otherwise have fallen exclusively on the tenants-in-chief, but these sub-infeudations also confused the picture by changing the records. It was possible for the Crown to lose track of a shower of small infeudations, of course, an especially useful device prior to the use of the 'Cestui a que' (Cestuy que), but vavassors then began to claim the right of inheritance as implicit in a 'fee' (sub-tenancy), so the chief lord might even find that his land had been barred or alienated from his possession! It may be that as the Crown began to pursue sub-infeudations (for example by supporting heritable tenure on a feoffee's behalf, if he made plaint against his feoffor),[81] until it finally closed them with the statute Quia Emptores (1290), the use of the Cestui a que was enlarged to comprehend 'feoffees to uses' (trustees)? Such devices allowed holders of land to avoid feudal incidents (payments) altogether by placing trustees in charge of the equitable uses (realties and interests) of lands. Thus although sub-infeudations had been proscribed the means of evading geld and scutage were not closed thereby, even after 1290, hence a further reason in the 13th century for the Exchequer to devise more comprehensive assessments of affluence than the old fashioned gelds and carucages. Human ingenuity is infinitely resourceful.

The problem which faced later Medieval tax resurveys was not only one of 'an ever more intricate web of sub-infeudation' which could not be captured in writing, not really. Jurists did their best, as de Zulueta observed,[82] to simplify the sub-infeudation structures (if only to create manors), an exercise which, in itself and at the peasant level, became socially divisive and aggravated civil disaffection, even contributing to events such as the (so called) 'Peasant's Revolt' which (as we have seen in chapter 9) was more of a 'middle class' revolt. There were, however, two problems of a strictly bureaucratic nature which hampered information gathering. The first was the need for participants, the collectors of information, inquisitors or commissioners (legati in 1086), to be adequately trained and disciplined in their circuit logic, what we would call task-specific training. There was, of course, no medieval mechanism for this and even had one existed too wide a dissemination of its particulars would have betrayed the covert nature of the enquiries. The social order required that those charged with affairs of state should be those with the largest stake in government, the magnates, yet these were the least likely to put state interests first: this was *the* paradox of feudalism. As it is we find the officers of great lords in 1279-80 instructing their tenants 'not to know' in more than an echo of the Kent folios of 1086 (see chapter 7). Word was spreading , did they now guess what was happening? When the Inquisitio Comitatus Cantabrigiensis was enrolled someone took the precaution of *including lists of jurors*, no doubt in order to identify any who subsequently proved to be foresworn? At every stage of the process there needed to be checks and it was essential that only a few, senior and dependable, scribes should understand the real purpose of any such survey if its aspect of 'divine revelation' was to be maintained. Those who might profit from 'insider' information, or be suborned, could not be given more than the most rudimentary of instructions (the 'commission instructions' and 'oath' in 1279) and even then adherence to their letter could not be emphasised without suggesting the real nature of the process. An ad hoc and part-time civil service is not an ideal structure for revenue collection. Domesday helped to change this. The second problem was in processing the information, for the larger the volume (or volumes) grew the less capable were a handful of Exchequer clerks of analysing and structuring it all! Even the system of arithmetic was against them (they really did need for nothing, for 'zipher' or 'O') and actually reading, re-sorting and restructuring the mass of detail would have required a massive *and* secure civil service headed by clerks with the status of great lords, but not with their social position and temptations. The hatred accorded to both Flambard and Becket had much to do with their immunity from the vulnerability of their humble origins.

Comprehension and ambition had outrun the means and techniques of analysis available, even by 1087. Domesday continued to be employed because, eventually, Exchequer clerks had acquired some grasp of it and some proficiency in its use. The enquiries involving Domesday tended to be specific and comparative and restricted to 'primary sector' economics, so the 'pocket version' (Breviatus)[83] was adequate. It is even possible that projects such as the Hundred Rolls foundered half way through, when the Exchequer realised it could not cope? The Winchester Domesday illustrates the enormously difficult task of encompassing cities, even *after* the rental (fee-ferme) problem has been identified. Where were the manpower resources with which to tackle London? Was it ever encompassed? After all, the purpose was to provide the King with revenues, not necessarily to achieve perfection, which does not mean that perfection was not perceived. It is a quandary still familiar to both civil servants and to military commanders, what matters most is the time limit. 'Right' and 'wrong' are inevitably subordinated to actually *making* a decision.

The hoax of Domesday was the indemonstrable hypothesis of an infinitely variable 'geld hide', the myth of an arbitrary impost exacted from an unresisting peasantry by an absolute monarch. Now, in all fairness, we cannot deny that there was a grain of intuition within this, even though it was never the fantasy world of 'toffs and workers' so beloved in historical fiction. The reality was (as we have proved) an attempt to change geld payments and to make them arbitrary *at the will of the payer*, that is not by any 'top-down' authority but rather by that 'bottom-up' which makes government by consensus and under equity essential to any culture's survival, as the French Revolution so eloquently proclaimed. Unfortunately, such theories did not fit the age in 1900 and so, perhaps driven by political imperatives, the author of the hoax sought to establish those solidarities which he supposed to be eternal verities, in particular the power of a ruling class to subjugate and exploit powerless masses by force rather than subtlety. It has proved a persistent fantasy and without it our Medieval legends might have gone unnoticed: Hollywood and many writers would then have been the poorer and 20th century European history very different.

What defeated and yet exercised administration after administration, commencing with Domesday Book, was the desire, even need, to tax a society for the benefit of all and of a few in particular. But human nature is infinitely resourceful and mendacious and it was only the gradual realisation that in order to control society one must collect all forms of information, practical or legal, whether useful for the immediate purpose or not, that information must be insidiously gathered for its own sake and, like a treasury, stored up against the day when it would become useful to an administration, which made later taxations possible. And so we developed a process of analysis for all aspects of society, one embodying practical knowledge of systems and of statistics and applying psychological force through selective revelation of that which was deemed hidden from all men. This process is rather like archaeology, we gather whatever we can see or recognise in order that it may be stored until a more expert review is possible and over the years we recognise and store more and more 'evidence'. Then, as with archaeology, the record is separated from the material archive and no one is left who can reinstate it, or reforming zealots purge the 'useless lumber room' and retain only that which appears to fit their present purposes. In this process of cleansing, ignorance and change for its own sake we discard that which would inform the future, except that now in our new millennium we appear to have an infinite capacity to store information. Let us hope that the mechanics of this capacity prove to be as durable as parchment and fero-tannic ink, less susceptible than Michael Wood's 'School's Domesday' of 1986.

We are the first to have an opportunity of using these many surveys and all this vast Domesday and satellite archive *according to the intentions of their originators*, for we are the first to have the means of accessing the end which they desired. In the end, maybe, we will understand enough to have a better idea of where we came from and, therefore, of where we are going? If the scientists are right, we may not have too much time remaining in which to make important discoveries and effect changes which might contribute to the survival of the human race? If we do avoid disaster with some sort of contribution from history it will be beholden to Domesday, of that I am sure, yet it may not actually be due to that gathering of verifiable information which Domesday Book initiated as much as to the landscapes and practices which it now allows us to access (if we wish) and the fresh evaluations we are then enabled to make of sustainability? But to do this we will need to change attitudes in our universities, or at least in their departments of history and archaeology, in order to reflect modern and scientific approaches to history. I suspect that there have been many researchers like the late Cecil Hewett[84] whose genius was largely sacrificed to a combination of academic jealousy and a lack of organs of publication. We must improve debate and review in historiography, in order to allow ideas to flow and to be respected, we must encourage, not stifle, innovation and we must use the concept of meritocracy creatively, not repressively. Ultimately we must change our system of education in order to engage and inspire rising generations with more than just a material ethic and an essential requisite of any such task must surely be a new determination not to become complicit in major and detectable errors through an indulgence in fantasy? May the Domesday hide be the salutary and last of academia's hoaxes.

THE END

FACTA EST ISTA DESCRIPTIO.NON SOLUM P HOSTRES COMITATUS
. SED &IĀ P ALIOS .

Certum Est Quod Certum Reddi Potest –
that thing is certain which is able to be rendered certain.

NOTES & SOURCES

† For those unfamiliar with these phrases, see Halliwell's Dictionary (1847) and Brewer's Dictionary (1894)

Φ Whether one accepts 'spoon' as spoony (lovesick) or as a silver spoon, and 'dish' as a bowl of wood or of clay, or as dished (cheated out of something), the allusion to a moral dimension still stands.

1   "Inventing the Middle Ages", Norman F. Cantor (Lutterworth 1992 and William Morrow and Company, 1991)
2   Total from the summary statistics on pp.51-52 of "Domesday 1086-1986" the PRO 900th anniversary exhibition guide.
3   For which see "The Norman Conquest of the North", William E. Kapelle (University of North Carolina Press, 1979)
4   "Dark Age Economics", Richard Hodges (New Approaches in Archaeology, 1982 and 1989).
5   'Herefordshire' in the Phillimore 'Domesday Book' series, vol.17, 25.7 (=187a) ,(1983)
6   'Middlesex', ibidem, vol.11
7   'Surrey', ibidem, vol.3
8   "The Hitch-Hikers' Guide to the Galaxy" by Douglas Adams (1978,1979,1986)
9   For relict landscapes see P. J. Drury and Warwick Rodwell (1980) in CBA Research Report No.34, "Archaeology in Essex to AD 1500", pp.59-76, figs 22 and 23; also unpublished research by A.C. Wright in Southend Museums archives, 1979.
10   White's "Directory of Essex" (1848)
11   Kelly's "Directory of Essex" (1894)
12   Kelly's Directories
13   "The Forest of Essex", W.R. Fisher (1887)
14   Ordnance Survey, 6 inches and 25 inches to the mile (pub. 1880, surveyed in Essex 1861-76)
15. For example Eastwood (Essex) in the Essex Record Office; Southchurch (Essex) in Southend Museums.
16. "Mersea Island: the Anglo-Saxon Causeway", Crummy, Hillam and Crossan in Essex Archaeology & History, Vol.14 (1982) pp.77-86.
     For Foulness Island see the 1309 Inquest Post Mortem of John de Rochford, which

included 1100 acres of marsh, and the Quo Warranto of 1285 giving "marshes within and without the walls" (seawalls).

17. "The History of the Countryside", Oliver Rackham (1986 & 1995)

18. "Feet of Fines for Essex", Edward IV, vol.iv (EAS, 1964) and in vol.v (1991) for Lord Riche's "fresh" and "salt".

19. "The Victoria County History of Essex", vol.1 (1903), J.H. Round in H. A. Doubleday and H.A. Page (eds) pp.424 and 440; also Phillimore's Domesday volume 32, 3.16 and editor's note. N.B. in 1980 this was denied again by a reader who said neither of these references existed!

20. Kelly's Directories for Essex

21. "A General Introduction to Domesday Book", Sir Henry Ellis (1833)

22. "John Norden's Description of Barley, Hertfordshire, 1593-1603", ed J. C. Wilkerson (Cambs.1974)

23. "English Historical Documents", (1955 and 1979), vol.2, (eds.) D.C. Douglas, G.W. Greenaway and D. Whitlock pp.483-6; also "Feudal England", J.H. Round (1895 and 1964), pp.124-130

24. "Domesday Book and Beyond", F.W. Maitland (1897 and 1969); also Douglas, Whitlock and Greenaway op.cit.

25. "The Tribal Hidage", C. Hart in Transactions of Royal Historical Society (1971), 5th series, 21, pp.135-57; also "The Contents of the Tribal Hidage" in Frümittelalterlich Studien, 8 (1974), H.Vierk and W. Davies.

26. "History of the English Church & People" by Bede, Sherley-Price (trans.), (1955) pp.181 (III.24)

27. "The Burghal Hidage: the establishment of a text", D. Hill, Medieval Archaeology (1969), vol.13, pp.84-92

28. "Anglo Saxon England & the Norman Conquest", Henry Loyn (1962) pp.135-6

29. F. W. Maitland op.cit. (1897 and 1969)

30. "Domesday Book Through Nine Centuries", E. M. Hallam (1986) pp.32-33 and 115-17; also Agarde's Exemplification of 1590, q.v. "Domesday Rebound" (PRO 1954) p.51. The view appears to be based on fitz Nigel's observation (Dialogue of the Exchequer) that it *was not to be questioned.*

31. "Dialogus de Scaccario", q.v. "Select Charters and Other Illustrations of English Constitutional History ", W. Stubbs (OUP, 1870-1960), ed. H. W.C. Davis. Also "English Historical Documents 1042-1189" (1953) vol.2, op.cit. Douglas and Greenaway

32. Kapelle, op.cit; "William the Conqueror", D.C. Douglas (1964)

33. Peterborough Chronicle, the "Anglo Saxon Chronicle" (E) quoted in D.C. Douglas & G.W. Greenaway "English Historical Documents", vol.2 (1953) p.161

34. A. le Prevost (ed.) "Historia Ecclesiastica" of Ordericus Vitalis, VIII.8 (1838-55)

35. "Chapters in the Administrative History of Medieval England", T.F. Tout, (1920, 1937, 1967), vol.1 in particular, pp.93-6

36. "Ranulf Flambard and the Early Anglo-Norman Administration", R.W. Southern, Transactions of the Royal Historical Society, vol.16, series 4 (1933)

37. "The Domesday Geography of Midland England" (CUP.1954), H.C. Darby & I.B. Terrett

38. Southern, art.cit

39. Eadmers' "Historia Novorum in Anglia" (1964), G.Bosanquet (trans.)

40. "The Lordship of Canterbury" (1966), F.R.H. du Boulay, pp.240-6

41. Bosanquet's Eadmer, op.cit

42. "Thomas Becket" (1986), F. Barlow; also Stubbs, op.cit I pp.500 and 623; from Grim's "Life of St.Thomas".

43. "The Domesday Geography of Eastern England" (CUP.1957), H.C. Darby, pp.122

44. Ibidem

45. "Victoria County History of Suffolk" vol.I, B.A. Lees, pp.412-16, after J.H. Round, "Feudal England" (1895) pp.98-103

46. "The Evolution of Settlement in Three Parishes in S.E. Norfolk", A. Davidson, East Anglia Archaeology 49 (1990)

47. q.v. "Domesday Book, A Complete Translation", A.Williams and G.H. Martin (eds.) (Allecto Editions & Penguin, 1992 and 2003), probably the best general (translated) reference available

48. "Medieval England, An Aerial Survey", M. Berresford and J. St. Joseph (CUP, 1958 and 1979) no.32, pp.86-94

49. "Two Saxon Land Grants" in Collectanea Londiniensis, London & Middlesex Archaeological Society Special Paper No.2 (1978), T. Dyson, pp.200-15. For Surrey see Phillimore's Domesday vol.3, for Middlesex see vol.11

50. Camden's "Speculum Britanniae, the First Parte" (Harleian Ms. 570) in Sir H. Ellis' "Speculi Britanniae Pars" (1840) ; also "The Tristram of Thomas", A.T. Hatto (1960) pp.345-6 and William fitz Stephen's "Descriptio Noblissimae Civitatis Londonae", trans. H. E. Butler.

51. "Five Hundred Points of Good Husbandry", Thomas Tusser, introduction by G. Grigson (OUP 1984)

52. Maitland, op.cit (1897) pp.179-80; Ellis, op.cit (1833) vol.2, pp.441 and 448

53. The Penguin/Allecto Domesday, f.191v – 192v. Learned philologists tell us that they have identified Whittlesey with "Witsie" and Whittlesley Mere with "Witelesmare" but the Domesday fisheries suggest that "Witesie" referred to the vill *and* the mere (or lake) while "Witelesmare" might refer to the Wash ("Mare") when both were one entity east of Peterborough? (viz. 5,660 acres of waters at "Witesie" in 1086, 5,600 acres at Whittlesley Mere in 1786 (and larger in the winter) and in 1849, yet only 3,000 acres by 1852.) The Wash would be about 71,000 acres of fen.

54. Penguin/Allecto Domesday f.192.

55. "English Medieval Industries", (1991), D. Parsons, J. Blair and N. Ramsay, p.8-9

56. "A Second Domesday: The Hundred Rolls of 1279-80", S. Raban (OUP 2004)

57. Penguin/Allecto Domesday, f.103v

58. Ibidem, f.121v

59. Phillimore's Domesday vol.7: 2.2, 4, 5 and 7

60. Penguin/Allecto Domesday, f.36 and f.164

61. Ibidem, f.64v

62. Ibidem, f.132v

63. du Boulay op.cit

64. The difference is between Ellis (1833) op.cit and the PRO "Domesday: Exhibition Guide" (Crown, 1986)

65. "The Medieval Essex Community: The Lay Subsidy of 1327", J.C. Ward, (ERO, 1983); "The Great Revolt of 1381", C.Oman, (1906), appendices II and III (Lord Treasurer's Remembrancer Rolls, Tax Accounts no.8, PRO)

66. "Essex at Work, 1700-1815", A.F.J Brown, (ERO, 1969)

67. Ward, op. cit.

68. Kelly's Directory of Essex, 1933

69. "The Annals of Roger de Hovenden" trans. H.T. Riley, vol.I (1853)

70. Stubbs (1870) op. cit. and Douglas & Greenaway (1953) op. cit.

71. Tout (1920) op. cit.

72. Columella, "De Re Rustica" trans. H.B. Ash, Loeb (Harvard, 1941 and 1967)

73. "Walter of Henley's Husbandry", E. Lammond (ed.1890). C. Cipolla examples 269 working days (in Lombardy) at best, q.v. "Before the Industrial Revolution, European Society and Economy 1000-1700" (1976 and 1981), while W. Abel in "Agricultural Fluctuations in Europe" (UP 1986) gives a 'working year' for artisans of 250-270 days.

74. "A Classical Dictionary of Biography, Mythology and Geography", W. Smith, (London, 1859) pp.219

75. "Winchester Studies .1. Winchester in the Early Middle Ages, an Edition and Discussion of the Winton Domesday", Barlow, Biddle, von Feilitzen & Keene, ed. M. Biddle, (OUP 1976)

76. Maitland op. cit (1897) pp.29 and 546, also "Henry Plantagenet", R. Barber, (1964), also "Taxation in Medieval England", S.K. Mitchell, (Yale, 1951)

77. Southern, art. cit.

78. Rufus was calling Domesday "meis brevibus...... in thesauro mea Wytoniae" and Henry I "liber de Wintonia in castello Wincestre".

79. q.v. "The Making of Domesday Book", V.H. Galbraith (1961)

80. q.v. "Regalian Right in Medieval England", M. Howell (London 1962)

81. e.g. Canterbury Cathedral Library preserves a writ of Richard I against the Prior and Chapter concerning the de Southchurch family.

82. de Zulueta in "Oxford Studies in Social and Legal History" ed. Vinogradoff (Oxford 1927) and Douglas, ibidem, "The Social Structure of East Anglia". For feudal concepts

of vassalage and benefice see F. L. Ganshof in "Feudalism" (1964).

83. For a brief summary see "Domesday Re-Bound" pp.47 (PRO 1954)

84. C.A. Hewett "The Development of Carpentry 1200-1700" (1969); "English Historic Carpentry" (1980) and other studies.

COVER IMAGE – courtesy of Mobile Museum

"And the booke that I hadde readde......
I fonde hyt in myn honde ful evene
Thoght I, 'Thys ys so queynt a swevene
That I wol, be processe of tyme,
Fonde to put this swevene in ryme
As I kan best, and that anoon'.
This was my swevene; now hit ys doon".

(Chaucer's "Book of the Duchess",
Durham & St. Andrew's Medieval Texts, 1982.)

INDEX

GENERAL

Account Rolls: 85
Acres: 11-12, 128
Actus: 128
Arabic numerals: 13,68
Black Book (of Bury St Edmunds): 76
Black Death: 114
Bordars:111-12
Bovate: 18,132
Brecklands: 81,83
Breviatus: 141
Burghal Hidage: 52-5,57-8,100,103,105
Camerarius/Camerarii: 17,74-5
Caruca: 14
Carucate: 13-14,76
Castles: 22,57
Cestui a que: 140
County Hidage: 50-1,104-5
Dane geld/Geld: 13,60,67,77-9,133-5
Dane Law: 14-5,50,108
Descriptio: 79,90
Dialogue of the Exchequer: 61,79,122-3,137
Domesday, origin of name: 61-3,138
Domesday Monachorum: 76
Dona: 134-5
Eels: 21,98
Excerpta of St Augustine's: 76
Exchequer: 74-5,106,133-6,141
Extents (leets): 80,82-9
Famine: 114,116
Ferding: 18
Fisheries: 21,83-4,97-8,100
Forests & Parks: 21,32,81,99,103-4
(The) Four E's: 7
Gersuma: 131
Governance: 89-91,92
Greater Domesday: 62,80
Harrying of the North: 10,63-4
Herrings: 82,84
Hide (unit): 12-13,122-3,129
Hoax: 1-9,46-7,138
Hundred Rolls: 107,132
Indemonstrable Hypothesis: 4,7-8,47
Inquisitio Comitatus Cantabrigiensis: 75,137,140
Inquisitio Eliensis: 76
Iugerum/Jugerum: 127
Jugum: 18,127
Landgable: 131
Lay subsidies: 114,117,132
Leets (see Extents): 83-4
Lesser Domesday: 62,80,89-90

Liber Eliensis: 136
Liber de Thesauro: 79
Liber de Wintonia: 79
Manors: 139
Maps: 46,51,60
Meadows: 18-19,100,129
Medieval Prairie: 69
Money Economy: 12
Northamptonshire Geld Roll: 50-1
Pasture: 19
Peasants' Revolt: 114-5
Permaculture: 19
Piltdown: 2-4,47
Ploughs: 16-17,127-8
Pole (Perch): 54
Poll Tax: 114,117-8
Preferred sizes: 95-7,103
Principal Inhabitants: 119-21
Purpose of D.B: xi,61-3,76,85,89-90,132,135
Quarries: 104
Quia Emptores: 140
Quo Warranto (writs): 76
Regalian Right: 138
Relict Landscapes: 25,31-2,35-6,128
Revised description of England: 74
Revised Hidations: 15
Sandlings: 81,83
School's Domesday: 43,142
Scribal Apothegm: 68,106
Scutage: 107,112,133,139
Selective Hidation: 15
Servicium Debitum: 112
Sheep Pastures: 19
Sokemen: 82,87,139
Speculum Britanniae: 93
Stick of Eeels: 21
Sulung (Solin): 17,72
Swine Pastures: 20
Swine Renders: 20
Swine Woods: 19-20
Tallage: 112
Tribal Hidage: 51,57-8
Tristan of Thomas: 93
Types of Hidation: 14-15
'Unfathomable Mystery': 85
Underwood & Wood Pasture: 20
Values: 22-3
'Variable Carucates': 76
Villeins: 112,116-7,122
Virgate: 17-18
Waters & Fens: 21,88,100
Winchester Domesday: 79,130-2
Woodlands: 20-1,25,100,103

151